LIVERPOOL
MURDERS

© Richard Whittington-Egan 2009

Published by The Bluecoat Press, Liverpool
Book design by March Design, Liverpool
Cover illustration by Tim Webster
Printed by Graham and Heslip

ISBN 9781904438885

RICHARD WHITTINGTON-EGAN

LIVERPOOL MURDERS

The Bluecoat Press

CONTENTS

THE HUNTING OF RAY BEECH

It was late afternoon when the telephone rang in Liverpool's Prescot Road police station. The desk sergeant picked it up.

"Hallo."

"Hallo. Hallo." The voice on the other end of the line was urgent. "Police? This is Jimmy Hatton speaking. I'm the landlord of the Princes Park Hotel in Upper Stanhope Street. I think I've seen Beech. Beech, you know, the bloke you're looking for the murders."

The desk sergeant stiffened to attention and clamped the receiver closer to his ear.

"Just one minute, Mr Hatton." Then, covering the mouthpiece, turned to the group of young policemen chattering away by the counter. "Hey! Shut up you lot," he snapped. "This is important."

The chattering subsided. "Hallo. Right Mr Hatton. Now what were you saying?"

"I had a chap in this afternoon the dead spit of Beech. I'm sure it was him. Had a girl with him. Young piece, about twenty-four. Now look, I don't want any trouble, I keep a respectable house, but I heard the bloke say to her that they'd be coming in again this evening. I reckon it might be worth your while looking in."

The instant he had put the receiver down the desk sergeant rushed round to the CID and told them what Hatton had said. Seconds later, Hatton's message was being relayed to the Murder HQ that

Superintendent Herbert Balmer had set up at the Lawrence Road police station.

Patrolling the Upper Stanhope Street area that afternoon, studying every face in the way that policemen do, were Detective Sergeants John Beaverstock and Joseph Gillbanks, and when they rang in a routine check call to Lawrence Road, they were told the score and ordered to "proceed forthwith" to the Princes Park Hotel. So they looked at their watches, saw that it was getting on for six o'clock, and wheeled round in the direction of Upper Stanhope Street.

Jack Beaverstock and Joe Gillbanks were both 45, a couple of old-timers, beginning, at least, to think in terms of retirement and pensions. Both, too, were family men. Beaverstock was the father of four young sons. Gillbanks had a lad of 16. They were big, burly men, tall, clean-shaven and, despite greying hair, not the type you'd choose to pick a barney with! Not that they were the sort to look for trouble – though they were not the sort either to shirk it if it happened to come their way. And now it had – with a vengeance. This was it. They knew that the man they were looking for had a partly-loaded revolver in his pocket. They knew, too, that he had already killed twice, and wasn't likely to be worried about notching up a third murder – particularly that of a 'Jack'.

It was just after 6pm when the two detectives with eyes in the backs of their heads reached the Princes Park Hotel. It was a very ordinary, rather shabby, public-house, all frosted glass and drab brown wood, just like any one of a hundred other slightly seedy Liverpool pubs. Quiet, too, at this time of the evening. It would be hours before it livened up.

The two CID men drifted gently in through the swing doors into the front parlour. No noise. No fuss. They fanned out slightly. At the same time their trained eyes took in the details of the six people in the bar. Five were eliminated in seconds. But the sixth ...

There, standing at a corner of the counter, a glass of beer in front of him and a girl beside him, was a dark, wavy-haired six-footer, with blue eyes and a fresh complexion. It was Beech all right.

Slowly exchanging a significant glance, Beaverstock and Gillbanks edged forward. You would have called their movements sluggish if you didn't know the reason. They didn't want to set off a shooting match. They didn't want innocent bystanders to catch a bullet, let alone catch one themselves. Very quietly then, they sidled up to Beech, one on either side. It was Beaverstock who spoke. "We're police officers. We'd like to have your name and address and some evidence of your identity," he said.

The tall young man between them hesitated. Old hands like Beaverstock and Gillbanks sensed that he was concocting a story. But that wasn't the point. The thing was, was he going to come quietly? Or was he going to go wild? At that moment there was one nasty, persistent thought ticking away at the back of both of their minds. If he chose to, the man could probably kill them both where they stood.

The hunting of Walter Richard 'Ray' Beech had begun a few minutes after the people who lived in Underley Street, Wavertree, had heard shots and screams coming out of No 32. That had been at about half-past six on the evening of 16 April 1951. Heads popped out of windows, women left their cooking, men in shirt-sleeves rushed out into the road. Respectable yellow-brick Underley Street suddenly buzzed like an upturned beehive.

The two boldest men, 56-year-old Arthur Barber and 42-year-old Gladwin Field, didn't hesitate. They rushed round to the back of No 32, up the entry, into the back yard, and peered through the kitchen window. Both blanched at the scene of bloodshed that met their eyes. Two women were lying close together on the floor. Both had been shot through the head. The face of one of them had been battered in. Beside her body lay the broken half of a gun butt. In a far corner was a little fat dachshund, piteously whining and whimpering.

Barber kicked in the back door. The two men tore through the house, every minute expecting another shot. But there was nothing. No one. Just those two splayed and very dead bodies in the kitchen. Stillness. Eerie silence, pierced only by the thin, high whinings of the dachshund.

The front-door of the house was swinging open. The killer had vanished into the network of alleyways which criss-cross that part of Liverpool. The jiggers ... a labyrinth of escape.

Within a matter of minutes, a cavalcade of cars had converged on normally quiet Underley Street, spewing out police. A cordon of uniformed officers had sealed off the street and a dozen grim-faced plain clothes detectives were shepherding the bewildered inhabitants back into their houses.

It did not take the police long to identify the murder victims. They were Mrs Lilian Harriet Parr, a 55-year-old widow who worked as a domestic servant at nearby Sefton General Hospital, and her 24-year-old married daughter, Mrs Lilian Beryl Beech. She was living apart from her husband, 29-year-old Ray, and was working as a night sister in the maternity section of the same hospital as her mother.

While detectives and forensic experts were going over the murder room inch by inch, searching for fingerprints and taking photographs of the bodies, others were questioning the neighbours.

It was Mrs Eleanor Barber who was able to give them the vital information that they needed. That day had, she said, been Beryl Beech's 24th birthday, and she had popped into Number 32 to see her. She had found Beryl and her mother in the back kitchen. They were very upset and both crying. While she was there Ray Beech came into the kitchen and told Mrs Barber that there had been a quarrel. He had wanted his wife, who was expecting a baby, to return to him, to leave her mother's and join him in the couple of rooms where he was then living, but she was refusing to do so. Upset and embarrassed by the family row, and not wanting to get involved, Mrs Barber had left. That was shortly after 6pm.

So, within an hour the police knew who they were looking for and why he had done it.

Out went the order – "Find Beech!"

In a teeming cosmopolitan seaport of some 800,000 people it is not hard for a man to disappear. There are a thousand out-of-the-way nooks and crannies to hide a fugitive. There is, too, a vast twilight world, a tight-lipped community that wouldn't raise a finger to help the 'scuffers'. But this time the police were in luck. Raking through the criminal records down at their Dale Street HQ, they found that they had plenty on file about Ray Beech. A former Merchant Navy steward, he was a known violence merchant. And he was no stranger to the feel of a gun. He had had one in 1946. With it, just three months after he had married Beryl, he had held up a house in Waterloo. He had got five years for that. And it wasn't his first conviction either. When he came out, a couple of months before the Underley Street shooting, Beryl had told him that she still loved him.

"I'll go straight this time, love," he swore.

He meant it, too. He even took a job as an acetylene welder with a firm of shipwrights. Then Ray Beech acquired another gun.

"Find Walter Richard Beech. Bring him in for questioning." Then, grimly, murder hunt chief Balmer added the ominous warning. "And be careful, he may shoot."

The massive manhunt was mounted. A cordon was thrown round all the roads leading out of the city. Sharp eyes watched from the shadows at rail and bus stations, and at the docks. Big, bulky men, treading like cats, moved through the night. Detectives with pictures of Beech in their pockets

11

visited the spielers, the sleazy clubs that he was known to frequent. In the back streets the constables shone their torches and peered through windows. The radio squad cars moved into action.

More than 300 detectives, uniformed police and tracker dogs raked the territory – the waterfront pubs, the midnight coffee stalls, the all-night cafes, the doss-houses of Sailortown. When dawn came they were still at it, still searching, footsore and weary from pounding the pavements. And all the following morning ... and afternoon ... a hopeless, needle-in-the-haystack quest ... in which they drew blank after blank after blank.

Until, in the late afternoon of 17 April 1951, the phone shrilled in Prescot Street police station.

And now the whole vast operation was to boil down to the quiet courage of two greying detectives facing death in a seedy, backstreet pub. Beaverstock and Gillbanks moved nearer to Beech. For a second or two he looked at them in silence. Then he spoke. "I'm off a Dutch ship," he said. "I haven't got my papers with me. They're just across the road. I'll slip over and get them."

But the CID men weren't falling for that one. "There won't be any need for that," said Beaverstock.

Over Beech's shoulder he caught the landlord Jimmy Hatton's eye. Almost imperceptibly a nod of understanding passed between them. Hatton gestured towards the back parlour. That was where the old dears used to settle down nursing their bottles of stout. At this time of the evening it was empty.

"Would you mind stepping in there with us for a minute?" asked Beaverstock, and they led him

12

into the unoccupied back parlour. Beech went quietly. "We're not satisfied with your explanation," Beaverstock told him. "We have reason to believe that you are Walter Richard Beech, and I must ask you to accompany us."

As Beaverstock and Gillbanks moved forward to close with him, Beech suddenly whipped a revolver out from under his coat. Pointing it at them, he shouted: "Stand back or you'll get it. You're not taking me in."

Beaverstock and Gillbanks froze. Their minds raced. What were they to do? Back away? Unthinkable. Stand their ground? Move nearer? Neither spoke, but as one man they began to edge nearer. "Stop! Stop!" Beech screamed. "It's loaded and you're going to get it."

Beaverstock felt the sweat prickle behind his ears. Gillbanks felt, like palpable blows, the punchings of his heart. "Don't be a fool, man. Put that gun away."

Beaverstock's voice sounded distant and unreal in his own ears.

"Don't be stupid," shouted Gillbanks.

Then, the gun pointing at their stomachs, the detectives advanced, stepped inexorably nearer, nearer. There was a flash. A terrific bang that echoed and re-echoed ringingly, deafeningly, in that tiny room. A wisping puff of blue smoke. An acrid burning smell. "I thought he'd shot Joe," said Beaverstock afterwards.

"I thought Jack had got it," said Gillbanks.

But, dropping his bluster, changing his mind in those final seconds, Beech had fired the sixth and last bullet in his .45 Colt into his own brain. Still dazed, not making much sense, Jack Beaverstock bent down to where Beech lay slumped on the floor, the gun still in his hand. The butt was broken in half.

It was precisely seven minutes later that the first big shiny car pulled in at the kerb outside the Princes Park Hotel. Out leapt Superintendent Balmer. He hurried into the pub. Balmer took from his pocket the half of a gun butt found beside the bodies of the women in Underley Street. He bent down, matched it with the weapon in Beech's stiffening fingers.

It fitted exactly.

"Call off the hunt," he said.

DEATH AT THE
GRAVEYARD OF CHAMPIONS

It was known in the elite circles of boxing and wrestling aficionados as 'The Graveyard of Champions'. Its official name was the Empire Stadium. It was situated at the top of Bixteth Street. The style 'graveyard' had come to be attached to it by reason of the slaughterings and 'deaths' that took place in the square – or squared – ring. The champs all seemed to take the tumble, lose their titles there. But for those *outside* the ropes it was a well-beloved sporting venue, and there are to this day, rheumy-eyed veterans who remember Friday nights as Jack Pye nights – Jack Pye, the 'Uncrowned King of the Mat', Jack Pye, the Doncaster Panther *v* Everybody.

Less happy, though, is the memory of one Sunday night in August 1961, and the death that occurred well away from the sporting arena of the Empire ring. The protagonists were unequally matched – a well-muscled 23-year-old man and a slender 19-year-old girl. He was John Christopher McMenemy, a labourer, who lived with his parents in Lorne Street, near Newsham Park. She was Valerie Sellers, who worked as a waitress in Rhyl, and lived, also with her parents, in the nearby hamlet of Gronant.

What was to turn into tragedy began as delight, joy in each other's company when Chris and Val first got to know one another in the summer of 1960. It did not take Val long to decide that the romantic young man from Liverpool was Mr Right for her. That July she took him proudly home to meet her parents.

Mr and Mrs Isaac Sellers found the pale, red-headed young Liverpudlian presentable and likeable enough, but they could not see much future in the relationship the way the couple's finances were. Nevertheless, not wishing to upset Valerie, when she sought their permission to marry Chris, her father gave her a qualified 'yes'. What occasioned his hesitation was his failure to see how the pair could possibly hope to set up house together on such low wages and with the slender resources they possessed.

Nothing discouraged, fully animated with the optimism of youth, the impecunious young couple carried on courting, toing and froing between their respective parents' houses in Liverpool and North Wales. Although far from wanting to precipitate things, nudge the youngsters into a rash marriage, by the time Christmas came, Isaac Sellers could not help feeling that it was a bit odd that Chris and Val were showing no signs of making any practical plans. He decided, however, to say nothing. Bide his time.

The first months of 1961 slipped by. Still no sign of any movement in the active sphere of matrimonial preparation and Isaac's misgivings returned to surface with even greater force. But Val seemed happy. The last thing that he wanted was to upset her. So he bit his lip and kept mum. In the end, though, he simply could not help himself. He had to speak out.

It was summer again. Almost a year had gone by. On Sunday 30 July, when Chris was spending the weekend with them, Mr Sellers raised the awkward issue. And yes, yes, they chorused, of course they still wanted to get married. And yes again, it was only the problem of money that was stopping them.

Taking Chris to one side, Mr Sellers had a quiet word with him, and, in response to his rather anxious questioning, Chris was bound to come out in the open and agree that there really was very little prospect of his being able to support a wife in the foreseeable future. Obviously thoroughly put out by that piece of home truth talking, Chris and Val had gone upstairs to her room, and Mr Sellers had heard Chris shouting angrily to his daughter, "I'll never marry you!"

She and Chris had been planning to have a night out in Rhyl, but that flew out of the window, and a bitterly weeping Valerie came rushing downstairs to tell her father what Chris had said. And Isaac Sellers told her: "It's probably all for the best." With exemplary tolerance, Mr Sellers told Chris McMenemy that he could stay the night. With placatory intent, no doubt, Chris told him that he was starting work at Mostyn Ironworks in the morning. He then betook himself off to bed. The following morning Mr Sellers gave him half-a-crown for his bus fare, and he left.

Nothing more was heard of him for the best part of a fortnight. Then, suddenly and unexpectedly, at ten o'clock on the evening of 12 August he knocked at the Sellers' door. He was received coldly. He said that he had come to repay Mr Sellers the three pounds and ten shillings that he owed him, and was about to launch into an account of how he was getting on at the ironworks, when he was told that he was no longer welcome in the house, was asked to leave, and told not to call again. After McMenemy had departed, Mr Sellers told his daughter, who had been upstairs in her room throughout, who it was that had called. He also said that he would wake her at 5.30 next morning to go to work in Rhyl.

But when he went in to give her that early call on 13 August, he found her bed empty, and no sign of her anywhere in the house. It was not hard to guess that she had gone off to join McMenemy. Indeed she had, and the pair of them were living rough, wandering about the rural outskirts of Liverpool, sleeping in the barns and outhouses of farms.

On Friday morning – 18 August – they were walking along the Liverpool-Warrington Road. It was at half-past eleven, when they were about eight miles from Warrington, that a car stopped, picked them up, and the driver, a Mr Edward O'Sullivan, took them to a transport cafe near Warrington. Over welcome cups of tea and a bit of a snack, O'Sullivan said that he would drive them up to Glasgow. They arrived there the following afternoon. It was while they were in Glasgow that McMenemy produced a sheath knife, which he carefully and secretively salted away under the dashboard of O'Sullivan's car. After spending only four hours in Glasgow the trio drove back to Liverpool, where O'Sullivan dropped them off. The sight of McMenemy quite openly retrieving his sheath knife from its hiding place, not unnaturally, gave O'Sullivan alarmed pause, and he decided that in the circumstances he was not sorry to see the backs of his late travelling companions.

The next recorded sighting of the lovers is at around 1.40am on Sunday 20 August, when two patrolling policemen saw a couple walking up Bixteth Street towards the Stadium. They had their arms around one another and the woman seemed to be distressed.

It was shortly after this that the lovers had a tiff that rapidly turned into a lethal quarrel. A stupid row over money. A fight for a very different sort of purse from the kind usually on offer at the Liverpool Stadium. It had less than three pounds 'prize money' in it. A fight that rapidly escalated out of all proportion, and ended in death.

The trouble started when Chris demanded some money from Val to buy rum with, and she wouldn't give it to him. "You can have your own [money], but you're not having mine," she told him.

But he was determined. "I am having it," he said, and grabbed her purse. She grabbed it back.

McMenemy, who had been trimming a match with his sheath knife, told Val that if she didn't give him the purse he'd stick the knife in her. The girl continued to defy him, hung on to her purse, and quick as a flash McMenemy plunged his knife into her stomach and seized the purse. She caught hold of his hand. The hand holding the knife. They were standing at the top of a flight of stone steps leading up to a side entrance to the Stadium. They struggled, and fell together, still struggling, down the steps. Val was desperately calling out his name, and, in a state of frenzy, he stabbed her again and again, until she lay still. Then, he took off his tie and wound it round her throat, before covering her head and body with her macintosh.

Leaving her there where he had laid her, Chris McMenemy walked smartly off into the night. He made his way down to the Pier Head and went to the coffee stall there, where he used the money in Val's purse to buy cigarettes and a succession of cups of coffee. Realising with horror that he was now a murderer, McMenemy thought at first of making a run for it, but he knew that it would be hopeless, he would be caught anyway. He walked round and round, frantically thinking what to do, and finally came to a decision. At precisely 3.48am, he stepped into a telephone box and dialled 100. An operator at Liverpool Central GPO exchange answered the call. "What number do you require?" he asked.

The man on the line told him that he wanted him to take a message: "There's a body by the steps behind the Stadium."

"Where are you speaking from?" asked the operator, but the caller hung up without another word. The operator contacted the police. The Post Office went into immediate action, and traced the location of the box from which the call had been made. Meanwhile, despatched by a radio message, Constables Smith and Walton sped in their Land Rover to the scene where the body was alleged to be. It had been no hoax call. There lay the heavily bloodstained corpse of Valerie Sellers, the raincoat draped over her legs. On the ground beside her was a man's tie.

It was now just after 4am.

McMenemy was still hanging about near the Pier Head coffee stall when Smith, Walton, and another police officer arrived there. As they approached, him, they instantly spotted that he was not wearing a tie. They noticed, too, a curious reddish coloured staining on his right hand, and a bloodstain on the cuff of his right sleeve. Constable Smith told him that they were making enquiries into the very recent murder of a young woman, and asked him to account for his movements during the past hour.

"I've been walking about," said McMenemy.

As he was being conducted round behind the coffee stall for further questioning, he suddenly blurted out, "She was my girlfriend. I stabbed her once and she groaned, so I kept on to put her out of her misery. It's in my back; in my waistband."

'It' was the sheath knife. The murder weapon. One of the policemen withdrew it from where it was positioned at the base of McMenemy's spine. Constable Smith, having cautioned McMenemy, arrested him, and he was whisked off to the bridewell in Dale Street. There, he was interviewed at length by Detective Inspector Wade. Searched, he was found to have several of Valerie's belongings in his pockets – a bracelet engraved with the words 'Chris and Val', a cigarette case, and her purse, which was empty. He explained, "When I knew I was getting picked up I didn't want to have any of her money on me, so I threw a note and some silver into the Mersey." Making a full confession, he told Inspector Wade, "It's my fault. I want everyone to know what happened. First, I didn't mean to kill her, I only meant to hurt her, but when she started gurgling, I decided to finish her off."

On 24 August, Mr Sellers was taken to the Liverpool City Mortuary, where he had to undergo the harrowing experience of identifying the body as that of his daughter.

John Christopher McMenemy came up for trial before Lord Chief Justice Parker at Liverpool Crown Court on 1 November 1961, charged with murder in the furtherance of theft, which was then a capital offence, so that he stood in danger of being hanged if found guilty. Even so, he offered no defence. Mr JS Watson, QC appeared on his behalf. Counsel for the prosecution was Mr David Carpmael, QC.

Opening for the Crown, Counsel described the discovery of Valerie Sellers' body, and disclosed the fact that she had been two months pregnant at the time of her death. He went on to outline the couple's aimless wanderings about the Lancashire and Cheshire countryside, after she had fled from home; their days of rough living and nights of rough sleeping. He told of McMenemy's confession to the police.

Isaac Sellers went into the witness-box to speak of his daughter's relationship with McMenemy. Asked if he knew what she was doing after she left home, he replied, "We did not even know where she was." He had, in fact, feared that the couple had gone off to Scotland, where the law allowed anyone over the age of sixteen to marry without their parents' consent.

Dr Charles Arthur St Hill, the pathologist who had carried out the post-mortem on Valerie Steers, gave the cause of death as multiple stab wounds. He testified to having found twelve stab wounds in the centre of her chest, one in the right side of her chest, and a five-and-a-half-inch-deep stab wound in her stomach. Four of her ribs had been severed. Great force, he opined, would have been needed to inflict some of her injuries.

McMenemy elected not to go into the witness-box, neither did he call any witnesses in his defence. He chose rather to rely upon his counsel's speech in mitigation. Mr Watson challenged the prosecution's contention that Valerie had been stabbed in the furtherance of theft and asked the jury: "Are you really satisfied that that was so? Because you have to be convinced of that before you convict this man of capital murder. He may have taken some of her property, but these two people were in love. They wanted to marry each other. Persons in love regard each other's property as their own."

The judge seemed to be summing up in favour of the accused: "The prisoner and the girl were loving friends. They intended to get married. Apart from one quarrel of which we have heard, they remained a loving couple."

But the jury were unimpressed. Doubtless they were appalled by the savagery of the attack. They

23

found McMenemy guilty as charged, pointedly making no recommendation to mercy, and he was duly sentenced to death.

He fared no better at the Appeal Court. His appeal was heard on 17 November 1961. Mr Watson asked the Court to substitute a verdict of manslaughter on grounds of diminished responsibility. He contended that evidence on that score had been available at the time of the original trial. McMenemy had, however, despite the pleas of his family and the strong recommendation of his legal advisers, refused to allow it to be heard. This conduct was surely, said Counsel, indicative of mental abnormality.

Their Lordships disagreed. Dismissing the appeal, Mr Justice Ashworth said that they could hear only new evidence. In this case the evidence had been previously available. It could not be regarded as new. McMenemy could not now be allowed to submit it. He had only himself to blame for his present predicament. But, Mr Justice Ashworth added, any misgivings that the Appeal Court might have were set at rest by the fact that McMenemy's mental responsibility would be carefully examined in other quarters.

And so indeed it turned out. Doctors appointed by the Home Office found that he was not fully responsible for his actions, and he was reprieved. After serving 12 years, John Christopher McMenemy was released in 1973.

THE STRANGLING TEDDY BEAR

"Oh, Teddy Bear," the widow murmured reproachfully, "I am dying. You must always take care of your Boofie."

She smiled up at the young charmer who had just strangled her. And expired. The cup of tea she had brought him minutes before sat, untasted and going cold, on the table.

Now it was Boofie's turn. He had to take care of her. He selected a knife from the sideboard. There was always the pyjama-cord in his pocket – just in case. As he slipped silently up the stairs of the little house in Liverpool's Northbrook Street, church bells, outside, were ringing, chiming for the Sabbath: inside, they were booming in his ears, calling him to a second act of murder.

Softly he turned the handle of Boofie's bedroom door, and saw that she was dressing for church. He put his hands on her shoulders, looked straight into her face, and said flatly, "You know how much I love you. That's why I am going to do this." He seized the girl by the throat. She struggled free and screamed for her mother. "You needn't call for your mother," he said, "I've already killed her."

The tragedy of which this was the awful climax had started six months before, early in 1928 ... It was one of those pouring wet days that every son and daughter of Liverpool knows so well. A ceaseless deluge. Coming down moggies and doggies, as if a gigantic hand had up-ended the Mersey and swamped the city.

Mary Agnes Fontaine, typist, aged 19, stood sheltering and shivering in a shop doorway. A pretty girl, rather frail looking, like a piece of porcelain, but below the frailty was a coolness, a resourcefulness, which was to save her quarter-spent life one nightmare Sunday in the following November.

At first she blushed and ignored the young man who dashed under the dripping eaves into the dry haven of the doorway beside her. They were alone, and she was embarrassed by his presence. He was like a drowned rat, or a sleek water vole. If only she had left him there shivering in the cold. Instead she took him into her home and her heart – and he devoured everything there within. It was like harbouring a stray puppy that grew into a wolf.

The young man, Joseph Reginald Victor Clarke, alias Reginald Kennedy, was decidedly not shy. He could never resist an opportunity of ingratiating himself with a pretty girl, and long before the fury of the rain had abated he had introduced himself in the name of Kennedy. By no stretch of the imagination could he be described as handsome with his slight build, clean-cut features, fair hair slicked back, and horn-rimmed spectacles. He soon confided that he was a wireless operator on one of the Atlantic liners plying regularly between Liverpool and New York. This was not quite accurate, but the seed of glamour was sown, and one thing followed another in time-honoured fashion.

Mary lived alone with her 47-year-old, widowed mother, Mrs Alice Fontaine, at 110 Northbrook Street,

Princes Park – oddly enough, almost opposite the house from which Victor Grayson, the vanishing MP, had disappeared almost a decade before. Life was somewhat bare for the two women, and they were only too willing to accept this well-spoken, lonely orphan of 21 into their home. He infiltrated their cosy cocoon like a deadly virus.

He came first for tea; then – it would have been about the June – he moved in as a paying guest, or rather as an unpaying guest, since it was soon Mary and her widowed mother who were not only doing all the paying out – he never paid a single penny towards his keep – but were also continually lending him sums of money which he never repaid. He finally achieved undisputed security of tenure as a suitor, when he and Mary became officially engaged. There would – or so the duped Fontaines believed – have undoubtedly been a wedding, if, that is, the gallant fiance had not been careless with an ardent letter from a former flame, who clearly believed that the fire was still burning brightly. It was Mrs Fontaine who found it.

The Fontaines should have shown him the door then. For their 'Teddy Bear', as they pet-named him, was really a grizzly bear of the most ferocious and evil *mien*. 'The boy with the hundred sweethearts', as the newspapers were later to call him, was in fact a highly experienced Don Juan. He lived by his wits, or other people's lack of them, and had made a career of sponging off vulnerable women. Like the mistletoe, that parasite of love, he clung and he sucked until his host was dry and empty. His laser-hard, unblinking gaze turned young girls, and older women too, to jelly. "Somehow I could not resist him, and would do anything he suggested," one victim confessed later. "I used to find myself feeling tired and sleepy when he looked into my eyes."

This sounds as if he had hypnotic powers – and that is exactly what he wanted people to think. Hypnotism was still a novelty, strange and exciting, in 1928. Amateur hypnotists abounded and party tricks were the fashion.

But Reginald Clarke had a head start over those who picked it up, like Pelmanism, from a pamphlet. He had learnt it scientifically in a psychology laboratory at Princeton University, in America, where he had acted as a volunteer subject. Do not, though, imagine that he was a student there. He was a pantry-boy. For Joseph Reginald Victor Clarke was a fraud from start to finish. Nor was he an orphan. He simply used the ploy as a sympathy-seeking ruse to ensnare his victims.

Like Münchhausen or Louis de Rougemont, he spun many yarns of adventure in steaming jungles and coconut islands, but the truth was that he was born in King's Lynn, Norfolk. His parents separated, and he was brought up by a female relative. When he was 16, she died, and he sailed to rejoin his mother in Virginia. His stint in the cool pantries of Princeton provided the needed exotic polish. He migrated to Halifax, Nova Scotia, and went too far with the daughter of a rich businessman there. Pursued by threats from her enraged father, in 1927 he worked his passage back to England – as a pantry-boy.

He scarcely had to leave the dockside at Southampton before entrapping a young girl shop assistant, who fell for his charms and chat line. Not only did she dole out money to him, but she also provided him with a becoming wardrobe out of her meagre savings. "Only the best is good enough when I am with you," he told her. Thus immaculately attired, he fed his new bevy of admirers with the old romantic lie that he was the 'sparks' on one of the big Atlantic greyhound liners.

Inevitably, it was not long before he managed to blot his copy-book yet again. Things became a little too hot for him, and, deserting his young benefactress, he migrated to Liverpool, whither his thoroughly starry-eyed Southampton admirer went on sending him money, her heart wrung, no doubt, by his puling letters:

> *Oh girl! Can you imagine wearing the same underclothes for six weeks with never a change? Of not having a bath for three weeks? Or sleeping in a nook of the wall of a warehouse with a sack for mattress, sheets, blankets and counterpane?*

Clarke knew how to write with a fine rhetorical flourish and his pleadings always had the desired effect. The tale of his ripest conquest in the new northern territory of Merseyside reads like a story straight out of the pages of *Decameron Nights*. He wooed four sisters at once, and such was his amatory skill and cunning that, incredibly, none of the girls suspected what was going on. Each thought that he was hers alone. He stole some of their mother's jewellery, including a valuable ring, which he gave as a present to the youngest girl, who was his favourite, and produced the purloined birth certificate of her 22-year-old sister when giving notice to marry the 17-year-old at the Birkenhead Registrar's Office.

His malfeasances discovered, he attempted to strangle the girls' mother, and was forthwith banished from his Mormonic Garden of Eden. Whereupon he waylaid his favourite betrothed in the street. "If I can't have you nobody else shall," he informed the shrinking girl, as he pulled a pyjama-cord from his pocket like a snake, and tightened it around her neck. But the rabbit broke free from the stoat and ran off screaming, "Police!"

The family, anxious to avoid unpleasant publicity, promised not to press charges against him providing that he made no further attempt to contact them, and he moved on. If only he had been stowed away safely then.

It was Mrs Fontaine's chance discovery of the letter from Teddy Bear's old sweetheart in Nova Scotia that shipwrecked his new idyll with the family in Northbrook Street. Outraged, his benefactors ordered him to leave at once. But he refused to sling his hook. He lurked sullenly upstairs and whiled away the time in his lair composing obscene anonymous letters to the Fontaines, mother and daughter. Uncuddly Teddy Bear had turned savage.

Mary and Alice Fontaine went to the police. Detective Sergeant Tomlin, having prosecuted 'certain enquiries', felt it his duty to warn them that their sitting lodger was notorious for 'other girls' and 'other things'. Meanwhile, a paranoid notion was growing fast, like a tiny cactus seed into a prickly plant, in Clarke's beleaguered head. It was that Tomlin fancied his girl, his very own Mary, for himself. If only the detective had been in a position then to eject this ticking bomb, lock, stock and barrel, on to the street. But he was not. And Teddy Bear stayed on, growling and licking his wounds.

The Fontaines, mother and daughter, tried everything they could to reform him. They nagged. They cajoled. They preached. Oh, how they preached!

It was the mother that he sprang at first that Sunday 4 November morning, as her voice, mingling with the clamour of the iron-tongued church bells, yammered on at him – "Get a job." "Pay your debts." "Face up to your responsibilities." "Improve." It did not take much resolution to respond to this demeaning tirade. He choked Mrs Fontaine to death in one minute flat. It turned out that her lungs were weak anyway.

Mary Fontaine was a tougher proposition. Like a Hydra with many heads, she fought back, defying this bloodied bear. He continued producing more and more weapons. He used his powerful thumbs … a pyjama-cord … some electric light flex. He seized her by the hair and repeatedly banged her head on the floor. She kept passing out. Imagine the horror of coming to and finding someone still trying to kill you. Once, he seemed to repent, and revived her. But she screamed again. She would keep screaming. He

31

cut her throat. There was silence – except for the gonging church bells outside, or in his head, he did not know which.

Then, suddenly, she was alive again, and this was probably her last chance of survival. For the moment he was exhausted. She thought hard: it had to be the right approach or it would all be over. She caught his hand and said quietly: "Let us sit on the bed, Teddy Bear. You know I love you. Why have you done all this?"

"I thought you meant to give me up."

"How can you think that?" she said, trying to keep her voice even. "I love you still. Let us go and see Mother."

"For God's sake, don't go now," he begged her.

"You must, Teddy Bear, and tell her you are sorry."

Very, very gently she inched out of the room. He shambled after her. She forced herself to go slowly down the stairs. The front-door came nearer and nearer. She ran at it. It opened. And she was out in the street, with people and the air full of bells. She was screaming and covered in blood, and they had to cut a cord from her neck.

When the police arrived, Clarke was calmly combing his hair in front of a mirror in an upstairs room. He made no attempt to escape. Nor did he defend himself at Liverpool Assizes, on 4 February 1929. He refused to plead insanity, pleaded guilty to murder and attempted murder, and was sentenced to death by Mr Justice Finlay. It was as if the violence of his crimes had sapped all his energy and with it his compulsion to deceive.

"Thank you, my Lord," he rapped curtly.

All who watched were struck by the coolness of his demeanour and his hypnotic gaze. His trial had lasted four and a half minutes.

Later, he wriggled and tried to appeal. He claimed that his full confession was false. His counsel, Basil Nield, sought leave to appeal against conviction. However, the three judges of the Court of Criminal Appeal – Mr Justice Avory, Mr Justice Horridge and Mr Justice Rowlatt – found nothing to justify interference with Clarke's conviction and sentence. In giving judgment, Avory J said that although since Clarke had been under sentence medical evidence had emerged which showed that Mrs Fontaine's lungs had been in a badly diseased condition, and that the prisoner's attack on her had only hastened her natural death, due to asphyxiation by causes beyond Clarke's control, that afforded no answer to the charge, and the application was dismissed.

Clarke made one last bid to save his own life. He decided to make a direct personal appeal to the Home Secretary, Sir William Joynson-Hicks. On the afternoon of 9 March, the news was brought to his cell that his appeal for a reprieve had been carefully considered but no grounds upon which to grant it had been discovered.

Joseph Reginald Victor Clarke was accordingly hanged at Walton Gaol on 12 March 1929. A crowd of some 200 people had gathered outside the prison gates, and most of those sighing figures that bleak Tuesday morning were young women.

Footman with a Handgun

Ambrose Bierce it was, the American author, who, in 1913, mysteriously vanished off the face of the earth, whose collected works were – quoting from the *Introductory Rubric* in *The Order For The Burial of the Dead*, in *The Book of Common Prayer*, – entitled *In the Midst of Life*. And nowhere is the implication of that sobering observation – 'In the midst of life we are in death' – better borne out than in the bizarre happenings which took place in the ancestral hall of the Earls of Derby on the night of 9 October 1952.

Four years before, on 22 July 1948, 28-year-old Lady Isabel Milles-Lade, the sister of the 4th Earl Sondes, had married Edward John Stanley, aged 30, who, earlier that year, had succeeded his grandfather as 18th Earl of Derby. The wedding took place in Westminster Abbey, and King George VI, Queen Elizabeth, and the Princesses Elizabeth and Margaret Rose, were present. And afterwards, there had been a glittering reception, with more than a thousand guests, at the Savoy Hotel.

The newly-weds took up residence at Knowsley Hall, the stately mansion standing magnificent in its great park, between Liverpool and St Helens. Crammed with treasures garnered-in and accumulated here by the Stanleys since the fifteenth century, their seat near the Lancashire village of Knowsley, had always been the place where, traditionally, kings and princes stayed when they visited the north of England.

Now, this October Thursday evening, Lady Derby was sitting alone in the smoke-room there ... and death was soon to enter unbidden through the door. The Earl was away that night, attending as a guest a Territorial Army dinner at nearby Altcar, and his wife was having her evening meal at a small table in front of the television set. The clock had just struck a quarter past eight, when, suddenly, betrayed by just the click of its catch, the smoke-room door slowly began to open. No knock. That was disturbingly unusual. It gave Lady Derby not only quite a start, but also a simultaneous irritation at the intrusion. She was not accustomed to people walking in on her without knocking.

Mild puzzlement escalated rapidly into acute alarm, when her eyes, initially dazzled by the brightness of the television screen, having adjusted themselves sufficiently to the circumambient gloom, she saw the young footman, Harold Winstanley, standing, tall and gaunt, framed in the doorway. From his lip a cigarette dangled insolently, in his hand he was holding a gun, pointing straight at her.

The startled Lady Isabel jumped to her feet.

"What are you doing?" she asked. "What do you want?"

He ignored her questions. All he said was: "Turn round, my lady."

Numbly, she obeyed. An instant later there was an explosion. She felt a violent blow on the back of her neck. It blasted her crashing to the floor. She lay there, beside the television set, feeling the warm blood running out and seeping into the rich pile of the carpet on which she was lying. Some life-preserving instinct, some sixth sense, made her lie there motionless, as one dead. It called for nerve, for rare presence of mind, but it was that brave, prolonged feigning of death that was to save her life.

A terrible silence descended upon the room. Gradually, her ears became attuned to the faint noise of Winstanley's breathing, and she could hear him moving stealthily around. A little while later, her anxiously cocked ear caught the sound of other footsteps entering the room, followed by a voice she recognised as being that of the butler, Walter Stannard, a 40-year-old Yorkshireman. He was asking Winstanley what he was doing in the smoke-room. In answer, he received a short burst of gunfire, and fell dead, thudding on to the carpet close to where, mouse-quiet, her ladyship stretched prone.

Winstanley's restless pacing resumed. In the midst of life …

Another eternity of stifling stillness passed. Then, from the adjoining room, the library, came voices. It was the under-butler, a 29-year-old Londoner, Douglas Stuart, who, worried by the noise of the unusual commotion, had come hurrying along to see what was the matter. Going first into the library, and finding there Winstanley, who had wandered in from next door, he was asking him, in rapid succession, what all the rumpus was about, where was Lady Derby, and, as the pair came through into the smoke-room, why had he a gun in his hand?

But seeing then with horror the bodies of her ladyship and his fellow-servant, Stallard, the chilling realisation of the nature of the situation came tardily to him, and, playing for time and opportunity, he turned to Winstanley:

"Take it easy, Harry. I'll do anything for you, and I'll not tell anybody what I've seen."

The verbal olive branch availed him nothing. Winstanley advanced grimly towards him. Panic rising from his chest into his throat, Stuart, galvanised, made a great leap over a sofa and crouched behind it. Winstanley tripped off a few shots, then stopped. Stuart, believing that the automatic's mechanism had jammed, made a bound for the library door. He was aware of Winstanley following him. He turned, and cried out a final pitiful appeal, "My wife … my wife!"

But the gun barked again, the fatal bullets lodged in him, and he collapsed, wounded, dying, against the door through which he had hoped to escape with his life.

Up on the floor above, His Lordship's valet, William Sullivan, busy tidying the place, had also been disturbed by what he recognised as the unmistakable sound of shooting coming from below. He ran out into the corridor, where he was joined by two frightened young housemaids. All three peered warily over the banister, and saw Winstanley emerging, gun in hand, from the smoke-room. Automatically, without pausing to think about any possible danger, Sullivan went rushing headlong down the stairs to confront Winstanley.

"What's happened? What are you doing with that?" he asked. "What was the noise we heard?"

"I'll tell you when the girls come down," answered Winstanley.

Anne Mitchell, one of the maids, called out to Winstanley: "Why do you want us to come down?"

"I'll tell you when you come down," he said.

The girls shook their heads. They weren't going to be caught like that.

Sullivan did not at all care for the way things were shaping, either. He knew nothing, in fact, of the fate of Lady Derby, Walter Stallard and Douglas Stewart, but having heard the shots and seeing Winstanley's agitated state, decided that discretion can indeed be the better part of valour, and took off as fast as his legs would carry him down the stairs, with Winstanley in hot pursuit and firing from the hip.

Reaching the ground floor, he scorched along the servants' corridor, an iron spray of death-dealing bullets whining and screeching and tearing splinters from the woodwork all about him, and found temporary refuge in a recess beside the lift shaft at the foot of the staircase – but not before one of the bullets had struck him in the hand.

During this phase of the uproar, Lady Derby's personal maid, Elizabeth Doxford, curious to find out the cause of the furore, came out of her room on the second floor. Winstanley was still prowling the servants' corridor, leading off from which was the housekeeper, Mrs Hilda Turley's, room, where she and the assistant-housekeeper, Miss Mary Campbell, had been peaceably watching television. After hearing what Mrs Turley described as a "fearful noise, as if the light bulbs were bursting", the two women had emerged into the perilous corridor just as Winstanley, chasing Sullivan, came hurtling towards them. As Sullivan went to ground in the corner by the lift, Mrs Turley and Miss Campbell ran across to help him. Mrs Turley was bent over the badly bleeding and hysterical man when she felt a sharp, tingling pain in her leg. Another of Winstanley's wild, ricocheting bullets had found its mark.

Winstanley himself approached, his pointing gun menacing the crouched and trembling Sullivan. Brave and cool, Mrs Turley stepped forward, interposed herself between them, laid a gentle hand on the gunman's shoulder and said: "Come on, Harry, what's wrong?" then adding, as surely only an Englishwoman would, "Would you like me to get you a cup of tea?"

Turning to her, Winstanley said: "I won't shoot you, you have been so kind to me." He turned then to Mary Campbell, nodded towards the shrinking Sullivan. "Pick him up," he said.

But Miss Campbell, too terrified, just ran helter-skelter off down the corridor, and Sullivan, by dint of a mammoth effort of will, rose to his feet and tottered unmolested after her.

The last person in that feudal stronghold to attempt to divert Winstanley from his fell purpose was the French chef, Monsieur Paul Dupuy. He walked along the corridor at Winstanley's side, chatting amiably and comfortingly to him, trying to introduce him to reason, until, yielding to impulse, he made his fatal mistake. He tried, as a tactic of surprise, to wrest the gun from Winstanley's grasp. An ill-judged act which triggered instant reaction. Winstanley lashed out, landing a pulverising blow on the Frenchman's head and releasing a nonuplet of bullets that pocked the wall around him like a circus knife-thrower's pattern of deliberate near-misses.

The time had now come for Winstanley's exit. He left by a side entrance to the Hall, walked with brisk movement and firm intention out of the park by Ormskirk Lodge, went into the Coppull House Inn in Knowsley Village, downed a pint of beer, bought a bottle and a packet of crisps to take away – and took them away, to an old barn he happened to know on a nearby lonely country road.

Brooding in the barn, reviewing the terrible events of the last couple of hours, Winstanley came round to the inescapable realisation that so gross and irreversible had been his conduct and its consequences, that no alternative was left to him other than to give himself up. Having, however, no wish to return to the scene of his engineered disasters, he headed for the main road and caught a late bus into Liverpool.

And there, at precisely 11.42pm, from a telephone box in North John Street, Harold Winstanley put a 999 call through to the Liverpool police, and within minutes a police car had sped round to the call box wherein the man who claimed responsibility for what he called "the Knowsley Hall affair" was still standing. He was arrested, lodged in Walton Gaol, and put up for trial before Mr Justice Jones at Manchester Assizes on 16 December 1952.

Defended by Miss Rose Heilbron, instructed by Mr Rex Makin, Winstanley pleaded not guilty. Called by his counsel, Dr Francis H Brisby, Senior

Medical Officer at Walton, testified that, in his view, Winstanley had not been responsible for his actions, being at the time unable to distinguish between right and wrong, or to know the nature and quality of his acts. He was, in Dr Brisby's diagnostic opinion, suffering from "a grave disease of the mind, in the nature of schizophrenia and gross hysteria."

Following the indications of the learned judge's summing-up, the trial jury, without leaving the court-room, found Winstanley guilty but insane, and it was ordered that he should be kept in custody at Broadmoor Special Hospital.

To discover the transaction whereby Winstanley became possessed of the gun with which he wrought so inordinate an amount of damage is of interest. The weapon in question was a Schmeisser 9mm automatic pistol, which was a type of hand gun issued to German paratroopers. On Tuesday 7 October 1952, Winstanley had gone over the water to Hoylake to meet a lad he knew. Well, this lad told Winstanley that he'd managed to get hold of "a smashing Schmeisser", and he was willing to swap it for a leather jacket. They argued and bargained and hummed and hawed, finally agreeing on the platform at Hoylake station to exchange the gun, about 400 rounds of ammunition, and some spare magazines, for £3 and a pair of grey gabardine trousers. The exchange took place the following evening in the toilets at James Street station, in downtown Liverpool.

There is good evidence that Winstanley was very proud of his new acquisition. Answering the front-door bell at Knowsley Hall at about a quarter past nine on the Wednesday (8 October) evening, Winstanley's fellow-footman, Terence Cooke, found Winstanley standing there clutching an expensive bottle of cocktail, which he thrust into Cooke's hand as a present, but Cooke said he did not want it.

A bit later that same evening, Winstanley had asked Cooke if he wanted to see a gun.

"Don't talk daft," Cooke retorted, "you've not got a gun."

"All right," said Winstanley, "I'll go and fetch it."

Which, to Cooke's surprise, he did. He said that he had bought it for £120 from a Pole, and that he would be selling it for double that.

The gun was proudly exhibited, too, to the housemaid, Anne Mitchell, at around five o'clock on the day of the shootings. She was told that he had paid £110 for it, and would be selling it on at a handsome profit.

Everyone was at a total loss to account for Winstanley's homicidal episode. All spoke well of him. He had been a very popular member of the household – "A normally very jolly and good-humoured man," was how Anne Mitchell described him. He was also thought well of by his superiors. Captain McKinney, Lord Derby's comptroller spoke of him as, "… an excellent worker who carried out his duties in a very efficient manner. [He] was jolly and he was easy to get on with. He was a very willing hard worker."

He was 19 years old when he arrived at

Knowsley Hall, in December 1951, as a trainee footman. He came, highly recommended, with a good reference from the Royal Liverpool Golf Club, at Hoylake, where he had worked as a wine steward before his brief military service with the Scots Guards, in which he had enlisted at the age of 17. He had been invalided out within a year, because his physical condition fell well below the promise of his impressive six-foot stature.

Winstanley said that he had been happy at Knowsley Hall. He had been well treated by Lady Derby and all the staff. "I have had no reason to do anybody any harm," he said.

The sole explanation he could offer for his outrageous outburst was panic. When he first went into the smoke-room he had, he said, intended to ask Lady Derby to help him to get rid of the gun. But ... "When she looked at me, I was frightened. I said, 'Turn round,' because I did not want to shoot her while she was looking at me."

The fact of the matter is that none of it makes sense. But there is one, surely significant, clue which emerged when the psychiatrists looked more closely into Harold Winstanley's family's medical records. They found a history of insanity on his mother's side. Lady Derby recovered from her injuries. She lived on to die a natural death at the age of 70, in 1990.

THE CLUE OF THE
THREE WISE MONKEYS

If at Christmastime, that festive season of the year when the pre-lunch sherry tastes sweet – or dry – upon your palate, and the brown and sizzling image of the turkey hovers on the near horizon, I were to invite you to play with me the old word-association game, I would hazard that the word 'sack' would bring to your mind a vision of that cornucopian bag slung traditionally over the broad, red shoulders of that beamingly benevolent, white-whiskered old gentleman, Santa Claus. Or, possibly, if the children are all grown up, and the stamp and patter of tiny feet no longer punctuate the pattern of your Yuletide, the word sack might ally itself in your mind to the word dry – and from this combination would flow the golden stream of a certain, and delectable, variety of sherry.

For myself, however, and no doubt the psychiatrists would draw some very sinister conclusions from this, I have only to hear the word sack and the theatre which lies beneath the vaulted white dome of my skull is instantly set with a very different series of images.

It begins, this grisly charade within my head, in total darkness. Then … gradually … out of the blackness grow glow-worm points of flickering light. They shape themselves into gas-lamps, and, in their fitful yellow radiance, I see a long, dark street. Along this street something is moving. It comes more clearly into focus. It is a hand-cart, and pushing it, two shadowy figures. My vision pans in, as the television people say, on to the hand-cart, and I see upon it a sack. There is something about the contours of that sack that shocks me. For a moment or two I am puzzled, then, suddenly …

But let me begin my winter's night tale at the beginning, for the shades that haunt this Christmastide reverie are no mere marionettes of fantasy. They are the ghosts of flesh and blood, who moved about their nefarious business through the murk of a long-ago December night in Liverpool. Let us turn back the leaves of the calendar. Back through other Christmases. Back beyond the anxious Decembers of the First and Second World Wars. Back to the night of Wednesday 10 December 1913.

It is a night of high wind. A full moon rides among the scudding clouds. A solitary figure is pacing slowly the deserted pavement of Old Hall Street. All around are locked, bolted and shuttered shops and offices. Tall, Dickensian clerks' stools stand forlorn in dark and empty counting-houses. Up and down the aeolian canyon of the wind-loud night street the patient sentinel moves.

He is Walter Musker Eaves, a young ship's steward on shore-leave from the *Empress of Britain*, and he has an appointment to meet his sweetheart, Miss Mary Catherine Shepherd. She is exercising the lady's privilege of being late. He glances at his watch. Half-past seven.

An extra violent gust of wind blusters up from the nearby river, sweeps along the narrow street and,

45

with a clatter, clouts a wooden shutter from the frontage of a shop that Eaves is passing. It strikes him a glancing blow on the head, denting the brand-new bowler he has proudly donned in honour of Miss Shepherd. And, as he stands there ruefully contemplating his damaged headgear, a boy emerges from the shop and picks up the fallen shutter.

"Hey! Just a minute," shouts Eaves. "Your shutter's ruined my new hat."

Quick as a lizard, the boy darts back into the shop. Comes out again seconds later accompanied by a young man in a grey suit. There is some conversation between Eaves and the young man in the grey suit. A reiterated complaint. An apology. Some talk of compensation. A florin is pressed into Eaves' hand. A cordial "Goodnight". The boy and the young man step back into the shop.

Eaves resumes his pacing. Presently he sees the shop-boy walking up the street, pushing a hand-cart. He is followed, several yards behind, by the young man in the grey suit. They disappear in the direction of the Lock Fields – and the Leeds and Liverpool Canal.

In the year 1913, the shop premises at 86 Old Hall Street was occupied by a Mr John Copeland Bradfield, a tarpaulin manufacturer, who also owned a factory in nearby Great Howard Street. Bradfield himself spent the greater part of his time at the works. The shop was managed for him by his 40-year-old spinster sister, Christina Catherine Bradfield.

Miss Bradfield exercised a sensible no-nonsense dominion over a staff of three: Miss Margaret Venables, a typist; George Sumner, a 22-

year-old assistant-cum-packer; and an 18-year-old lad rejoicing in the somewhat ornamental name of Samuel Angeles Elltoft.

When I met her, fifty-eight Decembers on, Miss Venables was an old lady of 79. As I sat with her and her husband in the bright living-room of their house in Maghull discussing the strange events of all those years ago, she told me that, although she was not exactly a tartar, Miss Bradfield was certainly a severely conscientious woman, on the prim side (as befitted a Sunday School teacher), dedicated to her brother's interests, and scrupulous in seeing to it that her tiny staff worked as hard and as honestly as she did.

The hours of business were from half-past eight to six o'clock, and Miss Bradfield was always the first to arrive and the last to leave. It was, said Miss Venables, about ten minutes past six on the evening of 10 December 1913, when, amidst the clutter of rope and twine and piles of horse-cloths and sacks, she put on her hat, coat, and mittens. She was in a hurry as she had a train to catch. She left behind Miss Bradfield, who was busy counting the day's takings, Sumner, who was sweeping the floor, and young Elltoft, who was putting up the shutters.

What was about to be done behind those shutters in that dimly lit shop after Miss Venables had gone safely home, was sheer *Grand Guignol*.

Had Miss Bradfield, one cannot help wondering, any inkling, any fleeting clue, as she sat there beneath the gas-jet, ranging the sovereigns, the half-sovereigns, the silver and copper in neat piles, of the awful thing that

47

hovered in the air of that dusty, old-fashioned shop? Did she, perhaps, glancing up as she shovelled the money – seven pounds and one penny – into the little leather satchel which it was her custom to take home with her each night to her lodgings over the water in Tranmere, see the glittering eye of George Sumner fixed upon her?

Or was it, when he pounced, a total and terrifying surprise?

Imagine, if you can bear to, the split-second of horror, the unspeakable terror, that must have gripped her as she saw that young man, over whom she had ruled with kindly severity for four years eight months, change without warning into a different, an utterly menacing, creature. It was as if the docile shop-cat had, by some nightmare magic, been transformed into a ravening tiger. The sudden and terrible unfamiliarity of the familiar must have nearly stopped her heart.

With ferocious bestiality, this 'quiet' young man fell upon her. He clawed the clothes from her back, humiliated her, assaulted her, and, in a frenzy that surely slipped temporarily over the border of sanity, beat her to death with a rope-splicing fid. It was only when the prim Miss Bradfield, half-nude, trussed up like an obscene, plucked chicken, had been reduced to a bloodied pulp that he finally came to his senses – and found himself standing athwart a corpse.

And where was young Elltoft while all this was happening? We do not know for sure. Nor do we know precisely how the labours of disposal – the cleaning-up, the packaging – were apportioned between the man, Sumner, and the boy, Elltoft. All that we do know, is that the roped and doubled-up body was sewn into a sack (Elltoft was a dab hand with a needle), laid upon the improvised hearse of a hand-cart, and trundled half or three-quarters of a mile through smiling moonlight and wind-rinsed streets.

Up Old Hall Street ... turn right into Leeds Street ... left into Pall Mall. Past lifeless warehouses, depots and manufactories. Not another living soul. Not a single moving vehicle. The universe empty – save for themselves, their dead-weight burden of meat, and a solitary starveling black cat streaking, startled by the rumble of their approach, under a railway arch.

Pall Mall narrows and becomes Love Lane – 'Sugar Land', dominated and overshadowed by the towering bulk of Tate & Lyle's. Then, Love Lane leads, straight as a die, to where, in 1913, the Lock Fields began. And across the clinging clay of this stark and rubble-strewn stretch of industrial no-man's-land they bore the body of Miss Bradfield. There stand the locks. White-painted. Heavy brown timber gates. Slabbed stone basins filled with dark and brooding water.

The moonlight boys tumble the corpse in its sackcloth shroud into the cold, wet grave of the Leeds and Liverpool Canal.

At five minutes to nine the following morning, when Miss Venables arrived, bright and neat, at the shop, she found Sumner and Elltoft already there, busily sweeping. But – unprecedented occurrence – of Miss Bradfield, the early bird manageress, there was no sign. She later told me: "When Miss Bradfield didn't come in that Thursday morning, I never in my wildest dreams thought that she had been murdered. And I certainly didn't think that the boys had anything to do with her disappearance. I always liked George Sumner. He was a good-looking, polite, cheerful young man, and very keen on music. He used to lend me gramophone records. I found it hard to believe he was a murderer. Young Sammy Elltoft was a good boy, too. Very much under George's thumb, though. They were both so calm and collected that morning Miss Bradfield was missing, you'd never have guessed they were involved."

There was still no sign of her when, around eleven o'clock, Mr Bradfield came into the shop in Old Hall Street. And to make matters even more mysterious, her landlady, Miss Holden, had telephoned from Tranmere. Miss Bradfield had not come home last night. Was she all right? Hearing this, Mr Bradfield thought that she might have gone to stay with her married sister, who lived in Wavertree. He made enquiries. No, she had not seen Christina. Worried now, he got in touch with the police.

Meanwhile, shortly after midday, Francis Robinson, master of the barge, *William*, was on the verge of picking the key to the mystery from the lock – No 3 Lock of the Leeds and Liverpool Canal.

Arriving at the eastern end of No 3 Lock, he found himself experiencing unusual difficulty in opening the gates. He put his boat-hook down to investigate, deftly snared the obstruction and drew it up – a large waterlogged bundle. Then, turned pale. Protruding from the dark and dripping sack was a black-stockinged leg. And when the sack had been slit open, and the body which it enshrouded fully revealed, there, suspended, like an identity disk, by a thin silver chain around the neck of the female corpse was … the Clue of the Three Wise Monkeys.

Later that day, Mr Bradfield and Miss Holden went along and identified the body at the Prince's Dock Mortuary. Among other things, there could be no mistaking the silver medallion on the chain. It was a Japanese charm. The Three Wise Monkeys:

> *Swazaru who speaks no evil;*
> *Mizaru who sees no evil;*
> *Kikazaru who hears no evil.*

Christina Bradfield had always worn that lucky charm.

That night, or rather at half-past one on the morning of Friday 12 December, the Liverpool police arrested young Elltoft. They found him sleeping peacefully in bed at his parents' house in Windermere Street, Anfield. They went also to Sumner's lodgings, in Boundary Lane, West Derby. But that young gentleman had already flown.

Throughout the next eight days the greatest manhunt that had ever been seen on Merseyside was mounted. Christmas was still a week or so away, but distinctly gathering its festive shape out of the murk of the December dusk. In the bright-lit streets and shops townsfolk were packing their shopping bags and baskets with gaily-papered parcels.

But while the people of Liverpool went merrily about their seasonal preparations, anxious policemen, with no time and little inclination for festal frivolities, went grimly about their vital search for the man they believed to be the killer. They combed the gigantic warehouses around the docks, the seamen's boarding-houses, the seedy Sailortown pubs and cafes. On the Saturday, squads of detectives mingled with the Christmas shoppers and the crowds at local football matches, for George Sumner was known to be mad about football. His photograph was projected on to the screens of the city's 'electric picture palaces'.

Rumour, that lying jade, had it that he had stowed away on the *Majestic*, bound for New York. The liner was searched at Queenstown, and, yet one more coincidence was uncovered in this chance-riven saga; a steward was discovered aboard whose name happened to be George Sumner.

Spurred on by the offer of £50 reward, Liverpool became a city of peeled eyes and bounty-hunting amateur detectives. But of Sumner – or Ball, as the police had now discovered his real name to be – there was absolutely no trace.

Christmas was only five days away now when, pure chance again, Ball (as we must now call him) was run to earth. It was an old schoolfellow who eventually spotted him in the street. Ball was disguised. He had shaved his thick eyebrows, bought himself a pink eye-patch and a pair of cheap spectacles. But his friend knew George's distinctive shuffling gait. He followed him and saw him go into the Mersey Lodging House Company's establishment at 84 St James' Street, where, it transpired, he had been staying for a week. Then George's friend told a policeman.

In the lodging-house hall, just before midnight on Saturday 20 December – his 23rd birthday – George Ball, alias Sumner, was arrested. His first question to the constable who took him in charge was as to the result of that day's big football match.

The trial of Ball and Elltoft took place in St George's Hall, and opened on 2 February 1914. The prosecution was led by Mr Gordon Hewart, KC, who, in 1922, was to become Lord Chief Justice of England. Ball was defended by Mr Alfred Tobin, KC, who, four years before, had defended Crippen. Elltoft was represented by Mr Lindon Riley.

Ball's defence was a complicated cock-and-bull story about a man with a dark-brown moustache who had suddenly materialised in the shop and held him at gun-point while he clubbed Miss Bradfield to death, then snatched her money-satchel before running off into the night. Left with a corpse on their hands, he and Elltoft had panicked: they had decided that the only thing to do was to get rid of the body.

But when Elltoft went into the witness-box he put paid to any faint chance that Ball might have had. The latter's story simply fell apart. It was a case of hanging together – or being hanged one by one! Elltoft testified: "I was just leaving the shop at about seven or seven-fifteen, when George said, 'Stand outside. I won't be long.' I waited a quarter of an hour on the corner of Virginia Street. Then I went back to the shop. George came to the door.

53

Just then a shutter fell. I put it back. Then George appeared with a hand-cart. I asked him what was in it, and he said a bag of rubbish. I wheeled it to the canal, and George dumped it. When I heard next morning of the disappearance of Miss Bradfield, I had not the slightest idea that anything was wrong."

The jury did not, however, have to rely upon these discrepancies alone. By any common sense yardstick the evidence against Ball was overwhelming. Accordingly, they brought in a verdict of guilty.

So far as Elltoft was concerned, they felt that there was some measure of doubt – a doubt of which they decided to give him the benefit. He was found guilty of being an accessory after the fact, with the rider of a strong recommendation to mercy, and was sentenced to four years' penal servitude.

While George Ball was waiting at Walton to be hanged, he made a full and frank confession of his guilt.

One of the things that weighted the balance in Elltoft's favour was the fact that not a shred of evidence could be adduced to show that he had in any way profited from the death of Miss Bradfield. However, a detective subsequently examining Elltoft's bedroom had a sudden hunch. He unscrewed one of the brass knobs on the boy's bed, and there, nestling inside it, glinted two and a half gold sovereigns. The price of his co-operation? Had the jury known about the cache, things might have gone very differently for young Sammy Elltoft.

It was pure chance that the money was

discovered at all. Indeed, so much in this extraordinary case boiled down to the workings of chance. It was pure chance that that shutter blew down when it did, and fell on Walter Eaves' new hat. If it had not, Eaves very likely would not have noticed, and been able to identify beyond any reasonable doubt, the pair who pushed the hand-cart with its macabre load, to the Lock Fields that night. And his evidence is vital. It was pure chance that Christina Catherine Bradfield's body fouled the lock-gates and lay there awaiting discovery, instead of being swept out by the swirl of the waters into the Mersey, as Ball had calculated.

But chance is a two-edged sword. While it saved the life of Samuel Angeles Elltoft, George Ball justly perished beneath its avenging blade.

Sammy Elltoft has been dead these many years now, but it is a safe bet that every Christmas of his life thereafter he must surely have remembered that long, long ago Yuletide, when, but for his youth and a prodigal gift of luck, he might well himself have ended up decorating not the Christmas, but the fatal gallows, tree.

THE BLOCKHOUSE MURDER

It was back in my fledgling medical student days that I first met Dr James Brierley Firth. He was not a doctor of medicine. Director of the Home Office North Western Forensic Laboratory at Preston, he held a doctorate in science, was a Master of Science, a Fellow of the Royal Institute of Chemistry, and a Member of the Institution of Chemical Engineers. All of these skills he brought to bear in the service of forensic science, which he defined as science applied to the interests of justice.

And very often Dr Firth's expertise was called upon to help in the solving of cases of murder. Among the celebrated ones in which he was significantly involved were those of Dr Clements, the Southport wife-murderer; Mrs Merrifield, the Blackpool poisoner; and that of the two larcenous Liverpool thugs, Burns and Devlin.

It was Firth's recondite ingenuity which contributed to the solution of the riddle of the Man in the Iron Cylinder, and that of the Girl with the Lungful of Diatoms. His assistance was also of vital importance in the unravelling of the mystery of the Blockhouse Murder.

At precisely 6.40pm on the evening of Saturday, 2 November 1940, James Hagan sent his 15-year-old daughter Mary out from the family home in Brookside Avenue, Seaforth, to buy him a packet of cigarettes and a *Liverpool Echo*, giving her two shillings to cover the purchases. The trip, to the newsagent's in nearby Sandy Road and back, ought not to have taken her more than ten or, at the outside, fifteen minutes. But as the time ticked by, and after two hours there was still no sign of Mary, her worried family contacted the local police, and PC Dixon came to the house. Friends and neighbours hearing of the Hagans' plight rallied round to help, and were soon organising search parties to scour the district for the missing girl.

It was a wild, wet night, and black as pitch, for it was wartime, and with the Great May Blitz etched in unforgettable flames in Merseyside's recent memory, the blackout in Liverpool was one of the most strictly enforced in the country. And very necessary that stringency was to prove, for a little over three weeks later, on 28 November 1940, came Liverpool's horror night of land-mines, 30 of them floating slowly down to earth, swaying sinisterly below green parachutes, one of them razing the Junior Technical School in Durning Road, Edgehill, in what Churchill was afterwards to describe as "the worst single incident of the war". Two hundred men, women and children died that Thursday night.

Very cautiously, then, with carefully doused torches emitting no more than an occasional glow-worm point of light, the searchers crept through the darkness.

At the spot in Seaforth where Brook Vale joins up with Cambridge and Sandy Roads, a railway bridge crosses the Waterloo-Lime Street line, and beside that bridge there had been erected at that time a small and rather ugly concrete structure, a miniature military pillbox-style fortress, or blockhouse, designed to function as an anti-invasion obstacle for *in extremis* use as a strong-point by the local defence unit of the Home Guard.

It was a search party led by a local ARP warden that came stumbling up to this dank, soot-stained, and rather forbidding-looking little building. Negotiating as best they could the ankle-deep puddle of dirty water standing in the entrance, they found themselves wrapped in an overwhelming, almost palpable blackness. Safely under cover, it was, however, all right to switch on a torch and rake the surrounding interior of the blockhouse with full beam. Its yellow radiance revealed a filthy floor littered with a detritus of old tins and cigarette packets tossed in through the gun-slits, bits of rag, crumpled sweet-papers, cigarette butts, spent matches and a carpet of myriad winds' sweepings of dead leaves. But ... wait ... there was something else. The hairs on the napes of the searchers' necks prickled. There, lying on the floor just beyond the circle of the torch's light, was a vague human shape. The hunt for Mary Hagan had ended. Her clothing was torn and disarranged. She had been raped and strangled.

It was 1.30am when Dr Firth, who had been summoned by the Seaforth Division of the Lancashire Constabulary, arrived by police car at the blockhouse. Pending the arrival of the forensic expert, nothing had been touched since the discovery of the body. Electric arc-lights had been installed, and after a police photographer had recorded the scene, Firth made a careful examination of the dead girl. She had, he decided, died at about 7pm. He found blood and dirt inside her nose and lips, and a bloodstained bruise and some dirt over the left eye. There were bruises on both sides of the neck. He noted particularly one bloodstain on the left side of the neck. It was composed of hard, dried blood. It seemed to him to be a thumb impression that had been made in fresh blood. It could, he thought, have been made by someone with a cut thumb from which blood was still flowing.

A soiled white handkerchief with a blue border, found under the body and marked with the name 'G Rimmer', was hailed by the detectives with considerable optimistic excitement. Rimmer is a very common name in West Lancashire – originating, so I have been told, in its application to those who lived and worked around the rim of reclaimed Martin Mere – but, disappointingly, all the Rimmers traced and interviewed after searches of nominal rolls, visits to Army camps in the region, and ships docked in the Mersey, yielded no result.

On the ground, underneath the body, was the copy of the *Echo* that Mary had bought, but of the cigarettes or the change from the florin which she had been given there was no sign anywhere.

With the aid of a stirrup-pump – such pumps were common wartime issue for dealing with incendiary bombs – the water was sucked up from where it had pooled on the blockhouse floor, and from the resultant quagmire a number of potential clues were recovered and carefully laid out for examination on blotting-paper.

Among them was a wrapper from a bar of chocolate. Significantly, as it was later to prove, it bore on it traces of zinc ointment and an antiseptic substance. A tiny matching piece from this wrapper was subsequently discovered in a fold of Mary's clothing, and particles of milk chocolate, found, *post mortem,* in her teeth, showed that she had eaten a bar of chocolate shortly before her death.

Also recovered from the water was what was described as 'a piece of soaked fabric'. It was this which, in Firth's skilled hands, was to provide the all-important key to unlock the mystery. He identified this piece of fabric as a strip of gauze made from materials very similar to those normally included in an Army field dressing. His analysis disclosed that it was impregnated with antiflavine. It revealed, too, a substance which he identified as a zinc compound. The gauze also exhibited bloodstains, the positions of which indicated that it had been used to bandage a wounded finger or thumb.

Everything about this fragment of bandage set warning bells ringing in Firth's mind. To begin with, the presence of zinc ointment puzzled him. No military medical orderly would have put zinc on a field dressing. It was quite unnecessary. He felt certain, moreover, that no serving soldier would have opened his field dressing packet to bandage something so slight as a thumb injury. Then there was the fact that he had found traces of zinc and antiflavine on the chocolate wrapper. They were sure proof that the wearer of the bandage had been in contact with Mary Hagan.

So, based on Firth's findings and deductions, the detectives reasoned that if they could track down the owner of the bandage, the chances were that they would also have found the killer. It would be a mammoth task, though, for there were literally thousands of troops stationed in wartime Lancashire.

A start was made visiting hospitals, doctors and chemists. No luck. No one remembered a serviceman with an injured finger or thumb. Next, a radio appeal was put out asking anyone who had seen Mary Hagan before 7pm that night of 2 November, or who had noticed anybody acting suspiciously in the neighbourhood to contact the police. Several witnesses came forward saying that they had seen a young soldier with a Lancashire accent and a cut face. One woman witness told of a soldier with a cut on his face who had approached her just as she was going into her house. He had asked her if he could use her bathroom to clean himself up, as he had been involved in a fight with another soldier. She had refused to let him in because she was alone in the house.

Detectives descended *en masse* to give saturation coverage to the streets around the Brookdale area, questioning people: "Were you in the vicinity of the blockhouse that night?" "Did you see a man thereabouts?" "Have you ever seen a man loitering near it?" This last question because there was reason to believe that the lock on the blockhouse door had been deliberately broken several days before the murder. Uniformly the answers to all the detectives' questions seemed to be "No".

61

Then, at last, "Yes" – from a young married woman. "Several days ago a soldier tried to trip me up on the bridge."

And "Yes" – from a schoolgirl. "There was a soldier on the bridge who looked at me and walked towards the blockhouse. I waited till some people came up before I dared cross the bridge."

And again "Yes" – a barmaid in a local pub remembered a soldier with a damaged thumb coming in on the night of the murder. A tallish young man in the Irish Guards, his right thumb was bleeding and there was blood on his cap. He looked as if he had been running and asked for a cigarette in an agitated sort of way. He had taken a field dressing from his tunic pocket and tried to bandage his thumb himself, but the witness had done it for him.

All this was good, sound, informative stuff, but it was still a needle-in-a-haystack operation trying to find the thumb-sore killer.

On 4 October, Anne McVitte had been cycling along the bank of the Leeds and Liverpool Canal, a mile or so from the scene of the Mary Hagan murder, when she was attacked by a young soldier. She had escaped from his menacing clutches by jumping into the water and swimming across to the opposite bank. He had stolen her purse, containing just under two pounds, and her bicycle. Other witnesses had reported seeing a soldier on the canal bank shortly before the attack. Their descriptions of him sounded uncannily similar to that of the soldier described by witnesses in the Mary Hagan case.

What the frustrated detectives needed was a stroke of luck. It came when they received a telephone call from the police at Streatham, telling them that, on 13 November, they had arrested a soldier who had been found loitering suspiciously in a doorway on Streatham Hill, and who, asked for identification, had run off. He was subsequently identified as Samuel Morgan, of Seaforth. Detectives hurried to London to interview the soldier. He was 28 years old. He was serving with the Irish Guards, and his home was in Berkeley Drive, Seaforth. He had a freshly-healed scar on his right thumb.

Morgan was brought back to Liverpool for questioning, and the police surgeon at Seaforth police station, who, on 15 November, thirteen days after the murder, examined the inch-long, semi-circular wound on his thumb, said that it could be anything from seven days to a fortnight old, and that it might have been caused by a blunt instrument, such as barbed wire, or possibly by a bite. A search was made at Morgan's mother's house, and there, in the bathroom, officers found a quantity of field dressing, which was being used as a face-cloth.

One is inevitably reminded of the case of the 11-year-old London girl, Vera Page, who, in December 1931, was found lying raped and strangled in the shrubbery just inside the driveway of the tradesmen's entrance to 89 Addison Road, Kensington. In the crook of the child's right elbow, detectives found a finger-stall covering a piece of lint smelling strongly of ammonia. Only one person who knew Vera had been wearing a finger-stall. His name was Percy Orlando Rush. Aged 41, married, he lived just a few minutes away from Vera's home, was employed at Whiteley's laundry, and worked with ammonia.

Rush, questioned by the coroner, Ingleby Oddie, stated that he had discarded his finger-stall two days before the murder was committed, and bandages and lint removed from his home were not identical with those of the finger-stall taken from little Vera's body. There were certain other clues, too, which seemed to point to Rush, but neither individually nor collectively did they present with the sort of secure evidence required for a committal. The murder therefore remains officially unsolved. Unofficially, Percy Orlando Rush is regarded as the killer.

In Samuel Morgan's case, the field dressing found at his mother's was sent to Dr Firth for comparison with the piece that had been recovered from the blockhouse. They matched exactly. Witnesses were able to identify Morgan as the soldier seen in the blockhouse area shortly before the murder. His boots were compared with a heel print that had been discovered in the blockhouse. Again, a perfect match. A soil sample collected by Firth from the blockhouse floor presented marked agreement, both spectrographically and microscopically, with soil removed from Morgan's clothing.

Put up at Liverpool Assizes in February 1941, Morgan admitted that he had robbed Mary Hagan of some cigarettes and a few pennies, but denied murdering her. The jury did not believe him. He was hanged at Walton Gaol on 9 April 1941, by Thomas Pierrepoint. He made no confession.

LETHAL BIRDS OF PASSAGE

For the delectation of those whose fancy, like that of Thomas De Quincey, tends to the appreciation of murder as a fine art, there was inaugurated in Edinburgh, in the fifth year of the last century, a wonderful sequence of volumes which was to become justly famed as the *Notable British Trials* series. Between their covers – scarlet for English, green for Scottish – are embalmed full accounts, complete with High Court proceedings transcripts, of what have come to be regarded by those learned in the forensic field, as classic cases of murder. By no means all of the famous trials of the past are, or indeed could be, represented in the series' 83 volumes, but there are sufficient to furnish an exemplary education in an acknowledgedly recondite subject.

In the annals of celebrated crimes, the name of Liverpool is writ large as the scene of two outstanding murder cases. The first is that of Mrs Florence Elizabeth Maybrick, tried at St George's Hall in 1889 for the poisoning with arsenic of her husband, James Maybrick, at Battlecrease House, in Riversdale Road, Aigburth. The second, is that of William Herbert Wallace, the Prudential Assurance Company collector, who, occupying the same dock as Mrs Maybrick earlier, was tried in 1931 for the battering to death of his wife, Julia, in the front parlour of their modest home at 29 Wolverton Street, Anfield. While

Mrs Maybrick's case is included in the *Notable British Trials* series, inexplicably, that of William Herbert Wallace has been omitted from the canon.

As it happens, I can boast personal connections with both of these affairs. The Maybricks were acquaintances of my grandparents, frequently dining at each others' homes, and my grandfather and grandmother actually went with them as their guests in the horse-drawn bus which they had hired for the occasion, to the 1889 Grand National, and were present when, on 29 March, gallant old Frigate, with Tom Beasley up, won, and the Maybricks had that quarrel on the course over Alfred Brierley which is alleged to have precipitated the murder.

I have myself been into Battlecrease House on a couple of occasions. Both were during the days of the Second World War when the place was standing empty, several of its windows bomb-blasted out and boarded-up. One of the window boardings was loose, and I remember clambering in on impulse, at dead of night, and exploring the empty, echoing house with its looming grand staircase throwing eerily moving shadows in the flickering light of my torch. My second visit was in broad daylight and was alarming in a different way. I had ascended to the floor where James Maybrick's death had taken place 53 years before, when I distinctly heard the sound of someone coming up the stairs. Thinking that it might be a tramp who had wandered in to find shelter in the deserted house, I went out on to the landing to look. No one. Nothing. I thereafter searched the place from top to bottom. There was no other living being anywhere in the house. But I did, I remember, find, in a small anteroom upstairs, a dressing-room to a bedroom I suspect, a quite extraordinary heap of dead moths, flies, and bluebottles, forming what looked like a thickish carpet on the floor, as well as a liberal deposit of their dried bodies on the window-sill.

Rather more tenuous is my 'connection' with the Wallace affair. It is simply this: that I was a small boy living in a house in Mossley Hill which Wallace passed closely by on the night of his Qualtroughean Odyssey, and six years before, Dr CG Mort, the Liverpool City Coroner, who held the inquest on Julia Wallace, was the doctor who brought me into the world. Later in life I came to know Mr Hector Munro, Wallace's solicitor, and the Wallaces' next door neighbour, Mr John Sharpe Johnston, with his amazing cupboard full of 57 assorted varieties of truss, still living in Wolverton Street, and still as firmly convinced as ever of Wallace's innocence.

Later still, with my old friend Jonathan Goodman, author of *The Killing of Julia Wallace*, I met, and subjected to severe cross-examination, Richard Gordon Parry, the man whom Wallace named as the killer of his wife. I was also, through the courtesy of the occupants of the Wallaces' old house, permitted to visit both the murder room and the kitchen, where night after night Mr and Mrs Wallace used to sit. Standing in the small front parlour, my feet beside the very spot where poor Julia's body had lain, I was surprised to find how little an after-shock that terrible event has left behind. Of course, the new owners have done a great deal of decorating, and brought about numerous changes in the place. The old gas-fire and the mantel-side gas-brackets have gone, but the contours of the room are as they always were. The kitchen and scullery, on the other hand, have undergone a complete face-lift. No trace of the old atmosphere of one's imagining remains.

And, finally, I found myself acting as defending counsel for Wallace in a mock trial, held under the auspices of the Merseyside Medico-Legal Society in 1977, at the Liverpool Medical Institution, where, arguing against the Liverpool barrister, Mr RH Montgomery, who appeared for the prosecution, I won my case.

What has struck and surprised me, thumbing through my collection of the *Notable British Trials*, is the considerable number of celebrated murderers who, in the course of their abbreviated passages through the world, have, in one way or another, come to rest, or nest, in Liverpool. The contact of some has been fleeting, using the city as a mere staging post.

Oscar Slater, for example – incidentally the subject of William Roughead's meticulous treatment in one of the early, green-bound volumes of the *Notable Scottish Trials* and treated by me in my *The Oscar Slater Murder Story* – is associated with Liverpool in this sort of way. He was the dandified German-Jewish immigrant, professional gambler and whoremaster, wrongly convicted in 1909 of the murder of the wealthy, 82-year-old,

Glasgow spinster, Miss Marion Gilchrist, and who was to languish for more than eighteen years in the bleak granite fastness of Peterhead Convict Prison, on the iron lip's edge of the German Ocean, before, in 1926, Sir Arthur Conan Doyle helped to bring about his belated release. Slater and his French mistress, Andree Antoine, spent the night of 25-26 December 1908, in Room 139 at the North Western Hotel, in Lime Street, before embarking for New York on the Lusitania.*

Then there is Crippen, who is to crime, as Sherlock Holmes is to detection, universally generic. He is remembered as the mild little doctor from Coldwater, Michigan, Hawley Harvey – Peter to his friends – Crippen. Leaving his filleted wife, the former Kunigunde Mackamozki, transmogrified into the latterday music-hall non-star, Belle Elmore, beneath the coal-cellar floor, at 39 Hilldrop Crescent, Holloway, North London, he set sail, with his *inamorata*, Miss Ethel Le Neve, hair cropped, decked out as Master Robinson, and himself posing as the 'boy's' father, Mr John Philo Robinson, aboard the *SS Montrose*, outward bound from Antwerp for Quebec.

Liverpool, in the shape of the ship's master, Captain Henry George Kendall, who lived when ashore at 8 Moss Lane, Aintree, brought about the capture of the fugitive. For his was the lynx eye that spotted the Robinsons', father and son, true identity as Crippen and Le Neve, and sent the first ever wireless message to catch a murderer. And it was to Liverpool that Chief Inspector Walter Dew, who had overtaken the *Montrose* in the faster White

Star liner, *Laurentic*, out of Liverpool, brought the wanted pair back to stand trial in London, at the Old Bailey.

They arrived at the Pier Head in the early afternoon of Saturday 27 August 1910, aboard the White Star liner *Megantic*, and travelled to London by the boat train. Le Neve was found not guilty of being an accessory after the fact, and was discharged. Crippen was sentenced to death, and hanged at Pentonville. I have in my 'Black Museum' collection the crucifix ring which Crippen, a devout convert to Roman Catholicism, wore, and the rosary beads which were entwined in his fingers when Mr Hangman Ellis came to fetch him.

A celebrated murderer who spent the earlier part of his career in Liverpool was Seddon the Poisoner. Frederick Henry Seddon was a greedy, grasping man. He was also a miser. He worked, and there are those who would say most appropriately, as an insurance superintendent, and in the first years of the last century he was practising the art and artifice of his calling in Liverpool, living, in 1900, at 60 Brunswick Road, and in 1901, at 88 Belmont Road, Anfield, just round the corner from where, in Wolverton Street, William Herbert Wallace, another insurance man, with whom Seddon has often been compared and likened, was to come to live fourteen years later.

The Liverpool period of Seddon's life was, of course, long before the time that fame, or, more accurately, infamy, descended upon his balding head. It was in 1910, that, diamond cut diamond, miser met miser, with ultimately mutually tragic results. The female niggard was one Eliza Mary Barrow, a 49-year-old spinster who came to lodge as top-floor tenant of the 14-room house at 63 Tollington Park, Islington, North London, where the Seddon family – Margaret, his wife, their five children, and his father – had taken up residence in 1909, and where Seddon ruled like a tyrant, everyone in the household being frightened of him.

Miss Barrow moved in July 1910, and throughout the succeeding 12 months, Seddon, playing upon her cupidity, systematically mulcted her of her assiduously garnered gold, promising mouth-watering future returns on handed over here-and-now hard cash.

Miss Barrow, it must be§§ said, was a decided oddity. Suspicious, selfish, quarrelsome, badly dressed, and exceedingly parsimonious. She was also densely ignorant, and had a previous history of overfondness for the bottle. She was fond, too, of a 10-year-old orphan boy, Ernest Grant, who lived with her. When, later, she became ill with the classic vomiting and diarrhoea of arsenical poisoning, she quirkily insisted that little Ernie should sleep with her in her distinctly noisome bed. There is small doubt that Seddon poisoned Eliza Barrow, and having done so, running true to form, gave her a cut-price funeral, not failing into the bargain to dun the undertaker for twelve shillings and sixpence commission for having introduced the business.

Miss Barrow's relatives, the Vonderahes, extremely put out at having received no intimation of cousin Eliza Mary's demise until after the funeral, came truffle-snuffling after her gold. Seddon superciliously dismissed them with the unwelcome tidings that she had parted with her scraped-together life-savings to him, in exchange for a guaranteed life-long annuity.

In these misfortunate circumstances, frustrated greed and need generated mistrust in the Vonderahe bosoms. Suspicion arose. So did Miss Barrow, exhumed from Islington Cemetery, and delivered into the probing scientific hands of Doctors Spilsbury and Willcox. They found arsenic. Seddon was arrested and put, with his 37-year-old wife, into the dock of star-rated Number One Court at the Old Bailey.

In the event, he scuppered himself by his demeanour in the witness-box. A hard-headed Lancashire man of business, flinty cool and callously clever, answering every question plausibly, he was described as 'cold and hard as a paving-stone'. He displayed such a jaunty, overweening self-satisfaction in regard to his fiscal acuity and business acumen, was so obviously preposterous and unsympathetic a character, that the jury's backs were arched like cats', and he seemed to them at least capable of being culpable insofar as the crime of calculated acquisition with which he stood charged was concerned. And that, when it came to it, was the verdict of them all. Mrs Seddon was found not guilty – upon hearing which, her husband exhibited his solitary demonstration of human emotion throughout the entire proceedings. He turned to his wife beside him in the dock and planted upon her a resounding kiss, loud and echoing through the tense stillness of the court.

When the time came for Mr Justice Bucknill, who was a freemason, to pronounce sentence of death, Seddon, making a secret masonic sign and declaring to his fellow-mason that "before the Great Architect of the Universe" he was not guilty, so upset the judge that the tears were coursing down his face as he spoke the words of the dread sentence of the law.

Frederick Seddon's overwhelming obsession with money stayed with him right up to the edge of eternity. On his last afternoon on earth he sent out from the condemned cell at Pentonville for his solicitor. He wanted him to tell him what sort of prices his furniture had fetched at auction. On hearing that they had fallen considerably short of his expectations, he showed great rancour, struck the table at which he was sitting with some viciousness, and said, "That's done it!"

To the end, which came on 18 April 1912, he went on insisting on his entire innocence, and met that end pallid but proudly erect, and refusing to join in with the chaplain's prayers.

My friend, Donald Rumbelow, showed me a copy he possessed of the *Notable British Trials* volume on the case. It had belonged to Sir Edward Marshall Hall, who defended Seddon. Beneath the photograph of Seddon which it contained, the Great Defender had written: 'Perhaps the cleverest and certainly the worst scoundrel I ever appeared for.'

THE FATE OF THE
GINGERBREAD TOWN SISTERS

Ormskirk, the little Lancashire market-town 13 miles north east of Liverpool, is a quiet place. Nothing much happens there. Births, marriages and deaths are the alpha to omega of its dramas. The neighbours are plain-speaking, kind-hearted, red rose folk. It is a good place to live. The town has long been famous for its gingerbread and its Church of St Peter and St Paul, which from a distance looks like two churches, because it has both a spire and a separate tower, side by side.

Two tales are told of how this oddness came about. One version is that the tower was added in 1540 to house the bells from Burscough Priory after its dissolution. The other is that there were two sisters of Ormskirk who bequeathed goodly sums of money to the church on the condition, said one of them, that a beautiful steeple be built; said the other, providing that a noble tower be raised. And the story goes that, animated by the greed of Vitellius and the wisdom of Solomon, the incumbent of the time, determined to lay hands on both ladies' legacies, erected both a tower and a steeple.

It is, however, with the tale of two other sisters of Ormskirk that we are here concerned, the Misses Margaret and Mary Ormesher.

In the late evening of Saturday 5 May 1956, Police Constable George Mellor, on duty, cruising alertly in patrol car Z-Quebec-Two, was somewhat

74

disturbed to spot his neighbour, 67-year-old Miss Mary Ormesher, walking home on her own, carrying what he knew to be the day's takings from her sweet and tobacconist's shop in Church Street in a battered brown attache-case under her arm.

It would, according to his reckoning, have been all of six years back that the police had advised her for her own good, either to put her money safely away in a bank, or, at the very least, to have someone walk with her at night the three-quarters of a mile from the shop to her house – Ivydene, 8 Asmall Lane. Miss Ormesher had, it turned out, a deep-rooted dislike and distrust of banks, but, heeding the detective's warning, she had arranged that henceforth Mrs Josephine Whitehouse, who lived over the shop, should escort her home every night. And so she had, each night for six full years, this May-time night an only and a first exception. She had been away visiting friends in Southport.

The following morning, in bright Sunday sunshine, Constable Mellor, off duty, was dutifully cleaning his car, when running along the lane came Tom Cummins, the Ormesher sisters' next-door neighbour at No 6, closely followed by a breathless Mrs Whitehouse.

Earlier that morning, at about ten o'clock, Mrs Whitehouse had carried round to Mary Ormesher – or 'Aunt Polly' as she was affectionately known by the locals – her usual morning cup of tea, and to her surprise had found the shop still locked up. Wondering whatever could be the matter, for Aunt Polly was a creature of disciplined and regular habits, Mrs Whitehouse had put on her hat and coat and set off for Asmall Lane.

Arriving at No 8, she had knocked repeatedly at the sisters' front-door, but could get no reply. There was something vaguely eerie about the unaccustomed shroud of sabbath silence in which the normally twittering little house seemed to be wrapped. Thoroughly puzzled, and with the first twinges of misgivings gradually acceding to alarm, she called at Mr Cummins' house next door.

He agreed that so profound an absence of activity seemed unusual, and deciding to see if anything was wrong, they had gone together through the unlocked side-entry door. Stepping into the back yard, they were disconcerted to see that far from being its normal neat and well-swept tidy self, it was, not to put too fine a point on it, a shambles. A dustbin had been up-ended. Shards of broken milk bottle were scattered about. Red flecks of what looked like splashes of blood spattered part of the whitewashed yard wall. Two unopened milk bottles stood, discreet among the chaos, on the back step.

But the worst was to come. Looking in through the kitchen window, they saw the bodies of Mary and Margaret Ormesher. They were lying on the floor on each side of the big square kitchen table in pools of blood, a vagrant shaft of morning sunlight illuminating their ghastly, ashen features. With one glance, and without more ado, Tom Cummins and Josephine Whitehouse took to their heels and went to spread the terrible tidings.

Arriving at the scene of the double murder, the police were greeted by the sisters' frantically tail-wagging black and white spaniel, Trixie. She had been hiding away when Mr Cummins and Mrs Whitehouse were at the window. They had heard her softly whimpering. She had been injured by a savage kick, probably when she tried to go to the aid of her mistresses. The officers noticed that the faces of the dead women were strangely clean. Trixie had tried to lick her mistresses back to life.

The sisters had both been hideously battered about the head. A poker, a heavy brass candlestick, a kitchen mallet, and a lemonade bottle, the weapons used to bludgeon them, had been thrown down near the bodies. From a trail of blood leading out into the yard, the detectives deduced that one of the victims had made a break for it, but had failed to escape and been dragged back into the house. The attache-case which had contained Saturday's takings lay upturned. It contained about fifty pounds in coins, but there were no pound or ten-shilling notes in it.

The Ormesher sisters belonged to one of the oldest Ormskirk families, and Aunty Polly was widely known in the town as something of a fairy-godmother. Not only was she ever ready with a smile and a sweet or two extra for her little child customers at the shop, but she, together with her 68-year-old sister, Margaret, had lent hundreds of pounds to help people who were in trouble trying to pay off their debts. These kindly-motivated acts of pure charity had inevitably given rise to widespread whisperings that the sisters were wealthy, and were sitting on a fortune hidden away in their house.

There was probably some truth in this, for notwithstanding that the sisters had no bank account, they were planning to spend about £2000 on alterations to the shop, and close friends knew that an old grandfather's clock was used as a safe in which to deposit the accumulated takings. It was searched and found to contain just a few shillings and to be full of empty boxes.

Chief Superintendent Lindsay, of the Lancashire County Constabulary, took command of the investigation. Later, there would be consultations between the Lancashire CID and the Liverpool CID, led by Chief Superintendent James Morris. Dr George Manning, the Home Office pathologist, estimated that the deaths of both sisters had taken place at around midnight on 5-6 May.

There were witnesses to be examined. Thomas Draper, who lived at 10 Asmall Lane, said that he had gone to bed at about 10.45pm on the night of 5 May. His wife, Joan, was in bed reading. He had just been dozing off when he was suddenly awakened by his wife. She had heard a noise. "Get up, Tom. There's someone in the yard." They both distinctly heard the "rattling, quivering sound" of a dustbin lid being disturbed.

Slipping into his trousers, Draper went down to have a look round. He found the dustbin undisturbed. He then checked the wash-house and the coal-house. Both were securely locked. Everything in the yard seemed normal. He was on the point of going back into the house when he heard a strange low moaning noise. At first he thought it was Mr Cummins' dog, two doors down the street. Then he heard the sound of breaking glass and a woman's voice saying softly: "Mr Cummins". This was followed by what sounded like someone tipping rubbish, either next door in the sisters' yard, or a bit further off in Mr Cummins' back yard. Rather puzzled by all this nocturnal activity, but satisfied that no prowler had been in his yard, Mr Draper returned indoors, and went back to bed, dismissing the whole incident as someone having a tiff.

Thomas Cummins, a shipwright, stated that he had heard similar sounds at his residence, 6 Asmall Lane. Earlier on, after visiting his wife, who was ill in Ormskirk Hospital, Mr Cummins had gone for a drink at the Eureka Hotel, in Halsall Lane. He had stayed there until closing time when, in company with a Mrs Allinson and his brother-in-law, Frank Halliwell, who was his lodger, he walked home. This would have been at about 10.45pm. Some ten minutes later, Cummins went over the road to Mr Ashcroft's house – No 17 – with a set of golf clubs.

Alfred Allinson, a miner, who lived with his wife in Brickmakers Arms Yard, off Asmall Lane, had spent the afternoon watching the Cup Final on television at Cummins' house, and, with his 3-year-old son had stayed on watching TV until Cummins got back from his night out at the Eureka. It was about 11pm when Allinson left to go back home. As he was crossing Cummins' back yard with his son in his arms, he heard what he thought was the sound of a milk bottle being broken. It was the sort of noise, he afterwards explained, that a cat might make knocking a bottle over. And then, just like Thomas Draper, he heard a woman's voice saying plaintively: "Oh, Mr Cummins". At first Allinson thought that the voice was that of Mrs Houghton, with whom Cummins had been having a drink earlier on, and that he must have said something to her of which she disapproved. Later, however, Allinson changed his mind, and said that he was practically sure that the voice was that of Miss Margaret Ormesher.

Two witnesses came forward claiming to have seen suspicious characters lurking around Asmall Lane. Eleven-year-old James Houghton, who lived at 37 Asmall Lane, right opposite the Ormesher sisters' house, said that on each of the three nights preceding that of the murder he had, at around 10pm, seen a tall man, wearing a fawn trench coat and dark trousers, in the lane. On the first occasion – 2 May – the man had been leaning on a blue bicycle against the hedge at the end of the block, some 30 yards from the Ormesher house. He had stayed there for the better part of a quarter of an hour, and kept glancing up and down the road. The boy had seen him again, at about the same time, on the Thursday and Friday nights. He did not see him on the Saturday.

Thomas Derbyshire, of Brickmakers Arms Yard, told the detectives that at about 10.20pm on the night of the murder he was walking along Asmall Lane. When he was a few yards away from the entrance to the Brickmakers Arms Yard, he saw a man on the opposite side of the road, just outside the house of his sister, who lived at 19 Asmall Lane, bending down, "as if he was looking for something he might have dropped out of his pocket".

A lad named William Brompton, who lived in Halsall Lane, and who had been out walking with his girlfriend on the night of 5 May, was interviewed. He had, he said, stopped for a while, around 10.45pm in the doorway of a livery stable, about 20 yards from the Ormesher house, but, possibly because their attentions were romantically directed to other quarters, they had, he unblushingly admitted, heard no unusual noises.

The detectives worked long and hard, and cast a wide net. An inch by inch search, involving the importation of tracker dogs from Police HQ at Preston, was carried out over the 1000 square yards immediately surrounding the murder house. The churchyard of St Peter and Paul's was scrutinised, as were the surrounding lanes and woods, for any bloodstained articles that might have been discarded by the killer.

Hospital casualty departments and doctors' surgeries in the district were checked to see if anyone had been treated for cuts and bruises. Inquiries were made at all laundries and dry cleaners' establishments in Ormskirk, Burscough, and Maghull, as to whether they had received any bloodstained clothing. From the disordered state of the kitchen, it was obvious that the sisters had both put up a fierce struggle with their assailant, and he must have been spattered with blood.

Notices were flashed on the screens of cinemas in and around Ormskirk. A patient who had absconded from a mental home on 5 May, and been picked up at Southport on 6 May, was interviewed. Twenty-two of the sisters' relatives, scattered all over the country, were traced, contacted, interviewed, and eliminated from the inquiry.

An Army camp at nearby Burscough was visited, and checks run on all the soldiers, in particular those who had been out of camp on the night of 5 May. Passengers who were regular travellers by bus and rail between Ormskirk and Liverpool were seen. Known local villains and Teddy boys (an unruly socio-sartorial phenomenon of the period) were accorded special attention.

Local shopkeepers and the staff in public-houses were asked to keep a sharp eye out for anyone passing bloodstained banknotes. People were also asked to make contact with the police should anyone offer for sale two valuable items which had been stolen from the sisters – a ladies' watch, platinum case, small face surrounded by some 40 diamond chippings and 20 emeralds, which cost £1,000 in 1942, and a gold ring, set with sapphires and diamonds.

On Friday 11 May 1956, several thousand lined the streets to watch the funeral cortege pass to where 500 sorrowing people packed the tower-and-steepled parish church of Ormskirk to await the arrival of the coffins containing the ill-used bodies of Margaret and Mary, the much-mourned Ormesher sisters. And Canon Redwood, the vicar, addressing the congregation, gave voice for them to their sentiments.

"Nothing," he said, "so dreadful has happened in our peaceful country town before. Most of us are here out of respect for the two gentle-minded souls whom we have known for so long."

The next day, Saturday 12 May, patrons of a drill hall, half a mile from Asmall Lane, where local youths attended Saturday night hops, were questioned, and that night Chief Superintendent Lindsay went along there and interrupted the jollification, casting something of a pall over the assembled dancers with the chilling announcement: "There is abroad in Ormskirk, a brutal murderer who should be put away."

And that is precisely the conclusion that police thinking had arrived at. The killer was a local man. They also thought that there was only one man involved. Whoever it was who had attacked the sisters must have had a good knowledge of their habits and movements.

Lindsay now let it be known that it was his intention to have every man, woman, and child of Ormskirk's 24,000 inhabitants questioned, and every male in the murder area fingerprinted. The detectives went back to square one. More house-to-housing. The forensic team began to fine-tooth-comb No 8 all over again, room by room, and to re-examine the back yard. But it all came to nothing.

George Mellor had a theory though. Long retired and keeping a pub, the Rowditch on the Uttoxeter Road, outside Derby, he confided to an old Fleet Street friend of mine, the celebrated crime reporter, Owen Summers. He was convinced that the old ladies knew their murderer.

"Once inside their house they would very seldom open their door to anyone. I never knew them to invite anyone inside. Only somebody living, or who had lived locally and knowing their habits well, could have somehow talked his way inside or trailed Aunty Polly home."

Whatever the truth of the matter, it all happened a long, long time ago. The years have cast deep shadows over the gentle ladies' grave, and the Beast of Ormskirk was never brought to justice.

THE CLOCKWORK CASK OF DEATH

When I was doing the research for my *Quest For Jack the Ripper*, I came across, a rare booklet, *Leather Apron; or the Horrors of Whitechapel*, compiled in 1888 by Samuel E Hudson, in which I read with some astonishment the following:

> *The mysterious murders of sailors at the great Canada docks, at the port of Liverpool, are today unsolved. Day after day the bodies of seamen were found either upon the bulkheads, or in the waters of the docks, with fearful gashes, until the number reached more than half a score. Then they suddenly ceased, and the police admitted they were baffled. Robbery was not the motive here. Then, what was? Was it killing for the sake of killing? Was it the work of a monomaniac, whose blood-craving appetite was finally appeased? Doubtless such was the fact.*

I must admit, I had never heard of any such series of murders on the Liverpool waterfront, and was intrigued. If they indeed took place, there ought to be some record of them somewhere in the city archives.

Strange birds of passage have come from time to time to roost in the port of Liverpool, blown in by the sea-winds of chance and, sometimes, by evil design. Surely one of the most sinister and mysterious of such ill-omened visitants was the man who called himself Mr W K Thomson.

The first to encounter him, upon the very threshold of his arrival, was a good-natured, amiable and hard-working Liverpool dock labourer by the name of Sullivan. Late one autumn afternoon in the year 1875, Sullivan was making his way home from his work on the quays, when he was approached by a tall, dark man whom he had never set eyes on before. "Forgive me for troubling you," said the stranger, who spoke with the educated voice of a gentleman, "but I wonder if you happen to know of anyone round these parts who has a room to let?"

It was not, however, any common or garden sort of room that he wanted. It had to measure up to certain very precise specifications. First and foremost, it had to be absolutely private and must not be in any way overlooked. Secondly, it had to be suitable to serve as a sort of workshop and bedroom combined. "You see," the stranger explained, "I am an electrical engineer, and I am working on an invention of mine, something to do with the docks, and it's still very secret. I hope to make a lot of money out of it eventually, and I don't want anyone to steal my idea."

Now it just so happened, the long, flexed arm of coincidence being what it is, that Mr Sullivan himself had just the very place that the stranger was looking for. And it just so happened that he had been looking for a tenant. The room was not everybody's choice. In fact, it was a sort of garret, large in area, but with a low ceiling, and lit only by two skylights in the roof. Only pigeons could look through and, in short, it was paradise for a secret-hugging inventor.

Highly delighted, the stranger, who now introduced himself as Mr W K Thomson, went home with Mr Sullivan there and then inspected the garret, expressed his entire satisfaction with it, immediately forked out two weeks' rent in advance without a murmur, and moved in, with assorted gear, the very next day.

The Sullivans nodded sagely to each other when their exotic lodger showed no taste for stirring out of his eyrie, and worked late into the nights. Hadn't he told them exactly what he was up to? Besides, he paid for everything on the nail, like a real gentleman. He sent Mrs Sullivan out for his food. She was glad to oblige, and only too happy to cook it for him. If the truth be told, the Sullivans were rather proud of having an inventor in their house, and they listened with awe to the appropriate noises aloft – hammerings, filings, and a peculiar whirring sound, like clockwork suddenly set off.

After two or three weeks, the symphony of sounds from the attic ceased. He must have finished his invention. Then … BOOM! It was like ten cannons. A terrible explosion rocked the whole house and filled it with choking fumes and thick smoke. Upstairs in the eyrie, shattered skylight glass lay like a snowfall of glittering, lethal-edged ice. Mr Thomson emerged from the smoke and smother unscathed, but with ruffled feathers, parroting frenzied apologies. Some chemicals had ignited accidentally, he explained. And, yes, of course he would pay for the damage, every last penny of the cost.

When their upright hair had settled down again, the reassembled Sullivans forgave their perilsome lodger. After all, inventors were eccentric, weren't they? And accidents would happen, wouldn't they? Thomson told them that he had nearly finished his work and would be off soon anyway. Meanwhile, he fixed a tarpaulin over the roof, to keep out the relentless Merseyside rain.

The explosion seemed to have summoned up strange creatures out of the pit! The Sullivans' hermit-like lodger turned out to have unsuspected acquaintances in Liverpool. A succession of furtive, unappetising figures slunk upstairs after dusk, stayed all night, and slunk away again before the sun was up. The Sullivans were hard put to find an explanation for all this sudden clandestine nocturnal activity, and could only suppose that these were secret-sharers with a vested interest in their extraordinary lodger's invention.

Mr Thomson's welcome was by now wearing a little thin. To make matters worse, gossiping neighbours were having a field-day, and the antennæ of the local police were beginning to quiver. A constable called. He half expected to find a coiner's den, but the tableau in the attic did not fit. Thomson was sitting at a long, low table on which were strewn pieces of clockwork apparatus in different stages of manufacture. There was a big tin trunk in a murky corner of the room, and the constable opened it both cautiously and hopefully. It was crammed with little packages of a substance that looked like compressed oil-cake. The constable picked some up. It was sticky. He sniffed it. It smelt terrible – like sulphur. He dropped it back in the trunk – obviously harmless – and took a civil leave of the stranger, with profuse apologies.

But birds disturbed in their nests never feel safe there again. That night Thomson decamped, taking with him most of his belongings, and the Liverpool garret lay bare and untenanted again, the only relic of its late occupant, a hole in the roof and a lingering smell of sulphur on the air. Mephistopheles had fled.

He went to ground in Preston – in a locality known as 'The Dust Hole', which, as its name implies, was a twilight world through which even a Jack the Ripper could have flitted without remark. When he felt the hounds were off, the foxy Thomson moved on to Southampton. There he donned a new mask. The explosive inventor was transformed into a rich American antique collector, a connoisseur of paintings, intaglios, old engraved gems, and suchlike costly collectables.

In this new guise, he strode confidently into a shipping agents' office, deposited with them several heavy cases containing, he said, valuable antiques, and arranged for them to forward them to New York, via the steamship *Mosel*, of the North German Lloyd Line. The *Mosel* was listed to call at Southampton on 12 December 1875, having set sail from Bremerhaven, Germany, on 11 December. The consignment of antiques to be put aboard at Southampton was heavily insured. That was the crux of the whole devilish plot.

Thomson then travelled to Bremerhaven, where he had had confederates take a villa for him on the outskirts of the town. His workshop this time was a coach-house attached to the villa. He ordered a puzzled local cooper to make a curiously-shaped oblong cask for him. Delivered to the coach-house, it was promptly filled with his clockwork apparatus and sulphur-reeking packages. On 10 December, he arranged for the cask to be shipped to New York on the *Mosel*. At the same time, he booked a passage on the *Mosel* for himself – but only from Bremerhaven to Southampton.

That December night, one of the worst frosts in living memory struck Bremerhaven. It spread an iron-hard glaze over streets and quays. A skidding, straining dray-horse arrived safely at the docks with his cart loaded with Thomson's cask. It drew alongside the *Mosel*. Then, as the horse leaned back in the shafts, his feet slipped from under him, the cart tilted, and the cask toppled out with a crash. The explosion which followed was like an erupting volcano. A dazzling white light plumed high up in the air like shooting lava. Horse, cart, driver – simply disappeared. Where they had stood, yawned a great crater, all of 30 yards in circumference. About 80 people on the docks, mainly relatives and friends seeing off departing passengers on the *Mosel*, were killed outright in the holocaust, and more than 100 injured. The *Mosel* itself was a listing wreck, its decks plastered with groaning victims.

Down below in his first-class cabin, Mr W K Thomson lay mortally wounded. He had shot himself when he realised that his elaborate plan had misfired. He died after five days of agony – a fitting end, surely, for this merciless dynamitard. For the mysterious packages in his clockwork cask of death were, of course, of dynamite, which was not so well understood here in those days as it was in the Wild West! He had manufactured an immensely powerful, primitive bomb, of the accuracy of whose clockwork setting he was so confident that he was prepared to travel part of the voyage, from Bremerhaven to Southampton, knowing that his infernal machine, stowed in the hold, was clicking away the minutes, until it was set to explode in mid-Atlantic, long after he had left the *Mosel*, and his bogus antiques had been loaded at Southampton. Then all he had to do was … collect the insurance money.

The magnitude of this little-known crime is amazing. What makes it all even more sinister is that the *Mosel* plot may not even have been the first trial run. A clockmaker named Fuch, who lived in the German town of Derenburg, told the police that two years previously, in 1873, he had made a clockwork machine to Thomson's order, which was so strange that he made a duplicate model of his own, and kept it. It was found that it could be set to go off up to ten days in advance.

Two machines to this specification, one after the other, had been delivered to Thomson by Fuch. And in that year of 1873, two fine vessels were lost without trace in calm waters. The *SS Ella*, bound from London to Hamburg, and the *Scorpio*, bound from Cardiff to Charente, and all who sailed in them, had been swallowed up as mysteriously as if they had been in the latter-day Bermuda triangle.

After the *Mosel* disaster, it needed no Sherlock Holmes to check out that both the *Ella* and the *Scorpio*, had carried aboard them cases of 'antiques' – heavily insured. In their holds, we may be sure, was a clockwork cask of death.

THE RIDDLE OF THE HANGING BOY

The radio was still on and the fire was blazing away merrily in the grate. A cosy kitchen scene in the big, comfortable house in Edge Lane, Liverpool. Except, that is, for one thing ... the body of a young boy dangling from the rope of a clothes-rack.

A lad named Ernest Johnson made the grim discovery. Passing the house of his relatives, the Greeneys, at about 10pm that February night in 1946, he was surprised to see the front-door wide open, and all the lights in the house on, their radiance streaming out into the garden. He decided to investigate. What he saw in that familiar kitchen sent him scampering, terrified, out into the night, racing wildly round the neighbourhood in search of Mr and Mrs Greeney. He ran them to earth at a local hotel, where they had been enjoying an evening out.

They rushed back to the house, but there was nothing they could do. Their 11-year-old son, Charles, was beyond help. There was a second shock for the Greeneys that night. Their house had been burgled. But in their grief at the loss of their son, the loss of a carpet, linoleum, jewellery, furs and a marble clock was a mere nothing.

The burglary had more significance for the police, because it seemed to them to provide a reason for the death of the boy. They were not prepared to accept that this death of so young a boy was suicide. It might, of course, just turn out to be an accident. Adventurous, experimental boys had been known to hang themselves by mistake. To support this idea, on the floor, under the body, lay a book about the exploits of Boy Scouts, which Charles had been reading when his parents left him on his own earlier in the evening.

But if it were an accident, was it not a huge coincidence that burglars should have selected that very evening, and precisely those two or three hours when the boy was on his own, to rampage through the house? Suicide or accident contemporaneous with burglary? It seemed most unlikely. Murder was the best bet. The burglar or burglars must have hanged him.

Two forensic specialists, Dr J B Firth and the pathologist, Dr W H Grace, were called in. Dr Firth's main area of investigation was the kitchen. He looked first at the clothes-airer. Before the era of the tumble-dryer, no kitchen was complete without one of those dodo-like contraptions. It usually hung from the ceiling above the fireplace, and consisted of half a dozen long wooden slats which rested at either end in an iron bracket. It could be lowered to waist-level for loading by a pulley-rope at one end, and would then be hoisted up to allow the washing to dry. Two knots, held by a cleat in the wall, secured the two positions – up and down. When Charles Greeney was found, the airer was in the up position, and his neck was strangled by the pulley-rope itself, his head in the loop above the higher knot.

How did he get there? Had he put his own head in the loop? In that case, he would have had to stand on something to reach it. There was a small fireside chair underneath. But there were no footmarks on either the seat or the arms. If he had stood on the arms he would have had to hold on to something else to support himself. He could only have held on to the mantelshelf, but this was thick with dust, and it was unmarked. Equally, if it had been an accident, or if someone else had elevated him, surely there should have been signs of a struggle, a fight for life? There was not.

But Dr Grace, who performed the post-mortem at the Royal Infirmary, had a perfect answer to that. He found evidence of recent bruising in the deeper tissues of the right temporal region, in front of the ear, as the result of a heavy blow, which could have incapacitated the boy before he was hanged. He could, in other words, have been unconscious. And so the police doctors worked on the theory that when the boy disturbed some burglars, they knocked him out, realised that he had seen them, and decided to finish him off by a method which involved no messy blood-letting, no weapon to dispose of, and no fingerprints.

The police anticipated that if the burglars were found, their defence against a charge of murder would be that the boy died by accident or suicide. Therefore, those two possibilities had to be eliminated. Dr Firth did some experiments. He established that even if he had stood on the chair, Charles Greeney could not have reached the rope above the higher knot. He could have taken the rope off the cleat and let the whole airer down, but there was then absolutely no way in which he could have hoisted the heavy airer – and himself –

to the up position. In order to do that, he would have to have been 'helped' by other hands. In which case, if the rope had first been removed from the cleat, it would have been difficult for only one person to manipulate ropes and boy. It would have been perfectly possible, though, just to part the double rope above the higher knot and insert the boy's head. The heavy tension caused by the loaded clothes-rack would have caused death in a matter of seconds rather than minutes.

A thousand sightseers crowded the streets for Charles Greeney's funeral: the Army was out in force to control hysterical scenes.

Within days, the police had arrested six men on suspicion of murder. All six were committed for trial on charges of house-breaking and theft, but only four of them – James Welsh, a seaman aged 25; Charles Lawrenson, also a seaman, aged 31; Henry Joseph White, a decorator, aged 24; and Thomas McGlynn, a ship's fireman, also aged 24 – were indicted for murder. Two of the men had admitted seeing the boy in the kitchen, and two others admitted knowing that he was in there. One of the accused, when arrested, was alleged to have said: "I can't understand what happened. They can't hang six for one, can they? Don't you think the kid could have done it himself?"

The four men pleaded not guilty to murder at their trial before Mr Justice Sellers at Manchester Assizes, and they chose not to give evidence in the witness-box.

The medical evidence suggested that the death could have occurred at any time between 8.30pm and 10.30pm. That meant that it was not beyond the realms of possibility that the boy was already dead before the men entered the house.

The Defence tried desperately to show that Charles Greeney was adventurous and accident-prone. Counsel for the defence, Mr Basil Nield, KC, had had the opportunity of examining a book which the boy had apparently been reading just before the tragedy, and he found in it one story about a highwayman called Brown Billy in which there were several references to hanging. But the boy's father would have none of it. His son was not accident-prone. He did did not enjoy reading thrillers. He was not adventurous by nature, and his ambition was learning to play the piano.

Well, said the Defence, suppose the boy for some reason climbed on to the polished arm of the chair, slipped, and clutched at the rope, thus pulling it down around his neck, fell, hitting his head against the mantelshelf, and was left suspended. This bruise could, of course, equally well have been caused by the boy's head having come into contact with the mantelshelf. Two of the intruders, in statements to the police, said that they had seen the boy apparently standing on the chair with his back to them and looking towards the mantelshelf. They had thought the lad was deaf, because he had not heard the noise when they burst panels in the door.

The Defence called only one witness, the celebrated pathologist, Professor Glaister. His credo was: "'Never jump to conclusions' must be a constant golden rule in forensic medicine ... All possible aspects of a situation have to be fully explored before an opinion is given. Even then, opinions can differ, and this is a healthy thing because it is right and proper that in evidence-giving such differences between experts open up a wide field of interrogation and afford the Court a broader consideration in the final judgment."

It was just such a difference of opinion which resulted in Glaister's coming down from Scotland, where, following in his father, John Glaister's footsteps, he occupied the Chair of Forensic Medicine at Glasgow University, to appear at Manchester, where, in the course of his expert witness testimony, he uttered the all-important words: "There is nothing specific to show in what way the hanging occurred. Everything is consistent with accident and there is nothing definitely indicative of homicide." As he subsequently wrote in his autobiography: "It was the first and still remains the only case in which I have been concerned where there was a charge of murder by hanging. The Crown had secured the evidence of several experienced medical men to support the theory that the house-breakers had, in fact, murdered the boy in this fashion. But I felt differently, for a number of reasons. The chair the men had mentioned had been present in the room, and, though its seat was a few inches below the level of the boy's feet, its wooden arms were on a rough parallel. The time of the boy's death was said to have been about 10pm, which came close to coinciding with the arrival of the four men. Yet I felt this was open to challenge if the boy had hanged himself. I had made some study of the incidence of various types of hanging fatalities, and sketched some of the details in my preliminary report to defence counsel.

"Statistically, suicidal hanging is by far the most common form and has been known to take place at all ages from boyhood to old age. It often occurs by accident. It is rare to find a case of hanging which is the result of homicide, but there is definite reason to believe that boys have unintentionally destroyed themselves by hanging from a strange principle of imitation or curiosity. Of all forms of murder, too, hanging is one of the most difficult. In most cases where a person has been hanged by others it has been found that this was done after death as an attempt to suggest suicide. The boy's body showed no evidence of a struggle, tearing, or even disarranging of clothing, and no significant injury. From all the evidence defence counsel put before me, the picture was perfectly consistent with suicidal or, more likely, accidental hanging."

Glaister's belief was that Charles Greeney's death was accidental, and that: "... probably, like so many others, while he was carrying out an adventurous experiment which was, by a quirk of fate, to end in tragedy just before the four men broke into his home."

There is an interesting corollary, provided by Glaister. He tells how, a couple of days after discussing with his sister the trial at Liverpool, arguing that it was impossible for the Liverpool boy to have slipped off a chair, and adding, "I'll prove it," a 16-year-old boy of Tonbridge, in Kent, was found dead in his bedroom. He was kneeling beside his bed, his chest against a chair, a noose round his neck, and the rope attached to the bedrail. Recording a verdict of accidental death, the coroner said: "I think it is quite likely, knowing his fondness for experimenting with ropes and following the remarks made to his sister, that this boy was experimenting with something on these lines and that, unfortunately, the experiment went wrong."

In his summing-up the learned judge hammered home the crux of the case. If the jury were to say to themselves, "Although we are not certain that it was an accident, we are not certain that it was not," then the verdict must be not guilty.

And that was the verdict they brought in. So ... the riddle of the Hanging Boy of Edge Lane remains – a riddle. Well, technically at any rate.

THE CAFFERATA POISONING CASE

There is, or was within living memory, a dark old house situated in the Vauxhall Road area of the fair city of Liverpool. The house, like many another in that quarter, had fallen upon evil times. It had seen change and decay. It flaked and peeled like some sick animal in a neglected zoo. But the darkness of that house was not entirely a matter of mouldering masonry and soot-grimed bricks. It came as much from the inside as the outside. For dark deeds had been done there, and it was, I believe, the legacy of those deeds, staining its atmosphere as surely as the smokes and fogs of a hundred years had stained its brickwork, that imparted to it the forbidding air with which it always seemed enwrapped.

The plain fact is that that old house was once the lair of a secret poisoner. Within those walls had dwelt merciless cunning, and therein had been enacted scenes of great cruelty and anguish, culminating in what it was the custom of those times to designate, 'murder most foul'.

Certainly there had been nothing sinister about the place in the year 1854, when Mrs Ann James arrived from the fresh-blown pastures of her native Devonshire, healthy, happy, and full of hope and ambition, to take up residence there. A clever, capable woman, Mrs James had rapidly transformed her new home into a thriving place of business. On the ground-floor she opened up a grocery shop, and a large room where meals and refreshments were served and several of the upstairs rooms were let to lodgers. Soon, the enterprising Mrs James found herself salting away a tidy nest-egg of savings.

Success brought in its wake a sizeable train of relatives. In next to no time Mrs James was joined by her married sister, Eliza Townsend. With her came her invalid husband and their three sons. Next to arrive were Ann James' married niece and her husband, a japanner by trade and Cafferata by name. And then there were eight ...

Nine, actually, for there hove upon the scene now a gentleman named Thomas Winslow. A former ironworker, he started off in the somewhat crowded James household as an upstairs lodger, but achieved rapid promotion – first, as *major-domo* of the lodging side of the business, and subsequently and additionally as manager of the grocery shop.

Predictably, this led to some degree of ill-feeling among the Jamesian relatives. They did not take to Winslow. They liked even less what they regarded as the disproportionate influence which he seemed to be exercising over Mrs James. It soon became a house divided: the Townsends and the Cafferatas on the one hand, Winslow on the other, and poor Mrs James fair and square in the middle.

The Townsend-Cafferata faction sustained a swingeing blow when, first, Mr Townsend, and then, in rapid succession, Eliza Townsend and two of her three sons, died.

That left only one Townsend – young Martin, a bit of a nuisance, forever joining, and having to be bought out of, the Army, but not rating as a very significant arms-bearing adversary in the internecine war – and the two Cafferatas.

Even by the high standards of Victorian mortality rates, the occurrence of four deaths in one family in so short a span of time was suspicious. In the light of later events, the arteries of suspicion harden into virtual certainty of the operation of compound foul play.

In the January of 1860, Mrs James herself was laid low by several mysterious attacks of illness, during one of which Mr Winslow somehow persuaded her to sign an authority, which he had written out, for him to withdraw the £130 which she had amassed in the savings bank. He also went to the Gas Company, where she had four gas shares valued at £200, and tried to get them entered in his name. On being told that this could not be done without a proper transfer, or by will, he arranged for the solicitor of the Gas Company to see Mrs James, and draw up such a will. In this document the business and the stock-in-trade were bequeathed to Winslow, and it was directed that the remainder of the property should be divided equally between Mrs Cafferata and Martin Townsend.

On 5 February, Mrs James suffered so severe an attack of the mystery illness that Dr Cameron, Physician to the Southern Hospital, was summoned. Three weeks later, Thomas Winslow wrote to Mrs Cafferata, who was away in Manchester, telling her that she must come at once if she wished to see her aunt alive. She came, and, for a fortnight, slept in the same bed with Aunt

Ann in the back-parlour. During that time she could not help noticing how exemplarily attentive Winslow was, showing great interest in Mrs James' fluctuating condition, and insisting upon bringing all her meals to her himself.

Very gradually, the invalid seemed to improve. Then, on 29 March, came a severe relapse, and Dr Cameron was hastily sent for. Again, his patient got gradually better. But further and worse relapses followed, with the worried doctor in attendance, on May 8th and 25th.

And, indeed, there were by now very tangible grounds for worry. Four times in less than four months he had been urgently summoned. Always the symptoms were the same – the patient in great distress, suffering from violent purging and vomiting. This time as he came out of the hushed sickroom he felt absolutely certain of it – a secret poisoner was at work in that house. Someone was trying to destroy Mrs James. When he left, the doctor had certain samples and specimens in his bag. He was going to have them analysed. Then he would know if he was right.

He had his answer on 10 June. The analyst had found indisputable traces of antimony.

Dr Cameron acted swiftly. He communicated with the police and with them, he went to his patient's home. The police took possession of all the medicine bottles and a number of cups that were in the patient's room, and Dr Cameron had Mrs James removed to the Southern Hospital, out of harm's way. Sadly it was too late, for there, on 24 June, she died.

A post-mortem revealed the presence of cancer in the intestine, and the pathologist gave cancer as the cause of death, but added that death had been accelerated by the administration of continual small doses of antimony. On the basis of this evidence, Thomas Winslow was arrested. He vehemently protested his innocence, accusing the Cafferatas of having poisoned Mrs James.

His trial opened at Liverpool on 20 August 1860. Testimony that he had been trying to obtain antimony was given by a Mrs Ann Foley, a woman who had once worked for Mrs James. She said that Winslow had given her tuppence and told her to go and buy some antimony, "for the dog". But the chemist would not let her have it.

More damaging was the evidence of a boy, Thomas Maguire, who had also lodged at Mrs James' house. He said that he had purchased a white powder from a bottle labelled 'Ant.' at William Miller's chemist's shop in Tithebarn Street, and had given it to Winslow. He had several times seen Winslow cutting bread in the kitchen for the mistress, take a white powder in a paper from his pocket, and sprinkling it on the bread before he buttered it.

In his charge to the jury, the trial judge, Baron Martin, told them that if the prisoner administered antimony with the intention of killing, and the deceased's death from a natural disease was thus accelerated, that was murder, but they must not convict unless the evidence satisfied their minds of his guilt.

Apparently it did not. Winslow's defence lawyers must have done their job well, for it took the jury only a few minutes to bring in a verdict of Not Guilty. So, officially at least, the Liverpool Poisoning Mystery remained just that – a mystery.

But if not Winslow, who? The Cafferatas? Young Martin Townsend?

The old dark house has kept its secret, but if stones could speak, I am pretty sure of the name that they would whisper ...

THE SKELETON OF BRANDY COVE

One day, in the year 1919, a quiet, very ordinary-looking little man sat down in the Compton Hotel in Liverpool and wrote a letter to the girl he called 'Wifie', and loved with all his broken heart: "I gave myself to you long ago, but you never seemed to care after the first few weeks ... I gave you my name and my love, and you trifled with both."

There are, I suspect, few people in Liverpool now who remember the old Compton Hotel. It stood in Church Street, just opposite where St Peter's Church stood until its demolition in 1923, and where Woolworths used to stand. Even eighty-odd years ago it was something of a relic, perpetuating in its name the glory that was Compton House – the vast building which has been described as 'a romance in brick and stone'.

The story of the great Victorian store known as Compton House began humbly, about the year 1832, when two enterprising young Liverpool men, James Redcliffe Jeffery and James Morrish, opened a small draper's shop on the corner of Church Street and Basnett Street. The bold affrontery conveyed by its *avant-garde* air, flatteringly combined with the tact and politeness displayed to its customers, and its outstanding business efficiency, speedily built up a first class reputation for the shop, together with a solid body of loyal and satisfied clients.

In what seemed like no time at all, the premises extended itself, adding department after department, where you could buy anything from a kitchen saucepan or an elegant ornamental clock, to a horse's saddle, household furniture or a travelling trunk, to the finest ladies' millinery, and the best quality gentlemen's clothing. One after another, adjoining premises were eaten up, new departments added, until the original little draper's shop had swollen into a huge department store with a frontage that occupied the entire block from Basnett Street to Tarleton Street, and stretched as far back as Williamson Square.

Then, on 1 December 1865, it all went up in smoke – literally. A shop-boy's carelessly jettisoned lucifer burnt the whole place to the ground. Since James Morrish had, in 1860, retired from the business, taking with him the tidy fortune that was his share, to James Jeffery, the sole owner, fell the daunting task of rebuilding. He set to work with iron will and steely strength of purpose, and amazingly, by 1867 Compton House had arisen again out of the ashes. But alas, the economic climate had changed, and the expenses of running the new Compton House amounted to more than double those which had been required for the smooth working of its predecessor, and after a Gargantuan struggle for survival, the final shutters were put up in March 1876.

Sadly, not long thereafter, James Jeffery, a man broken in health and spirit, faded away like a ghost – but his giant brick and mortar shadow was still cast over the Liverpool of 1919, and the Compton Hotel occupied the upper part of the old building.

The leaves of the calendar turn. Forty-two years flicker by. The scene changes. It is the year 1961. The month of December. We are in the Coroner's Court at Gowerton, Glamorgan. Gleaming, strangely white in the dusky twilight of late afternoon, there lie on the polished surface of an oaken table a pathetic little heap of human bones. For nearly eight hours the coroner and his seven-man jury have been trying to find the answer to a grim riddle. Was it possible that here, in that small bundle of crumbling bones, lay the answer to a question which for forty-two years had mystified the whole of Britain? – Where is Mamie Stuart? Today, the question that most people would ask is: *Who* was Mamie Stuart? But back in 1920, everybody knew the name of the 26-year-old ex-chorus girl who seemed to have dissolved into thin air.

Mamie, the daughter of James Stuart, master mariner, of Sunderland, had met, on 3 July 1917, a 37-year-old marine surveyor, Everard George Shotton, of Penarth, Cardiff. The couple fell in love and, on 25 March 1918, were married at South Shields register office. There was, although Mamie did not know it at the time, just one – or rather, two – small flies in the ointment. Shotton already had a wife, whom he had married twelve years before at Newport, Monmouthshire, and a small son. In blissful ignorance of these impedimenta, Mamie bore her new husband home to Sunderland, and triumphantly introduced him to her family.

It was in February 1919, that George and Mamie Shotton went to live in Swansea, where they took furnished rooms in the house of a couple named Hearn, at 28 Trafalgar Terrace.

Five months later, on 19 July, Mr Shotton left

Trafalgar Terrace, explaining that his job was taking him away from Swansea for a while. And on 22 July, Mr and Mrs Hearn saw Mamie off from Victoria Street railway station. She was, she told them, going to spend a short holiday with her parents in Sunderland.

The Hearns never saw her again. Mrs Hearn had a letter from her from Sunderland in September 1919, and that, so far as they were concerned, was the last of Mamie Shotton.

In fact, Mamie returned to Swansea on 5 November 1919. Shotton met her train, which arrived from Sunderland shortly before midnight, and took her to the furnished house which he had rented for six months. Situated close to the village of Newton, in a pretty seaside area called the Mumbles, five and a half miles south-west of Swansea, it was a detached two-storey villa, standing on the top of a hill commanding a magnificent view of Swansea Bay, and was named Ty-Llanwydd, which means 'The Abode of Peace'.

Exactly a week after her arrival, Mamie wrote a letter to her sister, Mrs Brass. That same day she also sent a letter-card to her mother and father, posted at Swansea, 5.15pm, on 12 November. But when, a few days later, they wrote back to her at Ty-Llanwydd, their letter was returned to them by the Post Office, marked 'House Closed'. Puzzled, the Stuarts promptly despatched a reply-paid telegram to their daughter. When this, too, was returned, marked 'House Closed', puzzlement turned to alarm.

Then, just before Christmas 1919, a telegram was delivered at the Stuarts' Sunderland home. It had been handed in at Swansea, purported to come from Mamie, and brought them 'the compliments of the season'.

The New Year arrived. Still no news. January … February … then, in March 1920, came the first confirmation of the Stuart family's steadily increasing fears. The manager of the Grosvenor Hotel at Swansea asked the police to examine a portmanteau which had been left for some months unclaimed at his hotel. When they opened it, they found that it contained a second, mutilated, portmanteau, in which were two dresses, cut to shreds, a pair of lady's boots, also cut to pieces, some small items of personal jewellery, a Bible, a rosary and a manicure set. It contained, too, a fragment of paper on which was written a Sunderland address.

Inquiries at Sunderland had soon established that the address was that of Captain and Mrs Stuart, and when the police went to see them, the Stuarts told them that the whereabouts of their daughter, Mamie, had been a mystery since the previous December. The mystery was further complicated by the circumstance that, although the portmanteau found at the Grosvenor contained clothing which had undoubtedly belonged to the missing girl, it could in no way be associated with her, for, so far as the manager could remember, the bag had been left behind by a man who had stayed at the hotel by himself.

Mid-March brought another sinister pointer. A local charwoman, a Mrs Bevan, engaged to clean up Ty-Llanwydd in preparation for new tenants, discovered a mildewed, brown-leather handbag behind the wash-stand in the front bedroom. In it was a sugar ration-card in the name of Mamie Stuart, together with cash amounting to about two pounds.

Weighing all these clues and circumstances, Chief Inspector William Draper of Scotland Yard, who had been called in to help the local force with the investigation, made no bones about the fact that he felt certain that what they were dealing with was a case of murder. He was equally sure that George Shotton, who by this time was safely back in the arms of his family, living with his legal wife and child at an isolated house named Grey Holme, at Caswell Bay, about a mile and a half from Newton, knew the answers to the many questions which plagued him.

Shotton, dapper, of medium height, with a shock of frizzy, jet-black hair, deep-brown, piercing eyes, and a dark face, which lit up on occasions with an unusually attractive smile, was all surface charm and co-operation. Yes, he had known Mamie. Yes, well – very well. And yes, (those dark eyes of his downcast in candid shame), they had lived together. Married her? Oh, no. How could he? He had a wife and child already, hadn't he? (Frank, disingenuous look.) "When did I last see her? Let me think. It would have been about the fifth or sixth of December – in Oxford Street, Swansea. We'd had a quarrel, you know. Separated. Finished."

Plausible. But the police were not satisfied. They began to dig. Slowly, meticulously, they uncovered the facts of the bitter-sweet romance between the gay, vivacious Mamie, and the dour, suspicious, and apparently violent man whom she had 'married'. From the lips of friends, family and acquaintances, from the mute testimony of letters, the picture of a stormy, jealousy-riven relationship emerged. Mrs Hearn remembered: "On one occasion Mamie Shotton made a very strange remark to me. She said, 'If I am ever missing, do your very utmost to find me, won't you?'"

Then there was a letter from Mamie to her parents:

If you don't hear from me, please wire to Mrs Hearn and see if she knows anything about me. The man is not all there. I don't think I will live with him very long. I am very much afraid of him. My life is not worth living.

That was in July 1919. And there were letters from Shotton. He had obviously begun to suspect that his "own little darling" was being unfaithful to him – as indeed she was.

Letter from Mamie to her boyfriend:

My dearest Dalbert – Awfully sorry, old Boy, for not writing to you sooner, only you must know how very careful I have got to be … I am leaving Cardiff, I think, tomorrow, so if you wire my fare to Sunderland I will leave straightaway and be with you very shortly, and we will make up for lost time … My old man seems to know quite a lot … but what the eyes don't see, the heart can't grieve … Am just dying to see you and feel your dear arms around me.

Convinced now that Shotton was their man, the police nevertheless went through the motions of circulating Mamie's description all over Britain.

> *Age 26. Of very attractive appearance. Height 5ft 3in or 4in. Well built. Profusion of dark brown hair, worn bobbed. Dark grey eyes. Four faint teeth marks on right cheek, the result of a dog-bite when a child.*

But, secretly, they were looking for a corpse. They searched every last inch of Ty-Llanwydd, and several times dug over the garden which surrounded it. They searched and dug up much of the adjacent countryside, too. They found nothing. Even so, on 29 May 1920, Shotton was arrested – and charged with bigamy.

By now he was admitting that he was the man who left the portmanteau at the Grosvenor Hotel: "After we had finally parted I went back to Ty-Llanwydd and found a whole lot of her things all screwed up on the floor. I put them in a small attache-case and took them to my office, and afterwards to the Grosvenor Hotel, and left them there."

He duly appeared at Glamorgan Assizes in July. His defence that it was not him, but someone impersonating him, who had married Mamie at South Shields, failed to impress the jury, and on 27 July 1920, he was sentenced to eighteen months' hard labour by Mr Justice Avory.

And that, had it not been for a millionth-chance twist of fate on a November day forty-one years later, would have been the end of the story.

On Sunday 5 November 1961, the precise anniversary of the day that Mamie Stuart travelled for the last time from Sunderland to Swansea, three young pot-holers, John Gerke, Graham Jones and Colin MacNamara, were exploring a disused lead mine sunk into the cliff top at Brandy Cove, on the Gower coast of Glamorgan. And there, in the dank and darkness of a bat-infested cavern at the base of an old air-shaft, 50 feet underground, they stumbled upon the secret tomb – and the perfect murder. There they found Mamie Stuart.

The lady had been sawn not in half, but into three. Her skeleton lay hidden behind artfully placed boulders and a three-inch-thick stone slab. Around the bones were swaddled the rotted remains of a sack. Nearby lay a black butterfly comb, a tuft of brown hair still attached to it, and two rings – a broad, gold wedding-ring, and an engagement-ring set with three stones.

At Cardiff's forensic science laboratory, Home Office pathologist Dr William Reginald James and Dr John Lewis Griffiths reassembled the bones into the skeleton of a woman: age between 24 and 28; estimated height 5ft 3in. Transparencies of the skull, projected on to photographs of Mamie taken during her theatrical career, showed indisputable corresponding features between the two.

Most of those who had actually known Mamie were either dead or doddering, but an elderly woman, Elsie Evans, who had been her intimate friend, was able to identify her rings. In all, 20 witnesses told their stories to the coroner and his jury.

The strangest tale of all was that of an 83-year-old retired postman, William Symons. He said that one afternoon in 1919, he had seen Mr Shotton struggling with a heavy sack outside Ty-Llanwydd. Shotton had glanced up and his eye caught a glimpse of the brass buttons on Symons' blue uniform. "Oh, God!," he had exclaimed. "For a minute I though you were a policeman."

Symons had offered to help carry the sack to Shotton's yellow van, which was standing outside the gate. "No, no, no," said Shotton, who then put the sack in the van himself, and drove off in the direction of Brandy Cove.

It did not take the jury long to reach their verdict: that the skeleton was that of Mamie Stuart, that she was murdered, and that the evidence pointed to George Shotton being her murderer.

But as it turned out, Shotton was beyond the jurisdiction of that, or any other earthly court. It had taken a three-week, country-wide search, involving Interpol, Scotland Yard and nine police forces to track him down to Bristol's Southmead Hospital, where, on 30 April 1958, aged 78 and penniless, he had died.

For nearly three years his body had lain in Grave Number 000405 in Arno's Vale Cemetery, Bristol. It is a weed-grown, unmarked grave. No headstone. No inscription. His only epitaph the words spoken by Mrs Edna Collins, the woman in whose home in Coronation Road, Bristol, he was during his last years a paying guest: 'He was such a perfect gentleman.'

Mamie Stuart's epitaph was spoken by Mr DR

James, a poetic Welsh coroner: "They found her, between highland and lowland, in a coign of a cliff; by a silver sea, without a grave, uncoffined, unknelled and unknown." But now her pathetic little ghost has risen to attain a kind of immortality as one of the legends in the murder-will-out folklore of crime.

In case you had not guessed, the ghost of Everard George Shotton hovers about the vanished writing-room in the old Compton Hotel.

THE CASE OF THE
FRIGHTENED WITNESSES

Marie Milne, June Bury, George McLaughlin, I remember their names like a litany – a trinity of shady characters, who, acting for once as upright citizens, helped to put the rope round the necks of two callous killers, Alfred Burns and Edward Devlin. Long after all that remained of the murderers lay buried behind prison walls, their evil influence lived on. That, at any rate, is what four – if we include old Tom Emery the blameless cabby – frightened people for whom friendly Liverpool became a place of bristling menace, believed.

The first attack was on George McLaughlin. It came from a man in a prison yard, armed with a length of lead pipe. A few days later, another prisoner tried to stab him with a pair of scissors. In a different prison, a gang of fellow-prisoners armed with shears went for him in the basket shop. After he had been released from jail, the attacks still went on. Married, and with a child, McLaughlin was severely beaten up in the street. For many a long day he walked in terror.

Next, Marie Milne. The underworld whisper at the time of the trial was that eight men in Borstal, friends of Burns and Devlin, had drawn lots. The man who drew the shortest match had to break out. His mission: to slit Chinese Marie's throat. Before he could do so, he was caught and taken back to Borstal. But still, when it was all over and Burns and Devlin condemned to die, she was far from safe. Coming home one night from a dance at the Rialto Ballroom, she was dragged into a dark alley off Parliament Street by three men, who gave her a kicking that needed 36 stitches to repair her injuries. And threatening letters kept dropping through her letter-box. One contained the sinisterly tinkered-with words of a popular song:

> *Some enchanted evening*
> *I was looking for a stranger*
> *And that stranger was you.*

After that, when Marie Milne went out she always rode everywhere by taxi.

June Bury took what she regarded as her first revenge beating in the Lighthouse all-night cafe. She was attacked for the second time in Manchester. She came back to Liverpool and was set upon twice more. When she came out of hospital, she fled to Manchester, and whilst in Piccadilly she was beaten up yet again. That did it. She left for London, to lose herself amongst the capital's anonymous hordes.

Even so, relatively small a bit-part player as Tom Emery, the taxi driver, who had been hailed by the murderers to drive them to the vicinity of their target, did not go unremembered. Although in 1956 he was 76 years old, he was brutally attacked in a dark street, beaten and slashed. For some time thereafter he gave up night-time driving, when the best money was to be made, and, plumping for discretion rather than valour, stuck to working day shifts.

A few months after the trial, Mrs Joan Downing, who had been only a minor witness, received a threatening letter warning her: *It is no use telling the police. Your number is up.* Thoroughly upset, she went into hiding, and while she was away, someone – the avengers, she believed – set fire to her house.

Such was the general level of alarm, that, mother of two, Mrs Joan Dudley, also a very minor witness, who lived not far from Mrs Downing, in another of those Manchester streets where the pale sunlight is trapped in the orange-red brickwork, was firmly convinced that she was a victim of the Burns and Devlin avengers. Their vengeance, she thought, caught up with her in Blackpool, 12 days before Christmas 1955, when she accepted a lift in a car. Five minutes later, she was lying dumped in the roadway. She had been shot. Happily, she did not die.

Did Burns and Devlin really manage, through a gang of their friends, to stretch out the arm of vengeance from their graves, or were the threatening letters really no more than unpleasant hoaxes, and the reported slashing, shooting, fire-raising, and beatings which befell the frightened witnesses mere flexings of the long arm of coincidence? That is the one abiding, unsolved mystery of the Burns and Devlin case.

It all began one summer's evening fifty-eight years ago in Cranborne Road, off Smithdown Road, when little Mrs Beatrice Alice Rimmer turned the key in the lock of her house, No 7, and stepped through the front-door into eternity.

It had been a really pleasant Sunday.

Mrs Rimmer had been on her usual weekend visit to her son, Thomas, and his wife's home in Madryn Street, Toxteth. Those trips were always enjoyable, but since the recent arrival of her new baby grandson, the weekly Sunday visit had been even better. It was about a quarter to ten when Tom, who had walked down High Park Street with his mother, waved her off on the No 27 bus, telling her he would call round to see her the following evening.

Small and plumpish, there must have been something about the 54-year-old widow. Perhaps it was that she managed to look stylish in her yellow floral-patterned frock, loose-fitting brown coat, and winsomely old-fashioned looking, dark-coloured straw hat, carrying an umbrella and a bunch of flowers in her neatly-gloved hands. Anyway, she had certainly impressed herself on the memory of Henry Bentley, the bus conductor. He distinctly recalled her alighting at the top of Lodge Lane, outside the Pavilion Theatre. He was the last person we know of to see Mrs Rimmer alive.

The next evening – Monday 20 August 1951 – Tom went over, as he had promised, to his mother's house. As a rule, she went out on Monday evenings to play whist at the Sefton Park Conservative Club. He was hoping to catch her before she left. Tom Rimmer was just approaching his mother's door when her next-door neighbour, Jack Grossman, appeared. He was, he said, a bit concerned. No one had caught sight or sound of Mrs Rimmer all day. That was unusual … and look … there was her milk untouched on the door-step, and the morning paper still sticking out of the letter-box.

Tom, who up to a few months before had been a policeman in the Liverpool Force, felt a familiar, worrying sense of suspicion switch on; a distinct fear that something might be seriously amiss. He knocked several times at the front-door. No response. With mounting unease, he bent down, pushed the newspaper in and the flap of the letter-box up, and peered through. The passage-like hallway inside was dark. He could just make out something that looked like a bundle of discarded clothing on the floor. Definitely alarmed now, he ran round to the back entry, dragged himself up over the rear wall, and dropped down into the back yard. He saw that the kitchen window had been broken. Punching out the remaining jags of glass with his elbow, he clambered through into the ominously silent house. It was in the hall-passage, just behind the front-door, that he made the discovery that he had begun to dread. His mother was lying there, white, ice-cold in a far-spread pool of congealed blood, and the flowers which he and his wife had given her the previous day lay beside her like a wilting funeral wreath.

He raised the alarm. His old colleagues arrived. The murder investigation machine creaked into familiar gear. Not that there was much to go on. The police surgeon on call put in an appearance at 10.30pm, made his grisly calculations, and placed the time of death as – delayed for a few hours after the actual attack – around 2am. At 11.30pm Dr J B Firth turned up, and set to work immediately carrying out a meticulous examination of the body and its surroundings. He reckoned that it had taken between 20 and 30 separate blows to produce the fifteen wounds which he found, mostly on the left side, on the head. Some of those wounds were clean-edged, others ragged, yet others were stellar-shaped. These diversities suggested to him that two different weapons had been used, one sharp-edged, the other blunt, perhaps a heavy torch. There seemed a likelihood that two assailants had been involved in the perpetration of the brutal savagery. Death had been caused by a combination of shock, a skull fracture, and loss of blood. A part of the skull, about two inches in diameter, was exposed. It had been a horribly lingering death, life slowly ebbing away in that dim passageway with the sluggish, but inexorable, draining of blood.

Detective Superintendent Hector Taylor, acting head of the Liverpool CID during the absence on holiday in Ireland of Chief Superintendent Herbert Balmer, and his team of detectives, worked heroically to try to break the case before the boss returned.

An appeal was put out asking anyone who had visited Mrs Rimmer's home in the past three months to come forward, and a mammoth search for the murder weapons extended even to the Edgar Allan Poeish scouring of the place of the dead – the ancient acreage of Smithdown Road Cemetery. Neither appeal nor scour produced any useful result. Bert Balmer, whom I knew well, and upon whom in those days I would often pop in for a chat, was a formidable police officer, who spared neither himself nor anybody else once he got his teeth into a case.

Returning from holiday, he at once took charge of the murder hunt. Now it so happened that at this very time there had been a spate of house-breaking and burglary in the Cranborne Road area. The police thought that they had struck gold on 4 September, when they found silver – stolen articles stashed away in a disused bakery in Spofforth Road. Two youths were triumphantly arrested, but, to Balmer's intense disappointment, proved on further investigation to have no connection with the Cranborne Road affair. Relying on that strange, powerful instinct which long-in-the-tooth veteran detectives develop, Balmer got it into his head that one or other of his 'regulars' stowed safely away in Walton Gaol might know something and might be persuaded to 'sing'.

And his hunch paid off. The songbird proved to be a 19-year-old Liverpool lad, name of George McLaughlin, just starting an 18-month sentence for breaking into his aunt's home, at 109 Cranborne Road. George's *curriculum vitæ* was not good. He had first come into what you might call disadvantageous contact with the police at the tender age of nine. Since then, he had notched up forty thieving convictions. As a change from breaking-in, he had broken out of an approved school, been recaptured and shunted off for Borstal training. His latest desertion had been from the Army, and immediately prior to being admitted to free board and lodging in Walton, he had been living rough in Liverpool, stealing for the wherewithal to keep body and soul together, and spending long hours of slow falling crumbs and bitter teas in the city's seedy all-night cafes. It was, indeed, in one of these out-at-elbow establishments – Bill's, at the top of Paddington – that George met Ted.

Ted, to give him his full style and title, Edward Francis Devlin, a dapperly apparelled, 'all-about', 22-year-old Mancunian, of externally superior, but morally identical, calibre to the shabby George, was a similarly shiftless and shifty character, convinced that the world owed him a living. He operated from a comfortable base at his mother's house, in Leinster Street, Hulme, Manchester, whence, mischief-bound, he ranged regularly forth bent on larcenous business. He had been at it since he was 13 and had, in the ensuing near-decade, matured into, to use a contradiction in terms, a pretty respectable villain. He had just emerged from doing half a stretch (six months) in Strangeways.

The two fell to talking about 'specs' for possible profitable jobs. McLaughlin reckoned he knew a peach. In Cranborne Road, where his aunt lived, there was a widow at No 7. The talk was that her husband had left her well provided for. She didn't go out to work and seemed to be able to fork out easily for everything she wanted. According to local gossip, she had a fair old sum of cash hidden away in the house. The meet between George and Ted had taken place on 27 July. They teamed up again the next day, and went out together to Cranborne Road to "case the old woman's job up", as George elegantly expressed it.

Having belligerently declared, "I'm no squealer", McLaughlin proceeded to furnish his jail visitor police officer with the lowdown that built

124

up the retributory case against Mrs Rimmer's killers. On the Thursday before August Bank Holiday, he had had another meet with Ted, this time at the Continental Cafe, off Lime Street. Ted had arrived with a companion, whom he introduced as Alfie. Like Ted, Alfie fancied his chances, all done up dandiacal in a smart brown pin-stripe. Alfred Burns, 21 years old, was also a native of Manchester, living there with his widowed mother in Medlock Street. And, like Ted and George McLaughlin, into crime, he was a young man prepared to work very hard at not working for a living.

Waiting on the plotting trinity at the Continental was 21-year-old June Bury, a young woman who divided her life between Liverpool and Manchester, where she had met Ted Devlin. Working as a waitress was a bit of a novelty for her. Mostly she used her charms and favours to extract money from men. Currently she was living with a Lothario by the name of Stan Rubin, in Canning Street, but she still nurtured a soft spot for Ted, with whom, previously, she had, for a while, shared a bed. Now, as plans for the Cranborne Road screwing were perfected, a role in them was found for June. George would give Ted and Alfie a leg up over the back wall. They would force the kitchen-window catch, and one of them would then climb through into the house, and open the back door for the other. June, meanwhile, would knock at the front-door, and when Mrs Rimmer opened it, keep her talking there while the others came through at her from behind.

The plan foundered when George was caught and sentenced for breaking into his aunt's house, further up Cranborne Road. He was in Walton serving the early days of his 18-month sentence when the screwing and its concomitant disaster took place.

June Bury was traced back to Manchester. She swore that in the end she had refused to take part in the robbery. She had last seen Burns and Devlin in Manchester on Friday 17 August, when they told her that they were going to Liverpool. She had absolutely no idea what they had got up to that weekend, but she knew of a girl who probably did. She did not know her surname – she only knew her as Chinese Marie.

Within three days, the detectives had tracked Marie Milne down in Liverpool. Aged 17, half-Malayan, she lived with her mother at the Great George's Place end of Upper Parliament Street. She was, like June Bury, a waitress and facultatively part-time prostitute, often to be seen picking up men outside the Rialto Cinema and on Princes Avenue. Superintendent Balmer never revealed what in the way of bargaining passed between him and Marie Milne, but the upshot was that she agreed to tell him everything she knew, and to give evidence in court. In exchange, she seems to have been granted immunity from prosecution in regard to any connection with the Rimmer murder. As a result of the statement made by Miss Milne, the police felt that they had sufficient evidence in hand to justify charging Burns and Devlin with the murder. All they had to do now was to find them.

Detective Constable Leslie Skinner, of Liverpool CID, who, like Bert Balmer, happened to be a very good friend of mine in my old journalistic days in Liverpool, was strolling along Stretford Road, Manchester, with Detective Constable Lynch, of the Manchester CID, when the latter recognised one of two men walking towards them as Devlin. The detectives watched the men disappear into a milk-bar, followed them in, and arrested Devlin. He was taken back to Liverpool by car, and charged at Allerton police station. During the journey from Manchester Devlin asked: "Have the girls been talking? Have you seen June and the Chinese bit?"

When it came to hunting down Alfie Burns, it proved very easy. He was already under lock and key in Manchester's Strangeways Prison, having been picked up as an abscondee from borstal. Burns and Devlin were reunited, standing side by side in the dock in the court of Stipendiary Magistrate, Arthur McFarland, at Dale Street, where I used to spend quite a bit of time in those days and saw a fair number of Liverpool's criminous celebrities on the first stage of their journeys – sometimes to the gallows. I was present there at the Burns and Devlin committal proceedings, and remember how insolent Devlin's attitude and behaviour were, whispering and sniggering to his companion in the dock. I never saw two people on a serious charge so unaffected by the circumstances in which they found themselves. I was later to see them at their trial. I expected that after the long weeks in custody there would be quite a change in their demeanour, but not a bit of it. They were still as cocky as ever. Neither the solemn atmosphere of the Assize Court, nor the impressive presence of the scarlet-and-ermined Red Judge, seemed to impinge upon them. I think they saw themselves as gangster heroes – just like in the films.

It was while these two dangerous young men were awaiting trial that things started to become very frightening for McLaughlin and the two girls; especially for Chinese Marie, whose testimony would be crucial for the prosecution. All three received threats, threats which, in view of the quarters from which they were coming, the recipients took extremely seriously. In fact, June and Marie went into hiding. I shall never forget Marie Milne's terrified face peering through the crack of a half-opened door the night that I tracked her to her secret hideaway to interview her. Even McLaughlin, in jail, was not safe, for criminals of the calibre of Burns and Devlin had friends and tentacles that found prison bars no barrier. And when I managed to find and talk with Tom Emery, the elderly taxi driver who had taken the murderers to Smithdown Road in his cab, I saw that the poor man was in a state of some terror, despite his insistence that he had not seen the faces of, and could not therefore identify, his sinister fares. But, be it to their eternal credit, the resolve of all the frightened witnesses stayed firm.

The prosecution solicitor, Mr J R Bishop, and those for the defence – Mr Harry Livermore for Devlin, and Mr Joseph Norton for Burns – set to work on their respective preparations. The full version of the story was now about to unfold.

On 3 August, Burns and Devlin had met June Bury by arrangement at the Rainbow Cafe, in Islington, and she had brought Marie Milne along with her. That night the four of them went down to the coffee stall at the Pier Head, and on from there to the Lighthouse Cafe, another all-night joint, where they remained until 7am. June had by then taken the decision to finish with Stan Rubin and move on, in the game of musical beds, to Ted Devlin. So the quartet hailed another taxi and set off for 39 Canning Street, where June peremptorily packed up her relationship with an angry Stan, packed a suitcase, and left.

Another taxi ferried them to 2 Verulam Street, where Burns paid 25 shillings up front for a room for Marie and himself for a week. And on that Saturday night (4 August), Devlin and June selected an hotel on Mount Pleasant as their somewhat seedy love-nest. On the Sunday the two couples went off to Manchester, where they spent the day, the girls returning that same night to Liverpool, June Bury having, before their departure, refused absolutely to play any part in the projected robbery. Marie Milne, however, agreed to act as look-out for the two men when they broke into the house.

At 4.45pm on Friday 17 August, Chinese Marie kept a date with Burns and Devlin outside the Rialto Cinema, at the corner of Upper Parliament and Berkley Streets, and the trio went along and had a meal at the Green Dragon Chinese Restaurant, in Leece Street.

On the Saturday, the three met again at 3.30pm on Lewis's corner.

So we come to the fatal Sunday, 19 August. June Bury had remained in Manchester. McLaughlin was in Walton Gaol. Burns, Devlin, and Milne foregathered at the usual spot outside the Rialto in the early afternoon. At around 2.15pm, they took a taxi to Smithdown Road, having it put them down outside Sefton General Hospital, at a point just about a 100 yards beyond the Smithdown Road junction with Cranborne Road. They walked those 100 yards back, and Burns told Marie: "This is where you wait for us at six o'clock tonight." And, pointing up the road, "That's where Mrs Rimmer lives." Then they caught a bus back into town.

Punctually at six o'clock, Marie was duly standing at the blitzed site spot by the Webster Road junction with Smithdown Road, where Burns had told her to be. She waited there until 6.30pm. No sign of Burns or Devlin, so she went back to the Rialto. The two men turned up by the taxi rank there, and took her into nearby Wilkie's Cafe, where the three of them dawdled, watching the evening slowly die, its lengthening shadows gradually merging with the descending clouds of darkness to weave that summer's day's shroud. Laggard-seeming night at long last fallen, it was at a quarter to ten that the villainous three emerged, blinking from the cafe's garish bright light, into the blindfolding dark, and boarded a bus that carried them up Upper Parliament Street and, veering right, down Smithdown Road to the corner of Cranborne Road, and an appointment with Fate.

Quoting now the subsequent evidence of Marie Milne, Burns and Devlin told her to wait on the corner there for five minutes, to allow them time to get into the house from the back. She was then to go to "the house four houses past the entry", and knock at the front-door. Once inside, she was to stand between the old lady and her front-door to make sure that she could not get out to look for help. This, she said, she did not do. What she did, was wait on the corner until half-past ten, then got a tram back to the Rialto. There she had met up again with Burns and Devlin, and, as the three of them walked down Upper Parliament Street, she had noticed that they both had blood on their clothes, and saw that Ted had a heavily bloodied handkerchief wrapped around his hand. She had also heard Devlin ask Burns: "Will the old lady live?" To which Burns replied: "To hell with the old woman; we'll be out of Liverpool before long, and we'll take little Marie with us."

We can, I think, never know for sure the detailed course of events between the time that the two men left Chinese Marie on the corner and met up with her again back at the Rialto. Only three people knew the whole truth; one of them was dead, the other two had a vested interest in peddling their own particular versions of how they had not been anywhere near Cranborne Road that night, let alone murdered Mrs Rimmer.

What the forensic evidence indicated was that Mrs Rimmer had been attacked in the hall, the moment she entered the house. There was blood on the wall behind the front-door, and a great deal

131

more between the front-door and the door leading to the sitting-room. Dr Firth noted that the formation of the blood splashes was indicative of the unfortunate woman's having received many of the injuries to her head as she lay on the floor. Her blood was Group A. He had found bloodstains on both Burns' and Devlin's clothing. Those on Burns', however, belonged to Group B. Those on Devlin's proved too slight for classification.

Burns and Devlin were put up before Mr Justice Finnemore at Liverpool Assizes, at that time held in St George's Hall, on 19 February 1952. The trial lasted ten days. Devlin was defended by Miss Rose Heilbron, Burns by Sir Noel Goldie, KC. Mr Basil Nield, KC led the prosecution. Both Miss Heilbron and Mr Nield were later to become High Court judges. Sir Basil, I came to know well. Dame Rose Heilbron I first met in her and her husband's flat in Verulam Buildings, just after her elevation to the Bench.

The defence case was beguilingly simple. Pure denial. No one – that is, of course, the prosecution witness, Marie Milne, apart – had actually seen either of the accused in the vicinity of, or to enter or leave, Mrs Rimmer's house. No one had witnessed the murder. No murder weapon or weapons had been discovered. The prosecution was, therefore, again Marie Milne's testimony apart, relying entirely on circumstantial evidence – which, incidentally, despite popular misconception to the contrary, can very often be the best. An alibi defence was offered. Devlin stated: "Round the time of the murder I was doing screwing jobs at Manchester,

132

Hulme, Deansgate and other places ... I was probably screwing a gaff on August the nineteenth."

And Sir Noel Goldie brought forward Burns' supportive claim that he and Devlin had been robbing the factory warehouse of Messrs Sun Blinds Ltd, in Great Jackson Street, Manchester, on the night of 19 August.

Devlin, called by his counsel, swore in the witness-box that he had never met George McLaughlin, and described how he, Burns, and a Manchester man named Allan Campbell, carried out a robbery at Messrs Sun Blinds Ltd, on the night of Sunday 19 August 1951.

Burns was also put in the witness-box by his counsel. He told of how he had gone to a football match, he thought at Maine Road, on the afternoon of Saturday 17 August. He said that he and Devlin had spent that night at his (Burns') mother's. At about 11am on the Sunday, they had "shot off" to a Mrs Downing's house, and then went on a lunch-time pub crawl. That evening, he, Devlin, and Allan Campbell, were at the Ship Inn. At about 11.30pm, they went to Great Jackson Street and carried out the robbery. He and Devlin had then returned to spend the night at Burns' mother's house in Medlock Street. Unfortunately for the prisoners, despite Allan Campbell's brave testamentary perjury, it could be shown that the details of the date of the break-in at Sun Blinds Ltd, in respect of which he was currently serving eighteen months, had somehow slipped his mind, for it had actually taken place on the night of the 18th, and not the 19th, of August.

February 27th. Verdict Day.

As dawn broke over the city a queue was beginning to form outside St George's Hall. By 7am, the queue had snaked to an inordinate coiling length. With a rattle of keys and bolts, the doors opened at ten o'clock. Two hundred trial-goers were disappointed. Finnemore J summed up for four-and-a-half-hours. At 4.15 the jury retired. Outside, the paving-stones of St George's Plateau were hidden beneath a quivering formicate mass. Those were the dramatic days of hanging, and the shadow of the noose exercised a powerful morbid fascination. A sussuration, almost an audible groan, swept along and over the teeming black ants. At 5.30pm the jury had returned, with a guilty verdict.

Appeals, petitions, special applications, dragged on over a period of eight weeks after sentencing. It all came to a full stop at nine o'clock on 25 April 1952, a morning of spring sunshine. Burns and Devlin, standing side by side on the Walton scaffold, paid the debt they owed for the cruel taking of Mrs Beatrice Alice Rimmer's life. It was Albert Pierrepoint who acted as society's debt collector. He was assisted by Syd Dernley. And it is Dernley who, in his reminiscences, has given us a last glimpse of the two hard men, and how, when it came to it, they who had so easily meted out death to the little old widow, faced it themselves.

Devlin spun round to meet his executioners as they came into the condemned cell to fetch him. Once described as 'handsome in a hard sort of way', he did not look hard, nor did he look handsome, now. He was white as a sheet, his face and brow creased with deep lines. He was clearly terrified. He put up no resistance.

Burns, the former couldn't-care-less tough guy, no longer existed. Also white as a sheet, and looking like a frightened lad, staring wide-eyed at the pinioned figure of his friend, white hood already over his head, noose around his neck, he walked meekly out on to the trap. Pierrepoint threw the lever. With neither prior protestation of innocence, nor final confession of guilt, Burns and Devlin were plunged into the Great Silence.

THE TERRIBLE DESPATCH OF JOHN CONWAY

When, as happens from time to time, someone – perhaps my shirt-maker or a shop-assistant who is obligingly calculating the correct size of bow-tie which I require – runs a tape-measure round my neck, I usually inform them, in jocular vein, that the last person who did that was the public hangman! This invariably produces a dutiful loud guffaw at what they think is a very ropy – in several senses – little joke.

Although offered as a jovial conversational gambit, it happens to be sober truth, for the former official hangman, the late lamented Albert Pierrepoint, did on one occasion, in a spirit of grisly gallows humour, pass his tape-measure round my neck. We had become acquainted at the time when another friend of mine, Joe Gaute, an editorial director of Messrs George G Harrap & Co, was arranging the acceptance of Pierrepoint's memoirs, *Executioner: Pierrepoint*, subsequently published in 1974, and my criminous advice had been sought in connection with one or two small points in the text.

The hangman, like the muffin-man, is an extinct, a vanished, figure. Some say good. Some say bad. Some, remembering the Moors Murderers, Brady and Hindley, and the Wests, of Cromwell Street, Gloucester, are not so sure.

As a matter of fact, I got to know Pierrepoint

quite well, and found him, as you might expect, a somewhat unusual man.

Albert was a Yorkshire lad, born in the village of Clayton, near Bradford, about the year 1905. He came of a family which, like the Sansons, the headsmen – master operatives of the guillotine – of France, boasted a tradition of providing their country's executioners.

Albert's father – Henry Albert Pierrepoint – and his Uncle Tom – Thomas William Pierrepoint – had both been well-qualified, long-serving hangmen before him, and Albert approached his work as a craft, a calling, a 'sacred vocation'. He firmly believed that he had been chosen by a 'higher power' for the task which he undertook, and that he had been put on earth especially to do it. Thus, he spared himself no pains in learning to carry out what he was truly convinced became in his hands the most humane and dignified method of meting out death.

In the course of twenty-five years, he had performed more judicial hangings than any other British executioner. His celebrated clients included such classic murderers as Heath, Haigh, and Christie, the controversial figures Timothy Evans, Derek Bentley, and Ruth Ellis, and Liverpool's infamous George 'Cameo' Kelly and Burns and Devlin. Each of them had, in the old-time hangman's phraseology, been 'turned off' with a dedicated craftsman's skill and pride, the appropriate drop calculated with the utmost care, the knot of the noose deftly positioned at the jaw's left angle, so as to break the neck neatly between the second and third cervical vertebrae and sever the spinal cord. What had at all costs to be avoided was the slow strangulation, asphyxiation, which would result from failure to dislocate the neck. Equally, it was vitally important to get the equation between the weight of the prisoner and the length of the drop allocated right, or the unfortunate man's despatch could turn into a very terrible disaster. What happened to John Conway at the hands of Mr Hangman Berry at Kirkdale Prison, in Liverpool, in 1891, would have appalled Pierrepoint.

Conway, also known by the name of Owen Gilbin, was a dark-bearded, 62-year-old stoker, or, as it was described in moments of aspiration, marine or ship's fireman. He was also the local delegate for his trade union, and it was to the office which he occupied in that capacity that he lured, and there murdered, 9-year-old Nicholas Martin. He had then stuffed the body into a carpet-bag, taken a cab to the riverside, and flung it into the water of one of the docks, where it was found floating on 16 May 1891. As well as the boy's mutilated body, the bag contained a knife and a saw, which proved to be the murder weapons.

The bag was traced to Conway, and witnesses came forward to testify to the police to having seen him and the boy together shortly before the time of the gruesome discovery. But why he had committed this dreadful crime was – and remained – a complete mystery. Certainly, there was nothing in the man's previous record indicative of any quarrelsome, let alone murderous, tendency.

Moreover, he himself was at an absolute loss to explain his uncharacteristic action.

He did, however, on the day before his execution, admit to Father Bonte, the priest who attended him in the condemned cell, to having done the deed: "In confessing my guilt I protest that my motive was not outrage. Such a thought I never in all my life entertained. Drink has been my ruin, not lust. I was impelled to the crime while under the influence of drink, by a fit of murderous mania, and a morbid curiosity to observe the process of dying. A moment after the commission of the crime I experienced the deepest sorrow of it, and would have done anything in the world to undo it."

Conway, Berry tells us, was a very superstitious man. He was a great believer in omens and witchcraft and all sorts of supernatural powers. He got it firmly into his head that if one really good man could be persuaded to pray for him, he would be saved from the gallows. For the efficacy of his own prayers he had scant regard, thinking that they would avail him nothing and that he was not fit to receive the last sacraments of his church.

The morning of the execution dawned. James Berry had done his vital calculation. The prisoner weighed 11 stone 2 pounds and stood 5 feet 7 inches high. That meant a drop of 4 feet 6 inches. And that was when Berry found himself in conflict with the prison medical officer, Dr James Barr. "The drop should be six feet nine inches," pronounced the doctor.

That was according to the 'official scale'. What he was referring to were the conclusions reached by the Aberdare Committee. This was a body which, as a result of the public concern about such 'incidents' as Berry's failure, after three attempts, to hang John Lee at Exeter Gaol, in February 1885, Berry's bungled hanging of Moses Shrimpton at Worcester, in May 1885, when his omission to take into account the weakness of the prisoner's neck muscles resulted in his head being torn clean from his shoulders, and the like decapitation of Robert Goodale, a 15-stone giant of a man, hanged by Berry, in what became known as the 'Goodale Mess', at Norwich, in November 1885.

By what route the committee reached its conclusions in the matter of recommended weight/distance of drop ratios is not clear. What is, however, apparent is that favourable ear was given to the purely theoretical views of the medical men rather than to the practical advisings of the experienced hangman, and after the Governor of Kirkdale had lent his support to Dr Barr's demand for a longer drop, Berry, very reluctantly gave way to the doctor. "All right, I'll do it as you like, but if it pulls his head off, I'll never hang another."

Actually, he had secretly reduced the drop by nine or ten inches. He adjusted the white cap. The prisoner's pale lips whispered the words, "Lord have mercy on my soul," followed by, "Oh, my God! Oh, my God!"

Berry pulled the lever.

Conway dropped from sight, as with a tremendous boom the two heavy wooden sides of the trap-door struck the stonework. Then, in the reverberant silence, a sinister sound came echoing up from the pit. The splashing of blood on the brick floor. Berry peered over into the blackness below and saw that the man's head was held to the body by the merest fragment of ragged neck muscle.

In high dudgeon and disgust, Berry left the prison immediately. He was informed that he would not be required at the inquest, nor would he be allowed to give evidence. The coroner told the jury that the governor of the prison had testified that everything had gone off as usual at Conway's execution, and Dr Barr had also stated that it had been "carried out in the usual way".

"Was there no hitch at all?" asked the coroner.

"No, so far as the execution was concerned," replied Barr.

The plain truth is that the Aberdare Committee had come down heavily on the side of risking decapitation rather than strangulation. Angry and resentful, Berry resigned his position as Number One Hangman after the Conway debacle.

Strangely enough, my paternal great-grandfather, Dr Richard Whittington-Egan, attended, in his capacity as Irish Crown Pathologist, an even more alarming hanging mishap at Dublin.

The case in point was that of an unfortunate Irishman, a native of Kildare, named Andrew Carr. A good-looking, well set-up, manly fellow, very sunburnt and pronouncedly hirsuit, with dark brown hair, beard, whiskers and moustache, he had joined the Army at an early age, seen rapid promotion to colour-sergeant, and served with the 87th Regiment for twenty-five years.

It was while Carr's regiment was quartered in Tullamore that he had first met Margaret Murphy. She was one of the five daughters of a farmer resident in that neighbourhood. An improper intimacy had developed between them, and when Carr was ordered abroad for foreign service, the girl, finding herself disgraced and rejected by her family, made her way to Dublin, where she became an outcast, taking to the streets, and sinking lower and lower.

It would be about the year 1860 that she became an inmate of one of the terrible dens in Bull Lane, situated at the rear of the Four Courts in a network of similar purlieus. Two years later, when the 87th Regiment returned from India, Carr went to live with Margaret in a hovel kept by a woman named Brien. He remained with her for a week. Then a quarrel took place and, vowing, it is alleged, that he would have vengeance on her, Carr left Margaret and returned to the regiment. For some reason which was never revealed, he was reduced to the ranks, and it was as a private that, at the age of 42, he took his discharge on a pension of eight pence a day.

That was in May 1870. He returned at once to Dublin, where he sought and found Margaret. She was living at 14 Bull Lane. Here, as long as the money lasted, Carr lived with her, a life of drink and vice, punctuated by vicious drunken quarrels.

On the morning of Thursday 16 June 1870, Carr handed Margaret sixteen shillings, which was

142

all that he had left. And she, finding that his means were gone, went blatantly to work making the acquaintance of other soldiers. Hardly surprisingly, this led to several violent quarrels in the course of the day, and by the evening they were both far gone in drink, and dark and threatening words were bandied between them.

It was between 10.40pm and 10.50pm that evening that Police Constable William Arthurs, while passing on his beat up Pill Lane, was accosted by a man "slightly under the influence of drink", who told him: "I'm just after murdering a woman in a house in Bull Lane by cutting her throat, and if you don't believe what I say, look at my hands." The constable looked. Sure enough, the man's fingers were liberally smeared with blood. Blood was also seeping from a cut in his left wrist. The man told him: "This cut I gave my wrist with the razor with which I cut her throat."

Constable Arthurs took the man – it was, of course, Andrew Carr – to Green Street police station. The constable, together with Constable Johnston, then made his way round to check at the house where the murder had allegedly been committed.

It was the first building on the left-hand side of the street, the ruin of one of those well-built, old-fashioned houses, erected perhaps a century before in the days when Bull Lane, now the terrain of the depraved and the lawless, was inhabited by respectable citizens. The place was in a terrible state of dilapidation. Every window from the cellar to the attic had been smashed, or had the sashes entirely removed. The banisters were wrenched off, and large portions of the old, greasy panelled woodwork of which the walls of the staircase were composed, had been removed, apparently for fuel. The whole house was in darkness.

The constables clambered gingerly up the rickety stairs, which were covered with layers of mud, brought in by midnight wanderers, brawlers, and the troops of bullies who haunted such dens of infamy to plunder and beat any drunken fool who might have been lured after nightfall into Bull Lane. Upstairs, the walls were covered with slimy filth, and the doors of every room – from which the old paint had long ago peeled off – were falling from their hinges, their broken panels showing the violent assaults to which they had been subjected. Everywhere was pervaded by a nauseous, fetid stench, which proceeded from the poisonous fumes of the noxious abominations which had been allowed to collect in the back yard.

The miserable top floor back room in which the murder had been committed, did not contain a particle of furniture, except two old wooden stools, and on the mantelshelf a few old cracked cups and saucers and empty bottles. The bars of an ancient grate were burned out from long use, and the dirty, slime-covered walls showed in several places where candles had been stuck against them. There was, too, a heap of old straw, ground into filthy chaff, and in a corner a tattered mattress black with grime, together with a few strips of old carpet.

In the centre of all this, in a pool of clotted gore, there lay the body of a young woman, her head nearly divided from her body by the desperate gash in her throat made by the open razor that lay in the blood beside her, her long brown hair protruding from beneath a gypsy straw hat, trimmed with blue ribbon and artificial flowers, saturated with blood, as was also the white dress trimmed with blue that she wore – the cheap finery recently purchased with the money given to her by he who had taken her life.

Carr was duly charged with murder.

At one o'clock in the morning my great-grandfather went along to the house in Bull Lane and examined the body, which, I see from his notes, he found lying on its back, the head turned over to the left shoulder, the lower limbs drawn up and apart, the arms extended by the side, the right hand clenched on a white handkerchief, bloodstained. There were no wounds on the hands, but there was some blood on them. The left eye was blackened, but not from recent injury. On the right side of the neck and forepart of the throat was a wound extending from the middle line behind, round to the anterior edge of the sterno-mastoid muscle of the left side, a few fibres of which were divided. This wound divided all the muscles, nerves, and blood vessels down to the spine, which had been in several places chipped by the weapon. The great blood vessels on the left side were uninjured. This wound was the cause of death, which must have been immediate, and it was not a self-inflicted wound.

The city coroner, Dr N C Whyte, held an inquest at Mr Crinion's public-house in Pill Lane. Carr was brought up in police custody by cab from the Green Street station house. He was wearing a plaid shooting coat, and the lower part of his trousers and Blucher boots were smeared with clotted blood. He looked most dejected.

Carr was committed for trial, found guilty and sentenced to death. The hanging was scheduled to take place at Richmond bridewell – the Dublin male prison in the parish of Rathmines, later re-named Mountjoy – at 8am on Thursday 28 July 1870. One of the windows looking out over the exercise yard was taken away and the bars removed. This window was to serve as a doorway to the rude scaffold platform of deal which had been built out some 22 feet up over the yard at the rear of the prison. The executioner, a man who sheltered behind the anonymity of the black crape mask which he wore covering his face, and obviously did not know his job, launched the prisoner on a 14-foot drop down the outside wall of the gaol. With a dreadful snapping sound, Carr's head, still shrouded in the white cap, was wrenched from his body, and both fell, spouting blood, to the rapidly incarnadined shingle of the yard, where body and head rolled over and over and for fully three minutes the wretched man's headless trunk continued to quiver and twitch in a horrible, obscene mockery of still-living flesh.

My great-grandfather wrote:

> *The last earthly thing Carr saw was the full-leafed tree with the top of Greenmount Brewery and its tall, smoking chimney.*

Great-grandfather knew, too, the identity of the masked executioner.

> *'The Finisher' of the Law was a tailor, an*
> *Englishman. His name was Fallon. He put on*
> *the crape on the stairs. He ran out of the jail*
> *immediately after the execution. It is hoped,*
> *like Judas, to hang himself, and with more skill*
> *than he did Carr. He got £5, and as a*
> *volunteer was a legalised murderer.*

That, I think, was a sentiment with which my friend Pierrepoint would have wholeheartedly agreed, for in the end his views on capital punishment underwent a quite extraordinary change. Listen to his *Confessio*:

> *The fruit of my experience has this bitter after-*
> *taste: that I do not now believe that any one of*
> *the hundreds of executions I carried out has in*
> *any way acted as a deterrent against future*
> *murder. Capital punishment, in my view,*
> *achieved nothing except revenge.*

Pierrepoint resigned his position as Number One Hangman in 1956. Ten years before that he had become 'mine host' at a public-house at Hollinwood, between Oldham and Manchester, curiously named the 'Help the Poor Struggler'. Wags were soon calling it the 'Help the Poor Strangler', and insisting that a notice was to be found inside reading: 'No hanging around this bar.'

Hanging was finally abolished in 1965. The last two men to hang were Peter Anthony Allen and Gwynne Owen Evans, the murderers of an inoffensive Cumberland laundryman. Evans was despatched at Strangeways Prison, Manchester, at 8am on 13 August 1964 – oddly enough by a hangman named Allen. And Peter Allen simultaneously dropped through the trap at Walton Gaol.

On my desk before me as I write lies an innocuous-looking piece of wood. But about it, in my imagination, there winds a procession of all those hooded figures who, over the years, dropped to their death on Liverpool's scaffold. They include among them George Sumner, or Ball, the Liverpool Sack Murderer; Lock Ah Tam, the Gentle Chinaman, who slew his family; George Kelly, the Cameo Cinema Killer; Alfred Burns and Edward Devlin, the murderous burglars who brutally did little Mrs Alice Rimmer to death. About it, too, flit the shades of those who might so easily have met their end in its shadow – Mrs Florence Elizabeth Maybrick and William Herbert Wallace. It is a portion of the hanging beam from Walton Gaol's now demolished gallows. It was presented to me by a reader of mine, a former warder at Walton, and a man who, more than once, had shared in the dread death watch of the last lingering hours of those whose fate or folly had brought them to the inescapable noose.

THE LIVERPOOL PIRATES

This is a story which begins in the bright sunlight of a palm-fringed tropical island ... and ends in the forbidding gloom of the Liverpool Assize Court in St George's Hall. It is a story which comes from the long-ago world of *The Onedin Line* – or, rather, its real-life equivalent. The world of the trade winds, the tall ships, laden with exotic spices and manned by the indomitable shellbacks. It is a tale of mutiny and piracy and murder most foul on the high seas, that thrilled and chilled all Liverpool, and set the old sailormen gossiping in the Sailortown pubs and grog-shops, and thanking whatever sea gods may be that they hadn't shipped aboard the ill-fated barque, *Veronica*.

On 28 December 1902, the steamship, *Brunswick*, owned by the Liverpool shipping firm of Hugh Evans & Company and plying mainly between Lisbon and various South American ports, sighted landfall and was presently dropping anchor at Tutóia, off the small island of Cajueiro, which forms part of the bar of Parnalba River, where it flows into the Atlantic on the north coast of Brazil, 150 miles south of the equator. She was to pick up a cargo of cotton and hides from the Evans Company's warehouse there.

Since the island was now an uninhabited one, Chief Officer William Thomas Watson, peering through his spy glass, was surprised to see a ship's longboat, the name *Veronica* painted on its bow, lying alongside the jetty. This was unusual, for the island was seldom visited by other vessels.

He was even more surprised when five men, clearly in the last stages of exhaustion, frantically hailed him and signalled that they were seeking permission to come aboard. This was granted, and they pulled out to the *Brunswick,* and clambered up to the deck. They were taken below, given a good hot meal and clean clothes.

Their spokesman, a 28-year-old German, Gustav Rau, had a sorry tale to tell. He and his four shipmates – Otto Monsson and Harry Flohr, both German, Dirk Herlaar, a Dutchman who called himself Willem Smith, and Moses Thomas, a black American – were the only survivors of a crew of twelve – a motley crew, said to have been recruited from the dregs of the Gulf waterfront, and two of whom, Rau and Monsson, had smuggled loaded revolvers aboard with them – who had set out from Ship Island, in the Gulf of Mexico, on 11 October 1902, on the 1,100-ton, three-masted barque, *Veronica*, of St Brunswick, owned by Robert and John Henderson Thompson of Liverpool, with a cargo of timber, bound for Montevideo.

To begin with, said Rau, the voyage had gone well. Then, it was as if a hoodoo had fallen upon the vessel. First, on 25 October, one of the crew, a Swede, Gustav Johansen, had died of a fever at sea. Then, on 23 November, the first mate, Alexander MacLeod, fell from the main topsail-yard and was killed. Finally, on 20 December, the *Veronica* had caught fire, and the order was given "Abandon ship!"

The ship's two longboats were lowered. In one, was Captain Alexander Shaw, with Fred Abrahamson, Julius Parsson, Patrick Durran and Alexander Bravo. In the other, was Rau with his four companions. Unfortunately, the two boats became separated, and Rau had no idea what had become of the captain and his party. After five days in an open boat, with only one cask of water and eleven ship's biscuits to sustain them, Rau and his men had reached Cajueiro.

The master of the *Brunswick*, Captain George Brown, agreed to take the men to Lisbon. And that would, in all probability, have been the end of the affair, had it not been for the strange behaviour of the black cook, who now made the most urgent request that he be berthed apart from the others.

That something was troubling Moses Thomas deeply, soon became evident. The calm of the tropical night was continually broken by his eerie howlings, groanings and lamentations. Nightmares, perhaps, brought on by his recent experiences? That notion was dispelled on the Monday (12 January 1903), when Thomas asked to see Captain Brown.

In consequence of what he told him, the captain communicated with the British consul at Lisbon, and was instructed to carry his five passengers on to Liverpool. The consul meanwhile got into contact with the Liverpool police, and when, on 28 January 1903, the *Brunswick* arrived here, she was boarded by detectives. After taking statements from Thomas and Flohr, who had by this time decided that the only sensible course open to him was to make full confession, to come clean, they arrested Rau, Monsson and Smith, and charged them with murder. Flohr subsequently turned King's Evidence.

The three accused promptly admitted that it was all true. Seven men had indeed been murdered. The ship had been set on fire – but it was not they who were guilty. It had all been the work of the black cook, Moses Thomas.

It was in May 1903, with the *Veronica's* longboat marooned low and dry as Exhibit A in the basement of St George's Hall, that, aloft in the Red Judge's Court, the true story of the last voyage of the *Veronica* emerged.

The log of the 13 days of horror and motiveless blood lust makes scarifying reading. It begins in the early hours of Monday 8 December 1902, when, at about 3am, Rau crept up behind Paddy Durran, the look-out, and felled him with a heavy iron belaying-pin. Flohr and Smith then crammed him, senseless, into the port locker.

This was the first act in a mutiny which had been smouldering in the mind of Gustav Rau from the day he walked up the gangplank. A savage, overbearing man of powerful personality, he had enlisted Monsson and Smith in his scheme, and Flohr, a somewhat weak and gentle-natured 18-year-old, had been terrorised into throwing in his lot with that of the menacing conspirators.

The mutineers' next victim was Alex MacLeod, who, Rau had said, had fallen to his death from the mast top. What actually happened was that MacLeod had come searching for the look-out man, Durran, who was by now the knocked-out man, reposing in the locker, and Rau struck the unsuspecting first mate down with his bloodstained belaying-pin, and flung him overboard.

Rau and Smith then made their way aft. Two shots. The second mate, Abrahamson, staggered, bleeding, from his cabin and lurched towards the captain's quarters. Captain Shaw was standing by the compass, looking at the topsails. Possibly because he was very deaf and his eyesight was no longer too good, he did not seem to realise what was going on. Rau, a frightening figure, revolver in one hand, belaying-pin in the other, shot him. The wounded captain managed to crawl into the chartroom, where he found Abrahamson. They bolted the door.

There was, at a later stage, some parley between Rau and the captain through the chartroom skylight. "I'll give you my gold watch," pleaded Shaw. "Please save my life. I have got a wife and children, and I should like to see them again. If you will let me go I will take you to any port you want."

Rau spared him – for the moment.

Meanwhile, Monsson had killed Parsson, and thrown him into the sea. Durran, who had come to, tottered out of the port locker, and begged Rau for a drink of water. "I'll give you a good drink," said Rau, who thereupon finished him off with his belaying-pin, and tossed him over the ship's rail into the 'drink'.

Now it was the cook's turn. Moses Thomas, only too well aware of the murderous business that had been going on, was cowering in abject terror in his cabin. "Come out, you son-of-a-bitch," shouted

153

Rau. Thomas' only reply was to barricade his door.

The dark hours of the night dragged by for the quaking cook in a waking nightmare. About 7am, Rau renewed his attack. He beat thunderously at the cabin door. "Come out, or I'll come in and kill you." And Moses came forth – trembling.

Rau did not kill him. Instead, he ordered him to the galley to make some strong coffee. Rau was a practical man and knew that they all had to eat.

The next murders were committed on 14 December. Abrahamson and Captain Shaw were shot, and consigned to the cradle of the deep Atlantic. Rau pocketed Shaw's gold watch. Now only seven men remained. Two more were to die. Johansen and Bravo.

Rau, now calling himself Captain Bungstarter, and his henchmen dressed themselves in the murdered officers' uniforms and strutted around the decks barking out orders.

On 20 December the *Veronica* was deliberately set on fire, and Rau and his four surviving fellow-mutineers cast off in the longboat, leaving her to sink to the sea bed. On Christmas Day they reach Cajueiro ... the first stage of their journey to the dry dock in St George's Hall.

The trial came on before Mr Justice Lawrance. Counsel for the Crown were Mr Alfred Tobin, KC and Liverpool's famous son and legal luminary, F E Smith, later Lord Birkenhead. The indictment contained counts of murder, conspiracy, fire-raising or arson, piracy and theft, but the charge proceeded on was that of the murder of Captain Alexander Shaw.

Young Flohr's evidence was used by the Crown successfully to support the testimony given by Moses Thomas. There was little difficulty in establishing means and opportunity, but the matter of motive posed a most perplexing problem. It has been suggested that poor food may have provoked a dissatisfaction, which, first voiced when, shortly after leaving Cajueiro, the *Veronica* was becalmed with sails idle in the Doldrums, had given rise to feelings of frustration that had escalated over the lengthening days of the voyage into a murderous frame of mind. But there is not the slightest reason to think that the food was significantly worse than that in many other sailing ships of the time.

Bullying and brutality by the ship's officers has been provisionally put forward as a potential source of the trouble. Again, there is absolutely nothing to support such a contention, although the first mate, MacLeod, was known to be a tough customer who did not hesitate to knock a man down if he didn't jump to it smartly enough when given an order. But in the declining days of sail, that relic of the far from unusual ill-treatment of the shellbacks of earlier days still persisted.

More persuasive is the theoretical explanation that several plainly belligerently-inclined, ill-disciplined and resentful Germans, possessing firearms, got together and, the balance of their temperaments being affected by the fierce Caribbean heat, embarked upon a senseless killing fest, just for the hell of it. Certainly, murder for gain was totally out of the question, for none of the murdered men left much money for their killers to seize.

As Crown Counsel, Mr F E Smith, was later to hazard: "This drama of the sea proves … that when men brood on trivial matters they may commit enormities so totally out of proportion to the provocation or hope of gain, that the only rational explanation is that they must have been insane. Yet these men were sane. Why they began, no one may tell. Once started, fear and the desire to save their own wicked and worthless lives accounts for what followed, but the mutiny remains and must remain for ever an unsolved mystery of the sea."

All three mutineers were sentenced to death, but Monsson's sentence was later commuted to life imprisonment.

On 2 June 1903, Rau and Smith were launched on the lonely sea of death, hanging from the 'yard-arm' of the gallows at Walton Gaol.

Flohr slipped quietly out of Liverpool, and, no doubt, set sail for his native land.

Moses Thomas, having issued a writ for libel against a newspaper, which action was settled for £150 and costs, became engaged to the daughter of a well-to-do Ormskirk farmer. The farmer's horrified family made the girl break it off. Moses once more had recourse to the courts, suing for breach of promise, and receiving a substantial settlement. He then retired to the West Indies, a devout admirer of the English judicial system.

THE CAPTURE OF
POLICE KILLER KENNEDY

It is twenty minutes to midnight. A small group of police officers are clustered in the vicinity of a house on Copperas Hill. One of them detaches himself from the rest. He has spotted a man walking rapidly along adjacent St Andrew Street. Swiftly and silently, he follows him. Drawing closer to the hurrying figure, the collar of whose overcoat is turned up, trilby pulled well down, and whose left hand is strategically positioned so as to hide his face, his pursuer nonetheless recognises William Henry Kennedy, and approaching him says, "Come on, Bill. Now then, come on, Bill."

Fast as a striking cobra, Kennedy spins suddenly round, faces Detective Sergeant William Mattinson, of the Liverpool Police Force, pulls a revolver out of his right-hand pocket, thrusts the muzzle into his ribs, and hisses, "Stand back, Bill, or I'll shoot you."

No empty threat. Mattinson would not be the first policeman that Kennedy had killed. Pluckily, the detective closes with him. There is a fierce struggle, in the course of which Mattinson is convinced that he hears a distinct click from the pistol. He manages, however, to wrench the gun from Kennedy's grasp, seizes him by the collar, and pushing and shoving, hustles him all the way back along St Andrew Street to Copperas Hill, where the others are waiting. They are Chief Inspector

Roberts, of the Liverpool Force, and Inspector Albert Kirschner and Sergeant Duncan, of the Metropolitan Police, who have come from New Scotland Yard to Liverpool to arrest Kennedy.

At Warren Street bridewell, Kirschner tells Kennedy that he is being charged with having been connected with a man named Browne, now in custody, in the stealing of a Vauxhall motor-car from Tooting, in south London, the previous November. Round about 4am, Kennedy is hied off to Police Headquarters in Dale Street, where he is lodged for what remains of the night in a cell. The following morning – Thursday 26 January 1928 – he is taken up to London. His wife is permitted to accompany him.

Let us now take a journey back in time to 27 September 1927. In the early hours of that Tuesday morning, PC George William Gutteridge, of the Essex Constabulary, set out from Stapleford Abbotts, about half-way between Romford and Ongar, where he was stationed, in order, in the line of duty, to meet up at 3am with PC Sydney Taylor, of Lambourne End, at what was officially known as a 'conference point', outside Grove House, at Howe Green, a quiet, rural locality on the Romford-Ongar road. After their 'meet', the two constables parted at around 3.30am, both heading for their respective homes, Taylor pedalling off on his bicycle.

Shortly before 6am, PC Gutteridge's dead body was discovered by William Ward, who, driving a touring car, was delivering mail to all the little local post offices between Romford and Abridge.

At first, Ward had thought that Gutteridge had met with an accident, been knocked down by a passing car. Then, to his horror, he saw that he had been shot. He was lying, half propped in a sort of semi-sitting position against a bank at the side of the road leading to Passingford Bridge, some 400 yards from his home at Townley Cottages, Stapleford Abbotts. His helmet lay on the ground close beside him. So did his notebook, open at a blank page, and his pencil was firmly gripped in his right hand. Obviously, he had been about to take down the particulars of some person or persons. The fact that his torch was still in his pocket, and the road was an unlit one, suggested that he must have been about to write by the light presumably provided by a vehicle. And, indeed, there were plain marks of the wheels of a motor-car that had run up against the bank where Gutteridge must have been standing.

Dr Robert Woodhouse, of Romford, was called to the scene to examine the body. He arrived at about 9am, and opined that death had taken place between four and five hours previously. The constable had been shot four times. There were two bullet wounds in the left cheek, and with incredible brutality his killer had shot out both his eyes.

Police Constable Gutteridge was just 38 years old when he was murdered, married, with two young children, a boy and a girl. He was given an impressive funeral, two hundred uniformed colleagues, headed by the Chief Constable of Essex, marching four-a-breast in the cortege, and he was laid to rest in Warley Cemetery.

Why had he been thus callously gunned down? Who could have done it? Here was a mystery indeed – and, to be frank, there did not seem to be much chance of its being solved.

The investigating officers did, however, get a lucky break. They learned that at about 2.30am on the morning of the murder a blue Morris-Cowley car, registration number TW 6120, had been stolen from the garage of a Dr Edward Lovell, who lived in London Road, Billericay. And at seven o'clock that same morning, Albert M'Dougall, a clerk, who lived at 21 Foxley Road, Brixton, South London, found what was obviously an abandoned car by his house. It was a Morris-Cowley bearing the number plate TW 6120.

The car provided two clues. On its floor, under the front passenger seat, a spent cartridge case. On its running-board, at the driver's side, marks of human blood.

The clue of the empty cartridge case was eventually to prove of enormous importance. Brought by the Chief Constable of the CID, Frederick Wensley, to the attention of the Assistant Commissioner Crime, Major-General Sir Wyndham Childs, who was something of an expert in such matters, it was immediately recognised by him as a Mark IV bullet, made at the Royal Laboratory, Woolwich Arsenal.

He also knew that it was a leaden flat-nosed type of revolver ammunition, which, issued to the British Expeditionary Force when it left for France in 1914, had been claimed by the Germans to be an expanding bullet, violating the terms of the Hague Convention. In protest, the Germans had begun cutting the tops off their nickel-coated bullets, making them effectively dumdums. The practice only ceased when the Mark IV ammunition was withdrawn from the troops in France – and either re-made or destroyed.

Examining the cartridge case under a microscope, he saw that what had appeared to the naked eye to be a little blister on the copper cap, was actually an elevation of the copper above the normal level of the cap, composed of a large number of minute bead-like facets. Other elevations in the form of lines and striations were also present. What they meant was that the breech-shield – that is the part of the weapon which takes the shock of the discharge – of the gun that fired the cartridge, would have depressions corresponding to the elevations or excrescences on the cartridge case.

It transpired that a bullet taken from PC Gutteridge's head was a Mark IV, and the revolver which fired the shot was a Webley. But where on earth, Sir Wyndham wondered, had the murderer got hold of such obsolete ammunition?

In fact, two different types of obsolete ammunition had been used in the shooting of PC Gutteridge. The second was spherical lead bullets, loaded with black powder instead of cordite; a kind which had not been in use since 1897.

Four months passed. Then, one day, Wensley came into Childs' room again with the news that a man had been arrested from whom four revolvers, including two Webleys, had been taken. The man was Frederick Guy Browne. He was the owner of the Globe Garage, at 7a Northcote Road, Battersea, where he combined legitimate work, repairing and so forth, with periodical profitable burglary and car theft.

Towards the end of December 1927, a letter had arrived at Scotland Yard. It was from an ex-convict who had known Browne, who, incidentally, could boast a very respectable criminal record, at Dartmoor. In it, the man said that he had been the driver of a car which had been the cause of a serious accident in Sheffield on 14 November. Browne had sold to a Sheffield butcher, Benjamin Stow, a Vauxhall car which he had stolen in Tooting.

The informant described Browne as a very dangerous man, adding that he had visited him the previous October at his garage near Clapham Junction, and seen hanging in the office there, a big Webley revolver. He had jestingly said to Browne and his assistant, Pat Kennedy: "I hope you didn't shoot Gutteridge." And received the reply: "We've been expecting them coming for us every day. But if they do come, we can prove we were letting cars out of the garage at 6am. We did go down there for a car the day before this chap was murdered, and it's a good job we weren't there the same day."

Later, in November, at the informant's home in Sheffield, Browne stood in the corner of the kitchen, a large Webley in each hand, and said: "If they come to my garage I'll let them in, even if there's half a dozen or a dozen, but there's not one that goes out alive." He is also alleged to have said: "The police aren't so fond of pulling a car up at night after what we did to Gutteridge."

The police came to Browne's garage at 7.30pm

on the night of 20 January 1928, and arrested him. He was initially held on the charge of stealing a car. After the discovery of two Webleys, one fully loaded with six Mark IV bullets, and the other with six rounds of the very old spherical, black powder ammunition, and examination by Childs confirmed that the breech-shield of one of the Webleys bore depressions which corresponded exactly with the elevations on the cap of the cartridge case taken from the Morris-Cowley, the charge was changed to one of murder.

Hearing on the grapevine of Browne's arrest, his friend Kennedy promptly took off for Liverpool, where, on Sunday 22 January, he and his wife, Pat, took a room in the house of David Staunton, at 119 Copperas Hill.

William Henry Kennedy was a man with a chequered career behind him. Born, thirty-six years before, in Ayrshire, of Irish parents, and taken as a lad to Liverpool, all his life he had affected the brogue of the Emerald Isle, and was used to answering to the name of Pat. Apprenticed to a compositor in Liverpool, he had the option of a good steady job with prospects 'in the print'. But, sadly, he lacked the vital ingredient of stability. He quit to join the Army, left the service with discredit in 1911, returned to Liverpool in 1913, and resumed his career as a compositor.

All might yet have been well, had it not been for a fatal flaw in his character, which seemed to make it impossible for him to conduct his affairs with anything remotely resembling honesty. His criminal career was scarcely Rafflesian romantic –

petty thefts, drunk and disorderly, indecent exposure, house-breaking and larceny. Several custodial sentences later, he went back into the Army, only to be discharged with ignominy. Again, Liverpool enjoyed the dubious benefit of his shady presence. He divided his time there between the practice of crime and the hawking of fruit.

A favourite watering-hole of his was Ye Cracke, in Rice Street. Joseph Thomas, the husband of the licensee, was an old friend of his, he and Kennedy having been out in South Africa together, bearing arms in the Boer War. As a matter of record, Kennedy had one of his last drinks in Liverpool at Ye Cracke, coming in there, according to Thomas, on either 23rd or 24th of January 1928.

According to his own account, it was in June or July 1927, when, after his latest release from prison in November 1926, he was working on a farm in Cheshire, that he had a letter from Fred Browne, whom he had got to know 'inside'. Browne wrote that he was opening up a garage in Battersea and invited him to come down as manager. He was glad to accept the job. In the course of his work he used to go out on occasion on motor rides with Browne. These trips would be in the nature of business journeys.

Sitting before Chief Inspector James Berrett at Scotland Yard at seven o'clock on the evening of 26 January, Kennedy was told that he was being detained with regard to the theft of a Vauxhall motor-car in Tooting, but, said Berrett: "I have been making inquiries for some time past respecting the murder of PC Gutteridge at Essex. Can you give me any information about the occurrence?"

Kennedy sat silent for a minute or so. Then said: "I may be able to tell you something, but let me consider. Can I see my wife?"

The two had been married only very recently. Kennedy had left London in December 1927, and gone off to West Kirby, where he had wed a young woman named Pat, with whom he had returned to London on 13 January 1928. He was still deeply entangled in the coils of love. His wife was brought in to him. He turned to face her. "When I was arrested in Liverpool yesterday I told you there was something more serious at the back of it. Well, there is. These officers are making inquiries about that policeman who was murdered in Essex."

She turned red … then pale. "Why, you didn't murder him, did you?" she asked.

"No, I didn't, but I was there and know who did. If I'm charged with the murder and found guilty, I'll be hanged and you'll be a widow. On the other hand, if I'm charged and found guilty of being an accessory after the fact, I'll receive a severe sentence of penal servitude and be a long time from you. Will you wait for me?"

"Yes, love, I'll wait for you any time. Tell these gentlemen the truth of what took place."

"All right, I will."

What follows is his version of events as set out in his statement, the gospel according to Kennedy.

He well remembered, he said, the day of 26 September 1927. Browne had suggested that he should go with him to Billericay to help him steal a car. They left the garage in Northcote Road together at half-past six, and went by train from Liverpool Street. They stole the Morris-Cowley from the doctor's garage. Browne decided that they would drive home by the byways, thus avoiding the main road to London. They sped through all sorts of lonely country lanes which led eventually to a kind of main road on the way to Ongar. They had gone some distance along this road when they saw someone standing on the roadside bank, flashing his lamp, signalling them to stop. They drove on, but Kennedy heard a police whistle and told Browne to stop. He did so, and when the person came up to them they saw that it was indeed a policeman. He asked Browne where he was going and where he came from. Browne said from Lea Bridge Road Garage, and that they had been called out to do some repairs. The policeman asked if he had a card.

"No," said Browne

"Have you got a driver's licence?"

"No."

He then asked Browne: "Is the car yours?" And before he could answer Kennedy said: "No, the car is mine."

The policeman had then flashed his light in both their faces, and asked Kennedy if he knew the number of the car. "Yes, TW 6120," he had replied.

"Very well, I'll take particulars," he said, putting his torch back in his pocket and pulling out his notebook.

The narrative now takes on a somewhat less than objective, less disinterested slant. Says Kennedy:

"I heard a report, quickly followed by another

one. I saw the policeman stagger back and fall over by the bank at the hedge. I said to Browne, 'What have you done?' and then saw that he had a large Webley revolver in his hand. He said, 'Get out quick.' I immediately got out and went round to the policeman, who was lying on his back, and Browne came over and said, 'I'll finish the bugger,' and I said, 'For God's sake don't shoot any more, the man's dying,' as he was groaning. The policeman's eyes were open, and Browne, addressing him, said, 'What are you looking at me like that for?' and, stooping down, shot him at close range through both eyes."

We can never know the true history of the events enacted on that lonely Essex road that awful autumn night, but it was Childs' opinion that: "Browne first shot the constable, and Kennedy subsequently blew the poor fellow's eyes out as he lay on the ground."

Childs had noted when studying a photograph of the dead man's face that the skin was punctured with minute holes and that the cartridges which had been used to shoot out his eyes had contained a granular black powder. The granules made puncture holes. Such black powder cartridges were found in Kennedy's gun.

Browne and Kennedy, both professional criminals, were jointly charged with the murder of PC Gutteridge. They were tried before Mr Justice Avory, the 'Acid Drop', at the Old Bailey in April 1928. Both were found guilty. Browne was hanged at Pentonville and Kennedy at Wandsworth, at 9am on 31 May.

Transmuted under the powerful impulsions of romance into a poet, the plausible Billy Kennedy, as he signed himself to his newish bride, was constrained to pen, with tardily acquired wisdom:

The follies of youth
Are the sins of old age,
And the ill-fated fool
Passes out with the sage –
They both pay the price,
With death as sin's wage,
A crimson-hued blot
At the end of the page.

A Georgian Puzzle in Venanation

"Sir, let me tell you, the noblest prospect which a Scotchman ever sees, is the high road that leads him to England." So declared the peerless fashioner of fine fancy phrases and maker of stout dictionaries, Dr Samuel Johnson. And in 1875, the year after Dr Johnson's death, suiting the action to the precept, Charles Angus, the ambitious, 18-year-old son of a barber of Stranraer, headed south across the border to seek his fortune among the Sassenachs.

Georgian Liverpool, where he found himself, was a place of excitement and promise. It bustled with activity. Sedan-chairs bearing the well-to-do through the streets. The rattling mails spanking, with flying hooves and steaming horses, into the coaching inns of Dale Street. The brawling Sailortown taverns and the fragrant coffee-houses. Places like the Slaughterhouse, officially George Bennett's superior wine and spirit purveying premises, with its inner sanctum, the Rat Pit. The massive warehouses of the Goree. Vessels from all four quarters of the globe, laden with tea and spices, teak and jute, cloves and rubber, cleave the waters of the Mersey, and drop anchor along its waterfront. And, riding the choppy river amid the forest of tall-ship masts, the dark outlines of the slavers, holds filled with innocent merchandise, but soon, on the middle passage of their triangular voyage, to be exchanged for crammed cargoes of human shame and misery. Black ivory. Black gold.

By contrast, the fine-clad merchants, many of them dealing, as Charles Angus one day would, in slavery, parading in their pomp and pride, and dignity-robed professional men, safe and comfortably insulated behind the bastions of the Athenæum, the exclusive gentleman's club, hard by St Peter's, in Church Street. The clean-limned, beautifully-architected houses of the prosperous, made gracious the town's rapidly expanding hinterland. The country poked green fingers in close above Shaw's Brow, where, no distance at all away, lay Everton.

Glenn Chandler lyrically describes the scene:

> *In those days Everton was a pretty village across rolling countryside where many of the wealthier merchants had their grand mansions, and where they kept their carriages in which they rode into Liverpool each day to do business. Once a barren sandstone ridge, it now flourished with tiers of well-kept gardens full of blossom and cascading greenery. ... on summer mornings, with the scent of hay and honeysuckle in the air [it] must have been ... idyllic.*

In this vibrant new and challenging town, Angus made a lowly start, well pleased at securing a position in a druggist's counting-house. Who should have guessed that this young man, tall, dark, curly-haired, tending towards stoutness, was to become the epicentre of a terrible life and death mystery that would puzzle the Liverpool citizenry down the years, and seems certain to remain unsolved over the centuries. A mystery concerning which, at my insistent instigation, my good friend Glenn Chandler, the creator of *Taggart*, television's celebrated Glaswegian detective, carried out a masterly investigation of his own, which resulted in his writing an outstanding book about the case, *Burning Poison*.

Time has washed away the records of Angus' first ten years in Liverpool, leaving only hints and whispers. Certain it is that as he sat like a coiled spring on the druggist's counting-house stool, it grew a progressively less comfortable perch.

There is evidence that this fringe-medical occupation stimulated Angus' interest in medicine and medicines. He appears to have taken the trouble to acquaint himself thoroughly with the contents of standard works on the subject, until he eventually reached the stage where he felt confident to prescribe and dispense for patients, and even to instruct young persons how to be doctors, and secure positions for them on Africa-bound ships.

At some point, as the century moved towards its close, Angus contrived a start as a general merchant in a small way of business. Before too long, he had his own counting-house, then went into mercantile partnership with a fellow ascendant Scot, Robert Copland, and the pair set up trading premises in Mersey Street, just off Canning Place. The partnership was dissolved in 1799.

The next milestone in Angus' life was his marriage into money. He was thirty-three. His bride was Maria McQuistin, the 13-year-old daughter of

Thomas McQuistin, a wealthy coffee plantation owner and livestock breeder, lately retired from Jamaica, and settled into a fine house, 2 Trinity Place, off St Anne Street, in a very good professional class neighbourhood. The couple were married on 5 March 1800, at St Nicholas', the Mariners' Church.

Angus' new father-in-law was in his eighties, and made it plain that he wished Angus to take over his affairs and conduct his business for him, both in Liverpool and Jamaica. It was in this way that Angus became profitably involved in the slave-trade, and the owner of two slave-ships.

A slight storm cloud blew up on the Angus horizon. Thomas McQuistin had decided to make a new will and sent a note round to his solicitor, Richard Statham, demanding the return of all his papers, and stating that he no longer wished him to act for him. As Statham rightly guessed, it was Angus, now living at Trinity Place, who was behind his dismissal. Mr McQuistin's revised will left the bulk of his estate to Angus, who must have intuited that Statham, a former executor, would have been strongly opposed to this. The resultant ill-feeling between Statham and Angus was to prove of subsequent significance.

Four weeks after signing the new will, Thomas McQuistin died. Angus was now a man of wealth and station. The seal was set upon his social acceptability by an invitation to join the Athenæum. In 1801 Maria bore him a daughter, Jane, and the following year a second daughter, Maria.

But now the first zephyr of an ill-wind began to blow. Angus lost two of his slave-trading ships, and as many cargoes, and things were going disastrously wrong with the Jamaican property, not a penny from which had thus far found its way home to the steadily diminishing coffers at Trinity Place.

In June 1804, Maria gave birth to a third child, a son, Thomas. She was still barely 18, and after all this child-bearing her health seemed to be failing. To ease the strain upon her, Angus decided to employ a governess who would take care of the children, and invited Maria's half-sister, Margaret Burns, to come to Trinity Place as governess-cum-housekeeper. For all these thoughtful provisions, poor Maria did not survive long. She died, on 25 June 1805, of tuberculosis.

Let it be said at once, and unequivocally, that Margaret Burns was in no wise attractive, either as to physical appearance or psychological temperament. It was no fault of hers, but she was pale and sallow of complexion, small and broad-chested of build, and a martyr to dropsy, her deliverance from the lethal effects of which, she ascribed to infusions of powdered Peruvian bark in wine, administered to her by the medically skilled Angus. Her temperament, in that it was 'pawky', which is to say 'mean-hearted', was very much akin to that of her half-brother-in-law. Indeed, taking into the reckoning their shared penuriousness and mutual delight in the practice of parsimony, there were those who would have said that Charles and Margaret were made for each other! It will come as small surprise then that not a great deal of time had passed before Miss Burns found her way into Mr Angus' bed. And not a great

173

deal more time passed before – at the beginning of March 1808 – it was observed that Miss Burns was getting larger. Could it perhaps be that Margaret was pregnant? This was to be a pivotal question.

There are some surrounding circumstances of which we need to take cognisance. About the middle of February 1808, Angus paid a visit to John Steele at the druggists' shop, Steele & Oakes, in South Castle Street, and asked him if he could let him have a quantity of Oil of Savin. Steele, who knew Angus quite well, was not worried about selling it to him, despite its being a potentially powerful poison. Its medicinal uses were in the treatment of chlorosis, the so-called green disease, an iron deficiency commonly found among adolescent girls, and in cases of menstrual absences or deficiencies. It is also an abortifacient, producing tetanic uterine convulsions. Administered in improper dosage, its characteristic symptoms are excruciating pain, accompanied by vomiting and diarrhoea, and climaxing in death. Steele would recall Angus' dismay at being told that *Oleum Sabine* cost five shillings per ounce. Pawky as ever, he settled for two drachms, that is a quarter of a fluid ounce, saying that that would probably answer his purpose. He did not, however, expatiate as to what that purpose might be.

A couple of weeks later, Angus betook himself to the shop of Thomas Richardson, cutler and surgical instrument maker. Saying that he wished for it to be sharpened, he produced a ten-inch-long tube with a three-edged point to it. It was an instrument designed for the purpose of causing a

174

miscarriage. On hearing that the sharpening would cost him ninepence, Angus, true to form, grumbled and growled before grudgingly paying up. He told Richardson that he would be using the instrument to pierce his children's ears.

With oil and perforator in the forefront of our minds, we come to the crucial days, the veritable Ides of March. At a quarter past nine on the morning of Wednesday 23 March, when the maid, Betty Nickson, came into the parlour at Trinity Place to serve breakfast, she saw at once that Margaret Burns was very ill. She lay down on the sofa, complaining of severe bowel pains and extreme thirst. She then began to vomit. The vomit was very black in colour. All that day she remained supine upon the sofa.

At eleven o'clock the following morning, Angus suggested that they should send for the family doctor. "You need not," he assured the ailing woman, "be afraid of the expense." But no doctor came, either that day or the next.

Friday, however, seemed to bring miraculous recovery. Miss Burns took some warm beer, which she kept down; later, a bowlful of gruel, which she also kept down; and later still, at about ten o'clock, she fancied some white wine. There was none in the house. Betty Nickson traipsed off to Mr Winstanley's, the wine merchant in Henry Street, near Duke Street, fully three-quarters of a mile away, right across the town, to buy a couple of bottles.

It would be coming up to a quarter past eleven by the time Betty got back from her long trek. The tableau that greeted her eyes when she pushed back the parlour door on her return was to haunt her for the rest of her life. It was a bizarre, horrific scene. Margaret Burns was "cowered in a lump in a corner of the room, her elbows on her knees, and her face pressed against the wall." She was dead. And there, in his easy-chair, a quilt pulled over him, was Charles Angus – fast asleep.

It was at the Liverpool coroner's behest that, at two o'clock on Sunday afternoon, the doctors plied their autopsy knives. The corpse lay in the upstairs bedroom immediately above the parlour, where, on that Friday afternoon, it had been carried.

A story was being bruited around that Miss Burns had been with child. The medical men, five of them, peered into the dead woman's uterus. Yes, they all agreed. She had recently given birth to a nearly full-term child. But where was the child? No one had seen sight nor heard sound of it. How had it, dead or alive, been disposed of? And of what had its unfortunate mother died? Neither of these questions was ever to be satisfactorily answered. The doctors found inflammation in the small intestine, on the edge of the liver and on part of the curvature of the stomach. In the latter there was also a hole, which, they suspected, could well have been caused by some sort of corrosive poison.

An inquest was held at the new Liverpool Exchange, in Castle Street. And who should turn out to be clerk to the coroner and solicitor to the corporation, but Angus' old enemy, Richard Statham. Another menacing shadow was cast by Mrs Sarah Lawson, Angus' sportive next-door neighbour, whose cupidinous advances it may well be that he had resent-triggeringly rejected. She was dedicating herself to a vengeful scouring of the town for former servants in Angus' employ, to testify to his sexual relationship with Miss Burns.

The Reverend John Vause, incumbent of fashionable Christ Church, in nearby Hunter Street, was adamant that he had encountered Angus at the Athenæum early on the Friday morning – the newsroom there opened at 7am, and Angus would often go there before breakfast to read the day's news – and walked back with him to Trinity Place. This was in direct contradiction to the statements of the servants, who said that the master had not left the house that Friday. The prosecution theory was that if Miss Burns had given birth to a child on the morning of her death, Angus had got rid of it on his way to the club.

Charles Angus was arrested and deposited in the Tower, the Borough Gaol, in Water Street. His house was searched from top to bottom for the body of a child and any poisonous substances. A vast array of bottles was found – one was marked 'Jacob's Water' and another 'Poison Water'. Both were submitted to Dr John Bostock, physician to the Liverpool Dispensary, for analysis. He found that the bottle labelled 'Poison Water' contained corrosive sublimate of mercury, saturated with a strong solution of arsenic. Angus was committed to Lancaster Castle for trial at the Assizes.

It seemed a long, long time from April to September, waiting in Lancaster Castle Gaol to be brought up to the dock, but at last, at eight o'clock on the morning of Friday 2 September 1808, he was led up the flight of steep steps from the cells and through the trap-door into the court. A prosecution witness of very great importance was a retired timber merchant, Peter Charnley, who, testifying to a conversation that had taken place twelve or thirteen years before, said that Angus had then shown him a silver, tube-like instrument. A slide ran up the centre, and it had a three-edged dart at its point. He had been told by Angus that by introducing it through the womb, and letting the air in, a miscarriage could be brought about.

The doctors then stepped up with their evidence. They were sure that Miss Burns had given birth. They admitted that no corrosive sublimate of mercury had been found in the dead woman's stomach. Dr Bostock, however, authoritatively asserted that the corrosive sublimate might be taken into the stomach in a state of solution, that following violent symptoms of vomiting and purging and the drinking copiously of diluted liquors, death might take place, and yet the most minute examination of the stomach and its contents might fail to detect the slightest trace of the corrosive sublimate of mercury. He, too, had examined Miss Burns' uterus. He had found it large enough to contain a quart of fluid, whereas an unimpregnated uterus had scarcely any cavity and was barely larger than a pear or a fig.

Mr James Topping, leading for the defence, asked Dr Bostock if he was aware of the perfectly innocent domestic use of a mixture of corrosive sublimate and arsenic as a bug destroyer, frequently employed for washing furniture. Angus had himself so used it, and he had requested the medical men to inspect the drawers in his house, when they would see a consequent whiteness about them. Angus pointed out that the 'Poison Water' in his possession was expressly labelled as such, and said that he had obtained the mixture in order to destroy moths which, seven years ago, were injuring his blankets, woollens and valuable carpets.

Referring, in the statement which he read to the Court, to the surgical instrument, Angus said: "It was never intended for any purpose relative to women. As I had studied Bell on the venereal disease, and had cured many venereal cases, it was in these instances that I applied it. The instrument was much longer, and as thin as a knitting-needle, and this probe was neither more nor less than to be introduced into men's urethras, in cases of stricture or warts."

'It was around midnight,' goes Glenn Chandler's evocative description of the scene, 'and the oil lamps of the Crown Court in the mediæval castle cast their eerie glow …' On to the stage stepped the last witness, Dr Carson.

So far as his medical brethren in Liverpool were concerned, James Carson was something of a maverick. Accustomed to taking up an opposition stance, the view which he chose to take in this case was, predictably, the reverse of that subscribed to by all the other medicos. The hole in Margaret Burns' stomach, he declared, had occurred *after* her death. He backed this diametric opinion by the provision of the details of three cases reported by

179

the great surgeon, John Hunter, in which such holes had been found post mortem. He did not, however, concur with Hunter in thinking that the holes had been produced by the action of the gastric juice. His startlingly idiosyncratic view was that water in the stomach at a temperature of 90 degrees, mixing with the common salt taken in food, could cause the stomach to dissolve!

As regards the alleged pregnancy, he put forward the even more bizarre diagnosis that the appearance of the womb was due to a 'dropsy of the hydatids'. In plain language: hydatids are largish vesicles or bladders containing either the larvae of a genus of tapeworms – *Echinococcus* – or sometimes simply sterile, fluid-filled cysts, which may develop as tumours or cysts in nearly all mammals. What Carson was hazarding was that Margaret Burns had 'given birth' to a huge mass of tapeworm cysts, which had grown pediculate in her uterus. An ingenious, but distinctly eccentric, notion.

The judge, Mr Justice Chambre, summed up with scrupulous accuracy and even-handed fairness. The jury, without leaving their box, found Angus not guilty.

The acquitted man's return to Liverpool was something less than a triumph. Stares, whispers, and hostility followed him. They confirmed his decision to show the town a clean pair of heels. In November 1808, he resigned his membership of the Athenæum, and took a coach for Scotland.

After he had gone, the Liverpool medics, piqued by what they regarded as Carson's audacity, got hold of the controversial uterus, still preserved in spirits, and took a close-focus look at the ovaries. To their delight and vindication, they discovered in one of them a *corpus luteum*; that is a yellow mass formed by a follicle which has matured and discharged an egg. If the egg has been impregnated, the *corpus luteum* grows and lasts for several months. If impregnation has not taken place, the *corpus luteum* degenerates and shrinks.

Charles Angus died at Turnberry Lodge, Turnberry, on the Ayrshire coast, on 21 May 1820, at the age of 53. He is buried in Kirkoswald churchyard.

In Liverpool, he has left no trace. The merciless waters of time have washed everything away. All that beautiful and gracious part of the town to which the young Charles Angus aspired, and eventually succeeded, has vanished into the limbo of lost things. The mansions of St Anne Street have long since crumbled, their once-lovely gardens have been crushed out of life beneath grey paving-stones. Number 2 Trinity Place survived – if you can call it that – as the Mohamed Sultan Lodging-House right on until the days of the Second World War. But for the rest, all that we are left with is old, old ghosts, hovering for just as long as there are memories to hold them, about the bleakly altered landscape of hinterland Everton, where once the lovingly cultivated roses and the wild thyme blew.

LIVERPOOL GANGS AND GARROTTERS

One of my earliest criminous memories is of my mother telling me of her father telling her of the Liverpool garrotters, and how they were put down by a fierce old gentleman called Mr Justice Day and his cat.

I remember looking up the word 'garrotters' in *Chambers' Dictionary* and finding that garrotting was a Spanish mode of putting criminals to death, originally by strangling them with a string around the throat, tightened by twisting a stick. *Garrote* is the Spanish word for a stick or cudgel. Later, the method was refined by the introduction of a brass collar, tightened by a screw, whose point was driven through to enter the spinal marrow.

What on earth, I wondered, could such barbarities have to do with latish nineteenth century Liverpool? But wait … a subsidiary definition in my indispensable dictionary: 'To garrotte: suddenly to render insensible by semi-strangulation in order to rob.'

There was, it seems, a severe outbreak in the Liverpool streets in the latter part of the 1880s of what we would today call by the infinitely less romantic and evocative, Americanised term of 'mugging', but which our grandparents' more refined ear and taste christened rather more exotically, garrotting. But, on the rose by any other name principle in reverse, there was absolutely nothing remotely romantic about being seized by a villainous scouser, half-throttled, and thus painfully separated from your purse or wallet.

And that is where, in 1886, the luminant Mr Justice John Charles Frederick Sigismund de Haren Day made his salvatory entrance on the darkling scene. The widely accredited intelligence at the time was that the garrottings were being carried out by a band of ruffians who called themselves the High Rip Gang. Some doubt has subsequently been cast on this. Sir William Nott-Bower, Head Constable of Liverpool from 1881 to 1902, recalled in his memoirs that Liverpool in his time was, in parts, a dangerous city. There were streets, particularly in the vicinity of Scotland Road, which were unsafe for respectable people to enter, and where the police habitually patrolled in pairs. 'This condition of affairs caused much concern and anxiety,' he confessed, 'and unfortunately some genius invented an absolutely unfounded cause for it.'

Sir William is referring to the suggestion that the large number of crimes in the Scotland Road area was due to a gang known as the Organization or, alternatively, the High Rip Gang, which existed for the purpose of plunder and violence, and the execution of vengeance on all who ventured to give evidence against them. He fulminated:

> *All this created considerable, and entirely unjustifiable, alarm ... There was never the very faintest shadow of foundation for the suggestions made ... But letters from all sorts of irresponsible persons, Press*

183

comment, and a certain sort of public opinion
assumed the impossible, and accepted the fact
of a High Rip Gang.

So ... Sir William was a sceptic. Why? Because: 'It was impossible, for such a gang could not have existed without the Police ever *hearing* of it.'

My friend of many years, the lawyer and author, James Morton, who is a leading authority on gangs and gangland, past and present, national and international, had this to say:

"Whether there was such a gang [as the High Rip Gang] may be open to question, but there were certainly a great number of robberies with violence and woundings in the list for the [Liverpool] November Assizes of 1886 presided over by Mr Justice Day."

John Day had been elevated to the High Court Bench in June 1882, at the age of 56. Nursing a profound distrust for 'the theories of penology built upon Lombroso and criminal anthropology', he placed his faith in deterring criminals from further offence against God – he was a zealous Roman Catholic – and society, by means of severe sentences coupled with the use of the lash known as the 'cat-o'-nine-tails'. His pity – he was not a cruel, sadistic, or unmerciful man – was always directed towards the victim. He regarded it as his duty to avenge the weak and innocent.

He was not, however, one of those remote judges of that ilk which enquires: "What is a Beatle?" When, at the time of the 1886 Assize, he came to Liverpool, he was not content to relax amid the judicial luxuries provided at Newsham House, the Judges' Lodgings, at Newsham Park, but decided instead that it was necessary for him to see for himself something of the night haunts and habits in their normal environment of the kind of social pests who were to appear before him. Accordingly, he requested Sir William Nott-Bower to arrange such a tour for him, and the other Judge of Assize then in Liverpool, Mr Justice Grantham, said that he would like to come along, too.

So, on the following evening, timing the excursion for after the public-houses had disgorged their rough habitues into the streets, the two judges, and Day's son, Frank, who was his Marshal for that Assize, escorted by the Head Constable, Chief Inspector Robertson, and another detective, sallied forth on an educational foray that included on its itinerary visits to such ill-famed nocturnal *loci* as the Loose Box and the Long Jigger. Both judges said that what they had seen that night was a revelation to them, and could not fail to be a help in the future discharge of their judicial duties.

The expedition does not, however, seem to have exerted any immediate influence over Mr Justice Day's normal sentencing procedure. Its mode went like this: "I shall not sentence you to a long period of imprisonment." The thug in the dock would give a self-satisfied grin of relief. The old boy was going to be lenient like Hopwood. Mr Hopwood was the Recorder of Liverpool at the time. He was renowned for his leniency, a factor which Mr Justice Day determined to counter by a deliberate policy of harsh sentencing, in the hope of stamping out, or, at the very least, drastically reducing, the prevailing social evil.

A piece of doggerel of the period enshrines a 'High Ripper's' view:

> *Oh, Mr Hopwood, what shall I do?*
> *They've sent me to Assizes,*
> *And I wanted to go to you,*
> *For though I may only get the sentence of a*
> *'Day',*
> *Oh, Mr Hopwood, the cat may spoil my stay.*

To return to the smirking thug in the dock ... Mr Justice Day continued addressing him: "I consider you a case in which the rate-payers' money would be expended to no good purpose; and so I shall not send you to penal servitude." The thug would by now be jubilant. "But I shall sentence you to twelve months' hard labour, with twenty-five strokes of the cat when you go in, and another twenty-five when you come out." Total collapse of thug. "Show your back to your dissolute friends when you come out."

In one case where the prisoner fell on his knees pleading for mercy, Day told him: "Get up, you cowardly rascal, and take your punishment like a man."

The policy, of inflicting a short term of imprisonment, balanced by the maximum allowance of the cat, sometimes misfired, the prison doctor declaring the man medically unfit to receive so many lashes. Observing this, Day made sure that a medical examination preceded his promulgation of sentence. What happened in practice was that the actual sentencing of those found guilty would be put back to the last day of the Assizes. It has been calculated that over a period of fourteen years, Day inflicted 3,766 lashes of the cat on 137 criminals.

Well, *did* the High Rip Gang exist?

There is no doubt that the *Daily Telegraph* believed that it did, for that newspaper reported in its issue of 15 November 1886, that two 19-year-old lads, said to be High Rips, had received fifteen years' penal servitude apiece for stabbing a member of the rival Logwood Gang. It also reported that one man had had to be given police protection because he had refused to let the High Rips use a goods shed belonging to the Lancashire and Yorkshire Railway Company, to which he held the keys.

Certainly Elizabeth O'Brien, an old lady of 86, who was interviewed in 1960, was in no doubt as to the gang's existence. Her recollections were quoted in the *Liverpool Echo* of 19 October 1960:

> *There were women in the High Rippers who identified themselves with a flower or plume in the hair. They were more vicious than men.*

She also remembered that the only person who could exercise any sort of control over the High Rippers was a policeman known by the nickname of 'Pins'. When he approached, the gang would scatter, with loud warning shouts of, "Pins is coming!" A quaint piece of social history folklore, from a woman who would have been a child of nine when Mr Justice Day was dealing with the gang – and doing it his way!

James Morton tells how, in the early part of the twentieth century, it was at one time estimated that fifty per cent of Liverpool's Chinese community was actively engaged in the manufacture of opium.

At that time, too, there were formidable gangs who were hard at it committing dock crimes of various kinds, including the 'rolling' of half-seas over sailormen. Paradise Street, Back George Street, and Park Lane, were gangland territory, and sailors were being lured out of such safe ports as the Sailors' Home and the YMCA with dangled carrots of shebeens and invitations tendered to the naughty parlours of willing girls. They would end up, not garrotted, but probably senseless, and certainly money-wad-less, in a dark alley.

THE WINTER GIRL

There are days in Liverpool when the sky lours darkly over grey streets, a nagging wind whisks the dust into tiny whirlpools and chases crumpled scraps of paper over the cobbles, and everything seems shaded with melancholy. I do not have the weather report for Monday, 6 January 1908, but that most surely sums up the 'reality' feeling of the afternoon of Madge Kirby's untimely death.

To our cinema-going grandparents Madge Kirby, star of stage and silent screen, was one of England's most successful exports. Leaving our shores at the age of nine, she was destined to become the American Biograph Studio's most popular comedienne. She started off her meteoric career when, reaching her fourteenth birthday, she went on the stage to become ingenue for Richard Carle and Lew Fields, before progressing to vaudeville and films, where she excelled in light comedy roles. A very decorative, fluffy girl, she used to play her parts in a blonde wig with tumbling curls, and won all hearts.

But it is with another Madge Kirby that we are concerned here – the seven-year-old, Liverpool-born Madge Kirby, from 55 Romilly Street, Kensington – who was playing on the wintry afternoon of Monday, 6 January 1908, along with her five-year-old brother, George, and her best friend, Annie McGovern, also aged seven, near the reservoir in Farnworth Street, just round the corner from her home. Through the gathering twilight, a stranger, a man in black, made his way along the pavement towards Madge and Annie. His approach was suave, genial. Smiling, well-spoken, he asked, "Would you like some sweets?" Annie resisted. Madge succumbed. Of course she would. What child wouldn't? He took her by the hand. Together they walked happily away. Both walked into oblivion. One of them into the oblivion of death.

Seven anxiety-racked months would pass before Madge was seen again. It was a labourer on his way to work, who, on the rainy Tuesday morning of 12 August, saw the sack. It lay, sad and forlorn, upon the rain-soaked pavement outside a condemned and derelict house – 15 Great Newton Street, off Pembroke Place. Despite the fact that there had been a heavy shower, the sack was bone-dry. It could not, therefore, have been placed where he found it more than a few minutes before. It did in fact transpire that it had lain hidden all those long months in the cellar of the empty house. Yielding to curiosity, he cut open the sack; a canvas sugar bag bearing no name or distinctive marks. Crammed within it was Madge's scantily clad and ravaged little body.

The pathetic remains, badly decomposed, bore small resemblance to the pretty blue-eyed, brown-haired, fresh-faced little girl in the black shirt, blue pinafore, black stockings, laced boots, and wearing a black velvet bonnet, who had vanished so softly and silently away. All that was left of her was conveyed to the Princes Dock Mortuary, where her father, unable to recognise her due to her condition, identified her by her chemise, stockings, and garters. A post mortem was carried out by Dr Nathan Raw and Dr Owen.

For months the police had been searching for the lost child, whose father, frantic with worry when she never came home for tea, had sought their help. His life had not been good of late. David Kirby was a journeyman plumber, thirty-eight years old, and a sorely recent widower, his wife, Jane having died only the previous September. Severely depressed, he had not been working as well and fully as he might.

Today, no doubt, the father would have been the first suspect; if only because of his known and demonstrable depression. Not so a hundred years ago. Then, it was willingly indeed that the police had come to his aid. Doors had been knocked on, bells rung, at scores and scores of doors in house-to-house enquiries around their Kensington and Edge Hill neighbourhood. Fanning out wider, 5,000 empty houses had been searched, parks and wastelands scoured, lakes, ponds, and pools dragged. No single stone, no matter how remotely possible it might seem of providing revelation, had been left unturned. And Heaven itself had been assailed with the daily prayers for her safe return of the children and teachers at Madge's school, St Michael's.

But there was to be no granting of a happy ending. On Thursday, 13 August, little Margaret Kirby was laid to rest in the same grave at Ford Roman Catholic Cemetery as her mother. Romilly and Farnworth streets were packed with mourners, many dissolving in tears as they watched in silence the funeral cortege move slowly by. The small coffin, heaped with wreaths, was carried gently into the chapel. Most touchingly, there was laid upon it a harp of flowers from her playmate of that fatal day, Annie McGovern.

With the finding of Madge Kirby, the police hunt switched to the search for her killer. Now, one of the most extraordinary, albeit very necessary, pieces of police deception was enacted. Such was the fever pitch of public interest and anxiety, that, on the evening of the Monday, 17 August, enormous, hampering crowds gathered around Prescot Street Police Station. Presently, two policemen came charging out, tugged by a [Great Dane] in apparent full cry, and off they went, an eagerly pursuing mob, estimated 2,000-strong, and including in its ragged ranks of hunt followers a fair number of riders on bicycles, two elderly men who had joined the chase in expertly manœuvred wheelchairs, and several brace of women racing along pushing prams, streaming down Prescot Street after them. What none of the excited pursuivants knew, was that they were zealously tracking a decoy, for, shortly after midnight, a second party of police, with a second dog, this time a bloodhound, had emerged into a now empty Prescot Street.

The bloodhound, named 'The Czar', lent for the emergency by his owner, a Mr Pakenham, was an especially sensitive performer. After taking up the scent from the murdered child's clothes, he set determinedly off upon his olfactory trail of detection. Its route led through the Botanic Gardens, across a deserted strip of wasteland on the eastern side of Edge Lane, along Wavertree and Tunnel roads, and ended up on the inner platform of Lime-Street-bound trains at Edge Hill Railway Station. There, standing stock-still, tail up like a scimitar, quivering nostrils busily sniffing the air, The Czar fixed his gaze on the dark mouth-gap of the Lime Street tunnel.

His handlers promptly hailed a cab, bundled The Czar into it, the driver whipped up his horse, and the group clipped off citywards at a brisk trot. Upon reaching Lime Street station, The Czar dragged them full tilt to Platform No 8, where it gave up the trail, and although Mr Pakenham thought that, since the trains from that platform went to Birmingham, this might well indicate that the murderer had left Liverpool for the Midlands, the police were unconvinced. Like the bloodhounds, Barnaby and Burgho, called in from Scarborough in 1888 to track down Jack the Ripper, The Czar had failed.

Echoing again an incident from the Ripper case – the 'Dear Boss' letter – there arrived at Prescot Street Bridewell, on 13 August, a letter addressed to Detective Inspector Moore, who was in charge of the case. On its envelope was written, 'From Madge Kirby's murderer'. It read:

> *Dear Sir,*
> *I should like to throw a little light on the murder of my victim, Madge Kirby. Some years ago I was a lodger at 15 Great Newton St. so*

that I know the house thoroughly. I am still in possession of a key to the front-door, which I used in those days.

On the night of January 6th at 8.45 I took the girl through the front-door, and it was quite dark. We had been over to 'World's Fair' (a public-house) before then .... That is the way I treated her; and then I did away with her. The way I killed her you will no doubt find out today. At 5.35 on Tuesday morning last I entered the house once more with my key, not with the intention of moving the body for good, but with the intention of letting the world know what became of the child. If I had not been drinking I don't suppose I would have attempted the task. It may lead to my arrest, and only the drink have I to thank for it.

I am now going to give you a real clue to work on. (I am a regular at the public house I mentioned). Since I have made this confession I will be obliged to say goodbye to ——— [a person's name is here given]. I suppose they have been good friends to me ...

I have given you a chance for your money now, so do your best, but I am sure your manhunt will be in vain.

If this letter is to be believed genuine, it appears that, after much thought and agonising, the killer had decided to let the world know of Madge's fate. He had, accordingly, returned to the cellar of the derelict house where he had left the body of his little victim, stuffed her remains into a sack, and put it out on the pavement. It was noted that the handwriting was plainly that of a person of education.

It may be that he was seen, for on the Wednesday (22 August) a man came forward saying that on the morning of the day that the body was found he saw a mysterious person, who struck him as a man dressed in woman's clothing, emerging cautiously and hurriedly from the back-yard door of the house adjoining No 15. There was no yard door to the house in which the murder is supposed to have been committed, but on the back wall between the two houses detectives found signs of its having been recently climbed over.

A number of witnesses gave evidence at the inquest, held by the Liverpool Coroner, Mr T E Sampson, at Dale Street Courthouse, but there was little of any practical significance that they could tell, and on 10 September 1908, a verdict of 'Wilful murder by some person or persons unknown,' was recorded.

The police were, in fact, presented with a suspect. He had been put in the frame by one Nathan Schwernsky, a bill distributor by avocation, who had lived at No 16 Great Newton Street until 31 August 1903. A tall, dark man with a black moustache, who had also lodged in Great Newton Street until about 1903. His name had been Thompson, and Schwernsky said that he had been rather eccentric. Every effort to track him down ended in failure.

In July, 1909, a certain Alfred George Noakes, who had been charged with the murder of Madge Kirby, was discharged, the stipendiary magistrate saying that there was no case against him. Conflicting evidence had been offered regarding the identification of Noakes as the man who was seen with the child on the night that she disappeared. The descriptions of this man as tendered by some of the witnesses did not, however, at all correspond with the appearance of the prisoner.

It is clear to us now that Margaret Kirby was the victim of a homicidal paedophile, but in those innocent days paedophilia was not recognised as the widespread affliction which it has since proved to be. Ordinary motives for murder were sought, even when the plain evidence showed the real truth of the matter. Incest, too, was thought to be extremely rare, and confined to remote rural areas.

Returning home at the conclusion of the inquest, David Kirby told his sister "This has finished me." Felled by grief and illness, he took to his bed, and never again rose from it. On 28 September 1908, only a matter of weeks after his missing child's corpse had been found, he died. The third member of that tragic little family to die within a twelvemonth, he was buried with his wife and daughter in the cemetery at Ford. They have lain there now these hundred years. Madge's slayer, too, must now be dead. He was never unmasked. He lies shrouded in anonymity for all eternity in his narrow earthen bed.

THE JAW KAY MYSTERY

Sadly, this cannot be a long piece, for the murder of Jaw Kay is a short and non-sweet story. It is, moreover, one of the very small number of cases that Chief Superintendent James Morris of Liverpool CID failed to solve.

In the bleak winter's weather of a February afternoon in 1946, a disgruntled, grumblesome, and puzzled knot of impatient people were gathered outside the firmly closed shop door of a small Chinese laundry at 44 Scotland Road. They were there, as it required no Sherlock Holmes to deduce, to collect their parcels of clean washing. As the numbers of those who waited increased, so did their restiveness, until one of them, more venturesome than the rest, broke away to tread a ginger exploratory path to the rear of the building – just to see what was going on. He found the back door swinging wide-open. And that was not all that he found. In a room at the top of the stairs, splayed on a blood-crimsoned bed, lay a man's body. It was the Chinese laundryman, Jaw Kay.

At the post-mortem examination, they counted 19 separate stab wounds, all on the left side, and varying in length from half-an-inch to two and a half inches, four contused gashes to the scalp, and ten abrasions on the back of the left hand. All those who knew Jaw Kay, the gentle Chinaman who always greeted his customers with a beaming smile, simply could not understand how or why anyone should have dealt him so savage and violent an end.

Examining the scene of the crime, the police found the rooms of Jaw Kay's house to have been ransacked; drawers pulled out, cupboards broken open, several suitcases forced, the contents of all strewn about the floor. It was impossible to tell if any money had been stolen. Everything pointed to robbery. But perhaps that was the intention. There was talk of Tongs, and Tong vengeance. The police dismissed the idea out of hand. But for all that, there *was* something mysterious about the little Chinaman who lived alone above the laundry.

Jaw Kay was born on 30 August 1889, at Kai-Hing, Canton, China. Perhaps in his salad days, the days before August, 1913, when he arrived in this country, he had done something to offend against the laws of a powerful Tong, or to arouse the ire of some other Chinese secret society. Perhaps it was flight out of the orbit of their dominion that brought him to Liverpool, where he settled down in about 1921. Here he was to stay for the remainder of his life, except for a period of five months in 1936, which he spent in Blackpool. It was there that, from 1931 to 1936, he co-habited with a woman who bore him two children.

When he first appeared in the Scotland Road area, he was regarded, as all novelties were in Liverpool in those days, with hostility-oriented suspicion. However, observed patting youngsters on the head and giving them sweets, softened hearts towards him. He became in the fullness of time a kind of adopted funny foreign uncle, remaining swathed in Oriental mystery, but no longer suspect. His way of speaking was, almost affectionately, described as "pidgin English flavoured with scouse." When at night he shut up shop and disappeared from the Scotland Road environs, speculation was rife as to what he might be up to. All he was, in fact, doing, was making his way over to Liverpool's Chinatown to mingle with his fellow exiled compatriots.

But why, the detectives wondered, with all this apparently innocent background, the frenzied knife attack upon him? More like the crazy lethal caperings of a maniac than the convenient killing by a beleaguered thief. Baffled, they called in Chinese interpreters, hoping that they might be able to throw some light on Jaw Kay's days and ways. And they did. They provided the useful information that, although he lived alone, he would from time to time give shelter to his fellow countrymen. This opened up new possibilities. Could it be, Detective Inspector (as he then was) Morris wondered, that one of these was his killer? Was it even remotely possible that a specially appointed killer had come, under orders, out of his Chinese past, to take his shelter – and his life?

"Round about that time," the Inspector was later to recall, "we had information that many Chinese returning home at the end of the war, were robbing other Chinese in the city to take cash or valuables back with them. We made many enquiries in that direction, but all proved negative. What surprised us, too, was that in murder cases such as this we usually got lots of information. But in this case we got scarcely a whisper. What we did learn was that Jaw Kay was a nice quiet fellow, very well liked by the people of Scotland Road. They were greatly shocked when they learned of his killing."

However unlikely it may seem that the hand of the Tongs wielded the instrument of 56-year-old Jaw Kay's murder, one must never underestimate their time-defying tenacity, or dismiss the malevolent power of the Tongs. They were first called into existence out of sheer necessity, back in the nineteenth century, when a great immigratory wave of poor Chinese flooded the Californian goldfields, near Marysville, and also provided coolie labour for railroad construction. The Tong was originally a secret society organised to safeguard members of the Chinese community from the terror tactics of hostile white American hoodlums who resented them and the effect of their intrusion into the labour market. The Tong offered physical and financial protection.

For the most part the Tongs victimised their own people, their fellow-countrymen. Each Tong had its hatchet men, killers, who, with razor-sharp hatchet, would split open the head of any foe or any resistant defaulter in the matter of the payment of demanded extortion money.

Gradually, the Tongs spread to the larger cities – San Francisco, Chicago, Baltimore, Pittsburgh, Boston and New York – and, as the years passed and the Chinese became more integrated, the composition of the Tong membership widened to embrace, not just wage slaves, but laundrymen, restaurateurs, shopkeepers and even merchants and their servants.

Other changes came along, too, notably in San Francisco. There and along the Barbary Coast, the Tong underwent a change of character; it was transformed from the single beneficent insurance and assurance body into a series of underworld gangs, despotic rulers over all the evils that the city could spawn; drugs, opium dens, gambling houses, brothels and prostitution. Bodies of hired assassins, known as 'highbinder societies', or *boo how doy*, to give them their proper Chinese appellation, provided their services, if the price was right. To assassinate a Tong leader cost $10,000; a hit on one of servant rank, $500.

The first bloody Tong war in America was set off in San Francisco in the spring of 1875. It was precipitated because of a slave girl called Kim Kum Ho. A member of the Suey Sing Tong, Low Sing, had claimed her for his own. This was far from all right with Ming Long, who was her lord and master, a member of the Kwong Dock Tong, and the notorious killer of at least fifty men. Low Sing and Ming Long argued. Ming Long settled the argument with his well-practised hatchet. Moments before he died, Low Sing named his slayer. That revelation triggered a terrible street battle between the Suey Sing Tong and the Kwong Docks. Twenty-five warrior men, the most skilled hatchets from each Tong, met at Waverley Place, and blood flowed in amplitude. Four men died. They were Kwong Docks. Their Tong formally apologised to the Suey Sings for Ming Long's transgression. He was ejected from his Tong and driven out of the country.

It was the murder of another one-time Chinese slave girl, Bow Kum, otherwise Little Sweet Flower, in New York in 1909, that started a war between the Hip Sing and On Leong Tongs.

Bow Kum came from Canton, where she had been sold by her father for a few dollars, and brought to America, where she fetched $3,000 in the San Francisco open market. Her purchaser was Low Hee Tong, who was prominent in the Hip Sing Tong. He lived with Bow Kum for four years, but when he got into trouble with the police and was unable to produce a marriage certificate, Bow Kum was taken away from him by the authorities and placed in a Christian mission. There she was discovered by Tchin Len, an industrious truck gardener of established probity, who married her and brought her to live in New York.

Tidings of Bow Kum's nuptials coming to his ears, Low Hee Tong made contact with Tchin Len and pressed him to make good the money that he had invested in Bow Kum. Obdurately, the gardener refused the refund. Whereupon, Low Hee Tong took his grievance to the Hip Sings in New York. Deciding that Low Hee Tong's was a justified claim, they made a solemn demand on his behalf to the On Leong Tong, of which Tchin Len was a member. The On Leongs also ignored the demand. The Hip Sings immediately unfurled the red flag of conflict, and set forth on the billboards of Chinatown posters of violent hue emblazoned with the declaration of war.

Within a few days, on 15 August 1909, a hatchet man slipped into Tchin Len's home at 17 Mott Street, and stabbed Bow Kum through the heart. He also cut off her fingers, and slashed her countless times across he body. Then the real killing began. Between them the Hip Sings and the On Leongs counted some fifty dead, several times that number wounded, and a considerable destruction of property by dynamite.

The Hip Sing leader was Mock Duck, whose technique as a fighter was thoroughly disconcerting. He would face his enemies squarely in the street, then suddenly squat, shut his eyes, and fire his pistol in all directions. The blind spray of his haphazard bullets would find dozens of victims, and he soon became the most feared man in New York's Chinatown. His lethal activities were halted when Judge Warren W Foster brokered a gang warfare truce in the first decade of the twentieth century. The truce did not last. The war between the Hip Sings and the On Leongs continued intermittently until 1925.

In the Chinese Masonic Hall in Nelson Street, Jaw Kay's friends stood beside his coffin, and, following age-old Chinese tradition, burned imitation Chinese money. And so it was that, with the upward swirl of the wisping smoke of the ritual burning, the spirit of the courteous little expatriate Chinaman passed into the lotus land of his ancestors, his most uneasy requiem spoken by an English coroner. ... "Murder by some person or persons unknown."

A SAMARRAN APPOINTMENT

DEATH SPEAKS: *There was a merchant in Baghdad who sent his servant to market to buy provisions and in a little while the servant came back, white and trembling, and said, Master, just now when I was in the market-place I was jostled by a woman in the crowd and when I turned I saw it was Death that jostled me. She looked at me and made a threatening gesture; now lend me your horse and I will ride away from this city and I will avoid my fate. I will go to Samarra and there Death will not find me. The merchant lent him his horse, and the servant mounted it, and he dug his spurs in its flanks and as fast as the horse could gallop he went. Then the merchant went down to the market-place and he saw me standing in the crowd and he came to me and said, Why did you make a threatening gesture to my servant when you saw him this morning? That was not a threatening gesture, I said, it was only a start of surprise. I was astonished to see him in Baghdad, for I had an appointment with him tonight in Samarra.*

W Somerset Maugham.

Liverpool was absolutely the last place in the world that Peter Allen wanted to be. But he had an appointment there with a Mr Robert Stewart – an appointment which he had no option but to keep. In order to understand the urgency of Mr Allen's appointment, it is necessary to travel up in space to the Cumbrian village of Seaton, on the outskirts of Workington, and back in time to the early hours of Tuesday, 7 April 1964.

Joseph Fawcett, a 65-year-old retired insurance inspector and his wife lived at 2 Coronation Avenue. The house was on the corner and actually next door to 28 Kings Avenue, the home of John Alan West. He was fifty-three, a bachelor, living there alone since the death of his 80-year-old mother the previous August. For the past 34 years, 'Jack' West, as he was generally known, had worked as a van man for the Lakeland Laundry. By no means a loner, he was a quiet man, enjoyed going to pubs, had belonged to a darts team, liked gardening, and was interested in motors and motoring. What does not seem to have been generally known was that Jack was a homosexual.

On the Monday (6th) night, the Fawcetts had come home on the ten o'clock bus from Workington, and as they passed Jack West's house they noticed a downstairs light on in his sitting-room. Nothing unusual about that. They had gone to bed at eleven o'clock and were asleep well before midnight. Suddenly they were jolted awake by a very loud noise, that they could only describe as though "something was hitting the foundation of the house," and they could "sort of recollect a shrill scream". It was exactly 3am.

Mr Fawcett got up and dressed. Peering out between the curtains, he saw, reflected in the windows of the house opposite, the lights go on in West's, first upstairs, then downstairs. He heard a car engine being revved up hard, but saw only the rear lights as it drove off, fast. Sensing something amiss, he and his wife went next door and knocked at both the front and back doors, but there was no response. Then they returned to their house, and knocked on the dividing wall. Still no response. Worried now, they went across the road to No 25 and knocked up Walter Lister. He opened his bedroom window, listened to the Fawcetts' uneasy tale, and telephoned the police.

At 3.30am Police Sergeant James Park and Constable John Rodgers received a message in consequence of which they drove at once to Kings Avenue and saw the Fawcetts. Sergeant Park was going to break down the front-door, but Mrs Fawcett knew that West kept a spare key hidden in a box of nails in the garage. And when the door was opened, what a sight awaited them. Blood, large slaughterhouse quantities of blood everywhere – splashes, smears, spots on floor, stairs, walls, ceiling, soaked stair carpet. A man, clad only in shirt and vest, lay stretched on his back on the hall floor, at the foot of the stairs, near the front-door. Horrendous head injuries. Smashed face. A hideously bloodied torso. And a stab wound to the heart. Lying on the living-room floor was a length of heavy metal tubing, about a foot long, encased in rubber, and half wrapped in a pair of pyjama trousers.

This cosh and a single fingerprint were at first the only clues that could be found to assist

Detective Inspector John Gibson, of the Cumberland and Westmorland Constabulary, who had charge of the investigation. There was no sign of a forced entry. The back door was locked and barred, as had been the front-door. All the windows were fully closed and locked. There was nothing to suggest that the house had been ransacked. On the upper landing Gibson found a metal poker and a set of lower dentures, which were established to have belonged to Jack West.

Then, in West's bedroom, the discovery of what was to prove the vital clue to the mystery. Laid neatly on the back of a chair was a short, off-white raincoat. In one of its pockets Gibson found a wallet, and in that wallet was a scrap of paper on which was written in red ink: 'Miss Norma O'Brian. 98a Upper Hill Street, Princes Road, Liverpool 8, Lancashire.'

Life was not looking good to 21-year-old Peter Anthony Allen. In fact, the outlook was bleak. Lack of money was, as it so often is, the root of all the trouble. His debts added up to £79, made up of £44 rates, £20 for a fine and £15 rent arrears on his house at 2 Clarendon Street, Preston, where he had received notice to quit. He had no job, having lost his position as dairyman with Preston Dairies because of absenteeism, after only one month's employment. He had a wife, Mary, and two boys, Mark Anthony (3) – not actually his child – and Richard (9 months) to look after.

Born in Wallasey on 14 April 1943, he was one of the six children of a journeyman shipwright. He had got off to a slow start because he suffered from defective hearing which had affected his speech. Between the ages of five and seven he had been regularly attending the Liverpool Ear, Nose, and Throat Infirmary as an out-patient, having his adenoids removed in 1950. He had left school when he was fifteen, not having done at all well there. Indeed, the verdict on him was 'not very bright', and his intelligence, labelled as below average, was rated as being, at fifteen, that of a thirteen-and-a-half-year-old. Physically, though, he was an impressive 6 feet 2 inches tall. He was in and out of jobs and spent some time in the army.

On 11 November 1961, he had married 18-year-old Mary Irene Hannett, a cinema usherette whom he had met at a fair at New Brighton. Blue-eyed, 5 feet 4 inches tall and slim, she was known to her friends as 'Mitch', which name she had spelt out in tattoo marks on the fingers of her left hand. Like her husband, who had two hearts tattooed on his left shoulder, and on his right, a knife and a snake entwined around his name, she had a clear penchant for tattooing, for on her left upper arm was tattooed 'Pete', on her left thigh the representation of a sword and bird, and on her right thigh a heart and the letter 'F'. She was uncertain as to her real identity, for she had come to know that she had been an adopted child. She had actually had four babies. Her first, born in 1961, when she was only fifteen, had died. Her second, Mark Anthony, also born in 1961, was not Peter's child, although he proved a kind and loving stepfather. Her third, born in July, 1962, also died. Her fourth, Richard, born 8 August 1963, was Peter's son.

Lodging with Peter and Mary Allen was 24-year-old Gwynne Owen Evans. He, too, was an unemployed dairyman. Less physically impressive than Peter, a mere 5 feet 4 inches, although it seems likely that he and Mary had some sort of special relationship, or, as he expressed it, "Me and Mrs Allen are more than just landlady and lodger." It must be remembered though that he was a fantasist. To begin with, his name was not Gwynne Owen Evans, but John Robson Walby. He said that he had been born at Innsbruck and that both his parents were German. Not so. He was born at Maryport, in Cumberland, on 1 April 1940. His parents, Thomas and Hannah Walby, were English, and, indeed, living at 6 Kirklands, Camerton, just three miles north east of Workington. He was the third child of a family of seven. Some concern having been felt as to his mental health, between the ages of ten and twelve he attended, as an out-patient, Dovenby Hall Mental Colony, at Cockermouth. Like Peter Allen, he had left his secondary modern school at fifteen, and was described as educationally well below average. His first job was in a factory at Carlisle. Then he was a page boy in a Carlisle hotel and an engine cleaner for British Railways. Four times he enlisted in the army and once in the RAF. It was his discharge from the Lancastrian Brigade that brought him to Preston, where he was briefly employed as dairyman and where he met Peter Allen.

It was Evans, who, acutely conscious of his friend and landlord Peter Allen's financial difficulties, had suggested that a chap he had known when he was working in Cumberland, and who had told him that if he ever found himself in any money difficulties he could count on him for the loan of a couple of quid, might come to the rescue. So it was arranged that, on Monday evening, 6 April 1964, he and Peter Allen should drive up to see him. They decided that Allen's wife, Mary, and the two children should come along also, for the ride.

Meanwhile, up in Seaton, the raincoat discovered in West's bedroom was yielding more clues. In one of its pockets was a Royal Life Saving Society medallion. It was inscribed on the back: 'G.O. Evans. July, 1961'. But what had seemed so potentially useful a clue fizzled out when a check with the Society's London headquarters brought the information that their records showed no such medallion ever having been awarded to any G O Evans.

The scrap of paper with the Liverpool girl's address on it, however, turned up trumps. Miss O'Brien (as she spelt her name) was a 17-year-old, unmarried machinist. She had a sister who was married to a soldier quartered at Fulwood Barracks in Preston. In the autumn of 1963, Norma O'Brien had stayed for several weekends in Preston with her married sister, and it was then that she had met a man named Ginger Owen Evans. He told her that he was from London and was staying at the barracks as an officer's guest. They had met three or four times before parting after a disagreement. He had been talking of getting married to her, but she was definitely not interested.

Norma's brother-in-law was interviewed. He remembered meeting, in September or October, 1963, a man named Sandy Evans, who had only just joined the army. He had asked him for Norma's address, and he had given it to him. He remembered, too, that Evans had told him that he came from Cumberland.

On Monday (April 6th) evening a car, belonging to James Cook, a moulder, was stolen from outside a Preston public-house, the Frenchwood Hotel. Just twenty-four hours later, the missing car was found parked in a lean-to shed in Knowsley Road, Ormskirk. It is hard to believe that Mary Allen can have been totally ignorant of what was going on. We know for a fact that she saw blood on her husband's jacket and shirt when he returned from his visit to Jack West's.The car had been 'borrowed' by Gwynne Evans and Peter Allen, not for joy-riding, but for the serious business of conveying them the 93 miles from Preston to Workington, to see Evans' helpful friend.

Here, according to the story they told, is what ensued.

They had arrived at Workington at 1.10am and drove to Kings Avenue. They parked the car by a roadworks a little way from West's house. Evans went in to No 28 to see his friend, and, hopefully, to borrow a hundred pounds. Allen, his wife, and the two children waited in the car. At about 2.50am Evans let Allen into the house.

Allen stated: "Sandy told him [West] that he wanted some fresh air and let me in without the chap knowing, but when he came down the stairs he saw me, so I hit him. Sandy had the bar and he gave it to me. Sandy put the light out and I was hitting out blindly. I only had my fists until Sandy gave me the bar. I only hit him twice with it, and then gave it back to Sandy. I went upstairs to see if there was any loose cash but there wasn't, but there was a bunch of letters and two bank books in the drawer and I just grabbed the lot."

Sandy Evans' version of events was somewhat different: "I knocked on the door, and he said, 'I didn't expect to see you tonight.' I told him I was up to see my mother. He asked me where I was staying, and I said I had a friend with me in the car. He asked me to go to bed with him. I don't know whether anyone knows it or not, but West was a homosexual. A knock came to the door, and West said, 'Who can that be?' I said I didn't know. He went to the door, and Peter rushed him and said, 'I want some bloody money.' I said, 'Well leave him alone, he hasn't got anything.'"

No better off financially for their savage adventure, they had driven off, leaving behind a battered corpse with a stab wound to the heart. They stopped briefly at Windermere, outside the Mountain Ash Hotel and bought a gallon of petrol at Smith's Garage, at 7.45am on Tuesday (April 7th). They stopped at Kendal, where, at 9am, as soon as the post office opened, Mrs Allen drew eight shillings family allowance. The next stop was at Liverpool, where, at 1.20pm they paid a visit to the Liverpool Trustee Savings Bank in Brunswick Street, and drew a total of £10 from West's two bank books. They then drove through the Mersey

Tunnel and went to New Brighton, where they had a meal at the Sheffield Restaurant, in Victoria Street. At Ormskirk, they left the stolen car in a lean-to shed in an abandoned builder's yard in Knowsley Road, and caught a bus to Preston.

The little party on the bus must have been quite a sight – two young men under twenty-five, one of them minus jacket and shirt; a young woman, with two children, one of them a babe in arms; and a tiny lamb, lying bleating beside her. The lamb they had found by the roadside on the moors between Clitheroe and Liverpool. Once safely back in Clarendon Street, Mrs Allen had telephoned the RSPCA, whose inspector, Richard Nairn, had called and collected the lamb.

Examining the recovered car, the police had found in it fingerprints which were identified as those of Evans and Allen.

Gwynne Owen Evans and Peter Anthony Allen were charged with murder at 1.15 on the morning of Thursday, 9 April 1964. Evans' defence was that Allen did it. Allen's defence was that Evans did it. But what they did not realise was that it did not matter who it was who actually *did* the killing. Engaged as they had been in a joint enterprise, *both* would be held to be guilty in law, no matter who it was who actually struck the fatal blow or delivered the mortal stab wound.

Their trial took place at Manchester Crown Court – Court Number 3. It lasted for six days, and the jury heard more than 40 witnesses, and viewed 119 exhibits. It took them three-and-a-quarter hours to find both men guilty of capital murder.

The trial judge, Mr Justice Ashworth, told them: "As both of you know, for the crime of which you have in my judgment been rightly convicted, the law provides only one sentence – that you suffer death in the manner authorised by law."

Mrs Allen was led, weeping, from the court.

On 20 July both appealed. On 21 July, both men's appeals were dismissed. Only one hope remained: that of the granting of a reprieve. On 10 August, the Home Secretary, Henry Brooke, intimated that he had found no sufficient ground to warrant his advising Her Majesty to interfere with the due course of law. Their final hope was gone. As it turned out, these two were the last in the United Kingdom ever to be hanged.

A dreadful scene was enacted when Allen's wife and baby Richard came to Walton Gaol to see him for the last time. As the visit drew towards its end, he went berserk and hurled himself bodily against the specially strengthened glass separating him and Mary, cracking and splintering it, and smashing his wrist.

At 8am on Thursday, 13 August 1964, Evans was hanged at Strangeways Prison, in Manchester. On the same day, at the same time, Allen kept his appointment at Walton Gaol with Robert Stewart, the hangman, who noted in his diary that he "smashed his head against the wall during his last visit and broke a finger. As I was strapping his wrist in the morning, he shouted 'Jesus!' That was it. Not another word."

Imprecation or invocation?

Nurse Berry and
the Dancing Hangman

The female of the species is, opined Kipling, more deadly than the male, and there is no more appropriate adjective than 'deadly' to attach to the bustle of Mrs Elizabeth Berry. The story that brought her to the dock at Liverpool Assizes, standing trial for her life before England's most feared judge, Mr Justice Hawkins – known to the criminal fraternity as ''anging 'awkins' – was not a pretty one.

It had opened on New Year's Day, 1887, in Oldham, where the 31-year-old widow was a nurse in the workhouse infirmary. Nurse Berry had spent Christmas with her sister-in-law, Mrs Ann Sanderson, at Miles Platting, on the outskirts of Manchester. For the last five years, Mrs Berry's daughter, Edith Annie, now aged eleven years and eight months, had lived with her Aunt Ann, Nurse Berry contributing £12 of the £25 *per annum* salary that she received towards Edith's keep. The Christmas holiday had been a very jolly few days, and when the time came for her mother to pack her bags and set off back to Oldham, Edith begged her to take her and a school friend to spend a bit of extra time together at the Oldham Workhouse infirmary. Although at first reluctant, her mother eventually yielded to Edith's persistent pleading, and on Wednesday, 29 December 1886, the three of them bade Mrs Sanderson farewell, and caught the train to Oldham.

A letter which Edith posted off to Aunt Ann told her how much she and her friend were enjoying their stay with her mother. The next communication Mrs Sanderson received from Oldham was a very different one. It arrived on Monday, 3 January. It was a telegram. 'Come at once. Edith is dying.'

According to Nurse Berry's account, the first intimation that all was not well with Edith came on the Saturday morning, 1 January, when she felt too ill to eat any breakfast; and later, while her mother was in the kitchen preparing sago for her patients, she was violently sick. Shortly after that, Elizabeth Berry was seen trying to persuade her daughter to swallow down a glass of milky-looking fluid. When, at midday, Dr Patterson arrived, paying his usual daily attendance at the Workhouse, she asked him to take a look at Edith, who, she said, had eaten something at breakfast that had made her ill. He duly examined the child, diagnosed a stomach upset, and prescribed a mixture of iron and quinine.

As the day progressed, the vomiting continued, and Edith's condition worsened. Dr Patterson saw her again in the evening. He found her no better, and was frankly puzzled to account for her symptoms. However, when he saw her for the third time at midday on the Sunday (2 January), he thought the girl was looking a little better, and told her mother that in his opinion she was on the mend.

It was at this juncture that Nurse Berry showed the doctor a blood and vomit stained towel, which, he noticed, gave off a distinctly acidic smell.

Deciding to give his patient some additional medication, he asked Nurse Berry for the key of the infirmary dispensary, which was next to her room, and the only key to which she held. The doctor had it in mind to administer a bicarbonate mixture. He wanted to add some drops of creosote to it, but finding the dispensary bottle of creosote to be empty, he wrote there and then an order for a fresh supply, and instructed Nurse Berry to dissolve eight drops in water and give Edith a tablespoon of this 'tar water' every two hours.

That Sunday evening the child was again violently sick, and Dr Patterson observed red marks around her mouth. They had been caused, Nurse Berry told him, by some lemon and sugar she had given her. Not satisfied, thinking it more likely that the child had been given a corrosive poison, Dr Patterson consulted with a second doctor. He agreed. By the next day, Edith's pulse was barely palpable, she vomited back any medicine they tried to administer, she was steadily weakening, and her lips were covered with blisters. She died at 5 o'clock on the morning of Tuesday, 4 January.

This sudden, swift decline of a previously healthy child did not sit well with Dr Patterson. In fact, the circumstances of little Edith's death led him to believe it to be likely that her mother had poisoned her. He suspected that Nurse Berry had given her the contents of the dispensary bottle of creosote on the Saturday, and another massive dose – from the second bottle which he had ordered – on the Sunday. It distressed him to think that had he not given her mother a second supply of undiluted creosote, the little girl would have survived.

Mrs Berry offered no objection to the carrying out of a post-mortem. Three doctors who performed the examination disclosed that the body displayed . no signs of natural disease. The stomach and intestines exhibited marks of blood, and the throat appeared black and corroded. Death was due to an intake of corrosive poison, quite possibly creosote which had an acid content, and which aforesaid poisonous substance had disappeared, as a probable consequence of prolonged bouts of vomiting; with the result that the presence of poison could not be proved by toxicological analysis.

Although a death certificate was issued stating acute inflammation of the stomach and bowels as the cause of death, rumour began to weave its sinister patterns, and, hardly surprisingly, suspicion crystallised around Elizabeth Berry, who, after all, had had sole access to the infirmary dispensary. And that suspicion grew sufficiently in strength to convince an inquest jury to deliver a verdict of wilful murder and send her for trial on the coroner's warrant. Elizabeth Berry was arrested and charged with the murder of her daughter. The Oldham magistrates had meanwhile concluded their hearing with the statement that, due to lack of motive, Mrs Berry had no case to answer.

She made her bow in the Assize Court dock in St George's Hall, Liverpool, on Monday, 21 February 1887. The trial lasted four days. The prosecution alleged that the prisoner had poisoned the girl in order to obtain £10 on a life insurance policy and, at the same time, to rid herself of the £12 per year upkeep cost of her daughter, which sum did amount to practically half of her total annual income. Somewhat significant may be held to be Nurse Berry's previous response when asked if Edith was insured, and she had replied: "Not a penny. I shall have to pay for the burial out of my own pocket." As a matter of fact, she had received £10 from a burial society in April, 1886, and had at that time tried to insure her own life and that of her daughter for £100, this amount to go to the survivor, when the first of the insured died. Although she had failed to pay the premium on this transaction, there are some grounds for believing that she fully expected this sum to be paid out to her.

Counsel for the defence averred that Mrs Berry had been a kind and affectionate mother, and said that the suggestion that she would kill her own child for money was a monstrous proposition. Mr Justice Hawkins, in the course of his summing-up, pointed out that the prisoner had made several false statements relative to the child's health and the insurance upon her.

The jury took little time to reach their verdict. Within ten minutes Elizabeth Berry had been sentenced to death for what Hawkins J described as a "cold-blooded, merciless, and cruel murder". What the jury did not know, although it would, of course, be known to the trial judge, was that the suspicions surrounding Edith Berry's death had led the police to investigate the death, in February, 1886, of Mrs Berry's mother, Mrs Finley. She, like her granddaughter, Edith, had died suddenly, and permission had been sought and granted by the Home Secretary for the body to be exhumed. Once again, the examination did not rule out poisoning, and the symptoms surrounding both deaths were disconcertingly similar. Mrs Berry had on that occasion also profited from an insurance pay-out, albeit small, but the circumstances were sufficiently weighted with suspicion for another coroner's warrant charging her with wilful murder to be issued against her.

There were other rumours, too. Her husband, Thomas Berry, had died in the summer of 1881, and her son, Harold, had followed his father into the grave in the autumn of 1882. Thomas had succumbed after a long illness. Harold had been taken ill and passed away after a trip to the seaside. After both events Elizabeth Berry was said to have benefited, but since she was already lying under sentence of death, there was no point in further pursuance of the accusations. Incidentally, it was immediately after Harold's death that she had placed Edith with Mrs Sanderson.

Although it has been reported that to the very end Mrs Berry continued to persist, even to the prison chaplain from whom she was receiving spiritual consolation, in her innocence, it has been said that she admitted her guilt in a memorial sent to the Home Secretary, in which she used the words, 'I must have been mad if I did it,' and mentioned tea as the medium in which the poison was given. Her execution date was fixed for 14 March 1887.

From the time that she received her death sentence, Mrs Berry's health seemed to have steadily declined, she became withdrawn, apathetic, expressing a desire not to see any visitors, occupying the handful of hours that remained to her in penitent mode – meditating, praying, and in the performance of devotional exercises.

Something of her state of mind is revealed by her demeanour when, two days before the carrying out of the sentence of the Court upon her, she was visited by her solicitor, who was to take final instructions from her in the matter of the settling of her worldly affairs. Attired in prison garb – a blue serge dress, white collar, and white cap – she was seated behind a steel mesh partition. No sooner did she see the solicitor, than she crumpled up in a swoon, and it took two doctors two or three hours to bring her round. Later in the day, the solicitor saw her again, and this time was able to conclude the necessary arrangements.

Now comes the strangest of codas to this strangest of stories. Stewart Evans' biographical study, *Executioner: The Chronicles of James Berry, Victorian Hangman*, tells how, when he arrived at Walton Gaol in the late afternoon of 13 March 1887. He was received by the governor, who gave him a peculiar smile. "I did not know you were going to hang an old flame, Berry?"

"What do you mean?" asked Berry, who thought the man must be joking, on account of the condemned woman's name being the same as his.

"She says she knows you very well," he replied. "You had better go and have a look at her tonight. I will make the necessary arrangements."

Later, Berry gazed curiously through the narrow slit in the cell door and recognised the woman inside as someone he had met in the past. Describing her as "a woman of not unpleasant appearance" whose "chief charm about her was her beautiful chestnut tresses", he went on to relate how he had once met her in a crowded ballroom while having some refreshment. She had approached him, asking if he was alone, and then, with a coy glance and a smile, enquired if he would dance with her. With his arm around the waist of "a young woman of charm and vivacity, who chatted gaily" to him about herself and her work (she told him that she was a nurse working in Oldham Hospital), he had trodden "the mazy dance". Then, after sharing refreshments together and another dance or two, they had discovered they were travelling home in the same direction, so he had invited her to join him in his cab, the two also travelling together subsequently for part of the train journey.

The following morning, Berry was early at her cell:

"I never liked to hang a woman. When I opened the door of her cell she looked up and nodded to me. 'Good morning, Mrs Berry,' I said. She came forward instantly and held out her hand.

'Good morning, Mr Berry. You and I have met before.'

'Where was that now?' I asked, pretending to have forgotten.

'Oh, at the ball in Manchester, given by the

police,' she said. 'Surely you can't have forgotten.'

'Oh, yes, I remember,' said I. 'It is a long time ago, and I did not realise that I was to officiate at the execution of a friend of mine.'

'No, I suppose you didn't,' she said.

'Well, I'm very sorry to have to do it,' I said.

She looked at me, and with a toss of her head said, 'You've no doubt heard a lot of dreadful things about me, but it isn't all true what people say about one.'

'Well, I've heard a great deal about you,' said I. 'But you must pull yourself together and die bravely.'

'Oh, I'll go bravely enough,' she said with a shudder. 'You need not be a bit afraid of me, Mr Berry. You don't suppose I'd want to give you any trouble, do you?'

'I hope you won't give me any trouble.'

'You'll be easy with me. You won't give me any pain. You'll be gentle with an old friend, won't you?'

'I shall not prolong your life a single minute,' said I. 'Have you made your peace with God?'

"She made no reply, and I besought her to make the most of what time remained to her. I went outside and caught hold of the arm of one of the warders. 'That woman is one of the biggest cowards in the world,' said I."

Shortly before eight o'clock Berry returned to the condemned cell to pinion her. She was wearing a black silk dress.

"'Now, Mrs Berry, I've come back again,' said I. 'Is there anything I can do for you before you leave the condemned cell?'

She shivered and shrank back.

'Would you like a drink of water?' I asked.

She shook her head again.

'All right, then. Time is getting on. Don't be afraid – I am not going to hurt you.'

"After I had pinioned her, the governor of the gaol led the way, followed by the chaplain, reading the prayers for the dying, and the rear was brought up by three doctors. The distance from the cell to the scaffold was not more than sixty yards, and along the roadway sand had been sprinkled freely. It was in the depth of winter, snow had fallen on the ground, and I was afraid that she would slip and fall. The condemned woman walked firmly until she turned the angle of the building and saw the gallows. … a cry of terror left her lips. 'Oh, dear!' she wailed, and then she reeled over and was just about to faint when I rushed up.

'Now look here, Mrs Berry,' said I. 'You remember what you promised me in the cell.' Her only reply was a deep groan. 'You promised me that you would give me no trouble. What do you call this?'

"I had caught hold of her arms to keep her from falling, and she begged me to unhand her.

'Let me go, Mr Berry,' she said. "Let me go, and I will go bravely.'

'All right,' I replied.

"She staggered along supported by two warders, and as she looked at the scaffold again a wave of terror came over her, and she shouted, 'Oh, God forbid! God forbid!' The warders helped her along and she repeated the responses to the prayers in a faint voice, but at last the ordeal was too much for her and she fainted. They lifted her on to the scaffold, and held her up while I completed my arrangements. She recovered consciousness while I was busy, and continued her responses, and at intervals she called upon her Maker to have mercy upon her. Just as I was about to pull the cap over her face she exclaimed, 'May God forgive me!' and she repeated the words just as I allowed her to go down.

"No sooner was the fatal act over than one of the wardresses came over, and, in bitter tones, spoke thus, 'There goes one of the coldest-blooded murderers – the worst species of womankind to carry out the deeds she has carried out.'"

Early that morning of the execution, a heavy hailstorm, accompanied by a clap of thunder and a flash of lightning, had passed over Liverpool. There followed a fall of snow. The flakes thinned and ceased shortly before the hour fixed for the hanging, but the snow lay thick. The air was like liquid ice, and a bone-stripping wind scoured the tree-bare, stony ground of the prison yard. Outside the massive prison gates, kept at a distance by a modest cordon of police, a small knot of people had gathered; mainly men on their way to work, and a sprinkling of cold-pinched women. Sympathetic souls, they hoped, perhaps, for the granting of a last minute reprieve. But the tolling of the prison bell sounded a tocsin of dashed hope, and the black flag, struck from the pole, bore fluttering witness to the ceased fluttering of

Elizabeth Berry's heart.

This was the first hanging carried out at Walton Gaol, and Berry found an odd way of commemorating the occasion. He cut two locks of her 'beautiful chestnut tresses' from Elizabeth Berry's corpse, and bore them triumphantly home to add to his grisly collection of gallows souvenirs.

THE PALE-FACED KILLER
OF WARBRECK MOOR

There was undeniably something distinctly Dickensian about Hugh George Walker. Seeing him in his rather old-fashioned Sunday best suit and well-brushed bowler making his way to St Peter's Church in Aintree, he was every inch a Dickens' character. And, with Dickensian appropriateness, he was the proud proprietor of 'The Old Curiosity Shop', at least that was what his neighbours in Aintree called 98 Warbreck Moor, his place of dwelling and sporadic commerce.

There is a Sherlock Holmes touch about his story, too. You will recall how, in 'The Adventure of Silver Blaze', Holmes calls Watson's attention to the curious incident of the dog in the night-time. But, Watson protests, "The dog did nothing in the night-time." "That," replied Holmes, "was the curious incident." In the sad case of Mr Walker, the dog, or rather dogs, did, as we shall see, plenty in the night-time.

When death, in the shape of the pale-faced man, came to Hugh George Walker he was eighty-two years old, a widower. A small, frail man, anguished by arthritis, who walked with a stick, and looked even older than the burden of years he carried. He had, before his retirement from the world of daily grind, been the master tailor at Fazakerley Cottage Homes, where he had taught generations of orphanage children the intricate art of professional cutting and stitching.

He lived, after his retirement, on his own in a large, detached Victorian house, where he set up in business as a second-hand dealer, with a Jackdaw-of-Rheims-like stock-in-trade assortment of bright bric-a-brac and ponderous antiques, much of it little more than junk. Cellar to attic, room after room of the rambling house was piled, floor to ceiling, with the re-sale detritus of vanished lives.

Mr Walker lived on the first floor. The ground floor had been turned into a tangled jungle of a shop. Slap-bang in the pride of place centre of the window, his trade mark as it were, hung an eye-catching old birdcage, a faded-plumed stuffed bird perched rakishly in it: a powerful symbol amid the hotchpotch of seedy merchandise.

A gradually developing eccentricity on the part of the increasingly eremitical Mr Walker, had been a slow-burgeoning reluctance to part with – that is sell – anything. Nine times out of ten, his door was to be found tight-shut, and would-be customers needed to hammer at it vigorously to attract the old man's attention and, after a longish wait, be admitted.

On a January afternoon in 1953, a young man came, directed by evil destiny, to knock for admission to Mr Walker's somewhat bizarre premises. The young man's aspect was not precisely engaging, but his manner was. At any rate, so thought Mr Walker. After poking around for a while, the young man made a purchase. He handed over one shilling and sixpence for a pick-up arm that had been wrested off an antique gramophone. In conversation, he conveyed to

Mr Walker that he was a dab hand at fixing broken clocks and watches; that tinkering with them was indeed something of a hobby with him, and asked if he had any work for him, repairing any of his timepieces.

Now it so happened that Mr Walker was harbouring upstairs a recalcitrant grandfather's clock, and this seemed to him a heaven-sent opportunity to have it brought to order. He accordingly intimated that he would be glad if the young man would care to match his skills against the aged mechanical rebel. The young man would, and agreed to return next day for that purpose.

The amateur clock-mender materialised, like a pantomime demon, at Mr Walker's shop door at around 2.30pm on 9 January. That Friday Mr Walker's sister, Mary Eliza Walker, came across from her home in Gloucester Road, Tuebrook, to see her brother. She saw, too, the young man. She didn't warm to him. Some sort of sixth sense seemed to switch on. What's more, she did not at all like the knife which she saw dangling in a sheath from his waistband.

The young man was there again when Mary Walker visited her brother on the following Monday, 12 January. Walker, who had obviously taken a shine to him, had allowed him to go upstairs on his own to a room over the shop, and work unsupervised on the grandfather's clock. Miss Mary did not at all approve. She noticed, too, that the man seemed very familiar with her brother, laughing and joking with him, and calling him 'Pop'.

Mary Walker was not at Warbreck Moor on Tuesday, the thirteenth, but the young man was. He opened the shop door in answer to the knocking of two young lads, Ronald Cole and Allan Lake. They wanted to purchase some valves for a wireless set. He told them to come back the next day.

The pallid young man turned up at Mr Walker's seedy antique emporium again on Wednesday, 14 January. It proved to be his last visit. After he had gone, the grandfather's clock remained unticking. And Hugh George Walker ceased to tick, too. Not that anyone knew that at first. The darkness and silence surrounding his brooding old house was simply interpreted to mean that he had set off somewhere for a brief break.

But there were those who knew ... a nine-year-old black Scotch terrier and a three-year old reddy-brown little mongrel. They had somehow managed to get locked out of their home. All night long they whined and barked and howled outside the shop door. Their instinct, which humans have lost, conveyed to them a sense of danger, a sensation that all was not well. They woke the neighbours, were roundly cursed, but loyally continued sounding out their warning and distress calls. They kept it up for two days.

At about 10pm on 14 January, a Mrs Lawson saw a thoroughly upset terrier barking frantically, clearly in unequivocal distress, outside Mr Walker's door. She rang and knocked for twenty minutes, then gave up, thinking that he must have gone away overnight, and did nothing about it, so far as the disturbed dogs were concerned. She was far from being the only one who, over the course of a couple of days, passed the dogs by, and, ignoring their obvious distress, likewise turned the other way. One is, incidentally, happy briefly to interrupt the narrative to report that Mr Walker's two faithful hounds, after being fed, watered, and lodged in Edge Lane's Dogs' Home, where, fit and well, they had been kept together and played together, were, in the following May, found new homes, near each other, far away from the scene of their bereavement and ordeal.

Finally, on the evening of Thursday, 15 January, a Mrs Marion Owen, who lived at 21 Hall Lane, the next street to Warbreck Moor, recognised that the dogs were trying to tell her something. She had been in the habit of giving them the odd bone, and one of them, it is not recorded whether it was the terrier or the mongrel, went round to her door. She saw at once from its demeanour and the distressed state that it was in – both the poor dogs were terribly hungry – that something seriously wrong had upset the animal, and was sufficiently sensitive to follow its lead to Mr Walker's front-door. There was no answer to her persistent knocking, no sign of life about the place. She did not like the look of things one little bit. He might have been taken ill or had a bad fall. At 9.30pm she telephoned the local police.

Sergeant Hosker, accompanied by a constable, came over from Rice Lane police station. Having satisfied himself that there were reasonable grounds for Mrs Owen's anxiety, the sergeant decided to force the lock of the front-door of No 98.

Shining his torch into the darkened hall, he saw by its light a figure lying spread-eagled on its back at the foot of the stairs, and quickly realised that Mr Walker was dead, murdered. His head was surrounded by a pool of blood, spicules of shattered skull bone spattered the floor and starrings of squirted blood stippled adjacent walls.

At 10.20pm, Sergeant Hosker wirelessed his report of the murder to Rice Lane. They, in turn, contacted Chief Superintendent Herbert Balmer, head of Liverpool CID. As soon as he arrived on the scene, Balmer ordered the cordoning-off of the area, and called in Dr Charles St Hill, of Huyton, the Home Office's chosen pathologist. He drove up at 12.30pm, conducted a cursory examination of the body and its surroundings, stated his opinion that the time of death would have been between 24 and 48 hours previously, and had the body removed to the city mortuary for a full examination. He began work there at once, and by 3am he had concluded the post-mortem. His findings: 32 blows to the head. Skull and left cheek-bone shattered. All the indications were clearly those of a brutal, prolonged and murderous attack.

The forensic expert, Dr J B Firth, Director of the North Western Forensic Science Laboratory of the Home Office, at Preston, and his specialist team, arrived as dawn was just about breaking, and set at once about a microscopic examination of the scene of the crime. They turned up the probable murder weapon: the head of an axe with a broken wooden shaft lying immersed in an enamel bowl of bloodstained water in the first-floor kitchenette.

The other piece of the shaft was found on the hallway floor. It looked as if it had been broken off by the savagery of the attack. An additional important discovery was that of a set of bloody footprints on the hall floor. They had been made by somebody wearing crepe-soled shoes.

From the testimony of Mary Walker and the two schoolboys, Ronald Cole and Allan Lake, Balmer was able to cobble together a fair working description of the man they were looking for "to help them with their inquiries".

He was "a travelling watch and clock-mender, aged about thirty, with thin pale features, a long pointed nose, with a distinct whitish wart at the side of his left eye. About 5 feet 8 inches tall, and last seen wearing a fawn gaberdine raincoat."

Miss Walker provided some useful additional facts. She had noticed that her brother's silver pocket-watch, which he always used to carry in his front waistcoat pocket, was missing. It was valuable, and had been of great sentimental value to him. She remembered that the knife that the wanted man had worn at his belt was single-edged, and carried in a brown leather sheath, which was pinned together with five metal rivets. The point of the knife protruded a little from the bottom of the sheath. She remembered that the axe that killed her brother was one that he had used to break-up large lumps of coal for the fire. She recalled, too, that the pale young man had said that he wanted to buy a big old wireless set from her brother. He agreed to pay him £2 for it, and said he would borrow a pram to carry it away with him.

Mary Walker's information about the suspect's planning to take the wireless set home in a pram, suggested to Balmer that they were looking for someone who lived within walking distance of the scene of the crime, and between 16 and 18 January, detectives carried out a daunting programme of door-to-door inquiries. But, as so often happens in these cases, in the end it was pure chance that snapped the net shut around the killer of Hugh George Walker.

On the morning of Monday, 19 January, Iris Tucker, was sitting in her home at 2 Park Gardens, sipping her breakfast cup of tea and flicking through the newspaper when she suddenly received the shock of her life. Interested, like pretty well everyone else in Liverpool, in the sensational Old Curiosity Shop Murder, she read with horror the description of the wanted man. Detail for detail, it coincided exactly and irrefutably with that of her boyfriend, John Todd. Moreover, the mentionings of watch-mending, the sheath knife, the old wireless set, and the pram, put the absolute seal upon her horrified realisation that the murderer had to be her own boyfriend.

Iris, twenty-two years old, had met Todd eighteen months before when she had been working as an usherette at the Bedford Cinema, Walton, where 20-year-old Todd had been the cinema fireman. They had become fond of each other. Every single evening since their first meeting, John had called at her home, just to see her and confirm that all was going well with her, for, because of ill-health, she had had to leave her job at the cinema, where she had worked for five years.

Unable to keep such appalling news to herself, Iris had immediately told her father about it. Come to think of it, he had never warmed to his daughter's boyfriend, hardly ever even spoken to him, and, after reading the newspaper account and listening to what Iris had to tell him, Walter Tucker had gone straight out to the nearest telephone box and rung the police.

Within minutes, Detective Chief Inspector Morris, Detective Sergeant Metcalfe, and Detective Constable Hall were on their way to Roxburgh Street, Walton, where Todd, an unemployed labourer, lived with his mother. Of course, he denied everything. They still arrested him, and, at 7pm at Rice Lane, charged him. His response was, "No. Only I know I didn't murder him."

As a matter of fact, the police had already had dealings with Todd. The previous Friday evening – 16 January – following an appeal put out by the police for people who had recently visited Mr Walker's shop to come forward in order to be eliminated from their inquiries, and perhaps to prove able to yield some useful clue as regards the identity of the unknown killer, Todd, prompted by his mother, had presented himself at Rice Lane, where he signed a brief statement telling of his recent purchase there of a gramophone pick-up arm, and went on his way.

When Todd paid his customary evening call on Iris at 7.40pm on 14 January, the fatal Wednesday, she had noticed that he was not wearing his habitual sheath knife, and asked him where it was. "I won't be wearing it any more, love," was his cryptic reply,

On the day after his arrest, 20 January, John Lawrence Todd was arraigned at Dale Street Police Court in front of the Liverpool Stipendiary Magistrate, Mr Arthur MacFarland. He was represented by his solicitor, Mr Harry Livermore. The prosecuting solicitor, Mr A E West, said that Todd had made and signed three different statements to the police. The first was that made on the occasion of his voluntary visit to Rice Lane police station on 16 January. The second had been made on 19 January, the day of his arrest. In it, he affirmed that he had been to Mr Walker's shop only once before, and that was with his mother, some two or three years previously. (It was, incidentally, to Mr Walker's house that Todd's mother used, as a girl, to go for dancing lessons.) Later, on 19 January, he made a third statement. In this, he told of how, on the afternoon of 14 January, Mr Walker had tripped over and fallen in the hallway of his house, just before opening the door to let him out.

As Todd stood in the Magistrates' Court dock, Hugh George Walker was at that very time being buried in Everton Cemetery. He was to make two further brief appearances at Dale Street, before being committed for trial at the next session of the Liverpool Assizes.

That trial opened at St George's Hall, on 8 April 1953, before Mr Justice Cassels. Todd was defended by Miss Rose Heilbron, QC. Edward Wooll, QC prosecuted. Todd pleaded not guilty.

Opening the prosecution case, Mr Wooll said that the police had discovered a heavily bloodstained fawn raincoat in Mr Walker's house. Todd had denied that the coat belonged to him. He claimed that he had lost his raincoat on 7 January, a week before the murder. He said that he had left it in a hut at Sandon Dock when he went to look for the shore captain, hoping to land a job. He had actually gone, on the evening of the day of the murder, to the house of a neighbour, a Mr Humphries, an ex-policeman to ask him what he should do about his lost coat, and was advised by him to speak about it to the officer on duty at Sandon Dock gate, but he did not do so. He subsequently admitted that he had not lost his coat at all. It was indeed the one found at Mr Walker's.

He explained the blood on it, on his navy-blue suit and his crepe-soled shoes by his account of Mr Walker's 'accident': "As I was leaving on the Wednesday, the old man tripped and fell against me. His nose hit my shoulder and started bleeding. His nose rubbed down the front of my raincoat as I tried to get my hands under his arms to try to stop him falling down, but I did not succeed. I then helped him up to see what had caused him to trip. I saw a type of adze or axe on the floor. I picked up the head as the handle was broken, took the head up to the kitchenette, and put it on the bottom shelf of the food cabinet."

This, said Todd, happened between two and half-past on the Wednesday afternoon. The old man, who had recovered from his fall, told him: "You've got blood all over you. Leave you coat and I'll get it cleaned, and you can collect it on Friday when you collect the stuff." The 'stuff' being the old wireless and some clocks. Mr Walker had said that he was expecting a visitor with whom he would be going away until Friday.

Dr St Hill had taken scrapings from underneath Todd's fingernails and found them to be stained with human blood. Todd's explanation was that the blood could have got there when he was scratching some sores on his leg.

At the end of his examination, Miss Heilbron asked her client: "Did you kill Mr Walker?" Todd replied firmly: "I did not kill Mr Walker."

Dr J B Firth went into the witness-box to testify to the finding of blood on the inside of both pockets, on both trouser legs, and in the seams of the jacket cuff, of a navy-blue suit. The blood was Group O, which was the same group as that of Mr Walker. Similar blood was found on the raincoat and on the upper part, but not on the soles, of the pair of tan-coloured, crepe-soled shoes.

Iris Elizabeth Tucker, pale, with long dark hair, and wearing a smart green coat, went into the box. She told the Court that on 9 January, Todd had said that he had been to a second-hand shop to mend some clocks, and that the shopkeeper was small and "only came up to about his waist". On 13 January, he had said that he would bring her "some clocks and an old-fashioned wireless", carrying them to her house on a pram. On 14 January, Todd had said that he could not get the things, "as the old man had gone away until Monday". She remembered that when they met on 17 January he was wearing a blue suit. But it was a different one from that which he usually wore.

In his evidence, Walter Tucker said that he had met Todd in the street shortly after the murder, and had asked him if there was anything in the paper about it. Tucker told him, "Yes, there's plenty. They're looking for a man discharged from the army suffering from a spinal injury and carrying a sheath knife." As Walter Tucker well knew, the description fitted Todd to a 'T'. Todd said: "Anyone who can do that to an old man wants hanging." The best reply that Tucker could manage was a grunt.

David Harrison, a jeweller and watchmaker with a shop in Paradise Street, said that he recognised the silver hunter watch which the police had found in Todd's possession as one that he had repaired for Mr Walker in September, 1951. He was absolutely certain of it. Todd, however, insisted that it was his watch. He said that he had got it some eighteen months before at the Bedford Cinema from a man named John Arthur.

Addressing the Court on Todd's behalf, Miss Heilbron, finding herself pretty well bereft of straw, told the jury of ten men and two women: "Todd comes to you not as a man with petty convictions or grave convictions against him, but as a man of sterling character, and if ever a character could be weighed in the balance, I am sure you will take that into account. Todd is a very ordinary young man living with his mother."

The judge, summing up, said: "No man is to be convicted on a charge such as this merely because he told lies, but you are not to leave out of your consideration the reflection as to why he told lies.

... If you are satisfied that his was the hand that struck those thirty-two savage blows on that defenceless old man's head, and thus battered the life out of him, you will return a verdict of guilty."

They did.

John Todd displayed no sign of emotion when the foreman announced the jury's finding. He stood unflinching to attention as the black cap was placed by the chaplain on the judge's head and sentence of death was solemnly pronounced upon him. It was carried out at Walton Gaol on 19 May 1953, my old friend the late Albert Pierrepoint despatching him with his customary expedition.

One cannot help but feel mystified by the crime. What was the point of it? Where was the motive? Surely it cannot have been the acquisition of an old and well-worn silver watch? What on earth can it have been that so suddenly released in the normally peaceable breast of a hitherto decent young man such a whirlwind of savagery upon a timid and harmless old man?

TIKI EVIL?

It, the evil thing, whatever it was, came out of the thick clinging winding-sheet of freezing fog that enshrouded all Liverpool that dulled December afternoon five days before Christmas, 1961. Fog is not usual in Liverpool. The Mersey wind, sharp and clean, generally sweeps it away before it has time to settle and coagulate. But Wednesday, 20 December 1961, was exceptional. The pathetic fallacy was made manifest: the weather set the stage for, and reflected, the horror.

That horror had been enacted in the living-room, transmuted by it into the dead room, of a little semi-detached house, trim, neat, smugly suburban, hitherto undistinguished, henceforth never to be the same again, No 14 Thingwall Avenue, Knotty Ash.

The tableau, resistant to effacement, is of that homely living-room, its customary well-ordered state disrupted. Lying on the carpet in a slowly oozing, inexorably spreading, crimson pool of blood, a fatally stabbed young mother, her dying watched in dazed bewilderment by her two-year-old son, and his 22-day-old baby brother, crying in his nearby cot.

That is the scene bequeathed to meet the anguished eye of 33-year-old Brian Dutton when he returned at 6.10pm that wintry evening from Widnes, where he worked as a research chemist with Imperial Chemical Industries, to find the house in darkness ... until he switched on the living-room light and flooded merciful dusky obscurity with immediate cruel revelation. Shocked virtually out of his senses, he robotically turned to the neighbours for succour and to the police for practical resolution. A doctor was also summoned.

The police arrived. Out came their notebooks, and on to their pages was painstakingly transcribed the disentangled chronology of the day's known events. At eight o'clock that morning Brian Dutton had taken a cup of tea upstairs to his 27-year-old wife, Maureen Ann, who was having a bit of a lie-in. She was still somewhat on the frail side after the birth of two-year-old David's as yet unchristened baby brother.

Maureen Dutton had been tentatively planning to take David over to Childwall Parish Church that afternoon to see the Christmas crib, and when her mother-in-law called in at about eleven o'clock she had asked her if she would be able to look after the baby for her while they went on the little expedition. Mother-in-law had said that she would, and left at around midday to go back home to her house in Broadgreen Road.

The fog meanwhile seemed to be steadily thickening, and at half-past one Maureen's telephone rang. It was Mother-in-law, saying that she didn't think she could come to baby-sit; the fog was getting too thick. So that was that, so far as the trip to see the crib was concerned. Maureen, mildly disappointed, set about preparing some lunch. It was afterwards found on the table, half-eaten.

And there the history of the day's doings, and the policemen's notebooks, snapped shut.

Upon closer examination, Maureen Dutton's body proved to have 14 stab wounds – a savage attack on her throat and chest. It was calculated that her unknown assailant had used a sharp, narrow-bladed knife. Oddly, there was no evidence of there having been any struggle. Nothing had been stolen. And there were no signs of a forced entry.

The investigation was taken over by Chief Superintendent James Morris, head of the Liverpool CID, and Deputy Chief Constable Herbert Balmer. The murder squad headquarters was set up at Old Swan police station.

An intensive road check of all vehicles in the area was instantly ordered. Result: negative. The help of tracker dogs and their handlers was enlisted. They drew a blank. Concentrated efforts were directed to the finding of the knife that dealt the fatal blows. A thorough probing of all the drains in the district ultimately yielded more than a hundred knives, but the murder weapon was not among them. All Christmas leave for those working on the case was cancelled.

A daunting schedule of house-to-house inquiries was embarked upon, and by 17 January writers'-cramped police officers had scribed more than 20,000 statements. Out of this forest of paper stepped a curious figure. A stranger in a leather jacket, seen looming through the fog by a significant number of witnesses. A young man, he was spotted walking along Thingwall Lane towards Thomas Lane at about 1.50pm on the day of the murder. Resisting all entreaty, 'Leather Jacket' never stepped forward.

Anxious to be of help in any way that it could, the *Liverpool Echo* printed on its front page on 18 January 1962, a full-colour identikit picture of the man in the leather jacket. It brought in more than sixty claims from people who thought that they recognised him. Most of them were mistaken, but one woman stated that, on the afternoon of the day that Mrs Dutton had been murdered, she had seen a youth in a shiny black jacket being violently sick near the Methodist Church at the corner of Court Hey Avenue. She had noticed that all the time that he was vomiting he had kept his hands in his pockets. That had struck her as odd.

Another woman, who lived not far from Thingwall Lane, told of how, just before 1.50pm on the day of the murder, a youth in a leather jacket, identical to the lad in the identikit picture, had called at her house, and when she opened the door he just stood there with a half-smile on his face, never speaking a word, and tap, tap, tapping his left hand on his right. It was quite eerie. Before slamming the door on him, she had observed his hands. They were well-kept and sun-tanned, and had slender fingers.

Morris and Balmer cast out several nets. They released a press appeal for any bus conductor who had been on the Thomas Lane route between 1.30pm and 6.30pm on 20 December, and happened to have noticed anybody acting in a suspicious manner, to contact them.

This brought in an account of a woman, wearing a pale pink coat, black stiletto-heeled shoes, and carrying a white, envelope-type

244

handbag, who, at 4.30pm on the afternoon of the murder, boarded a No 10D, Longview to City Centre, bus, at the East Prescot Road stop, opposite Eaton Road. Tall, buxom, 25-35 years of age, she spoke with an Irish accent. She seemed agitated and out of breath, as if she had been running for some considerable distance. She was talking constantly to herself, saying that she had to get out of Liverpool immediately, and that she was going to London to catch an airplane All through the journey she kept muttering, "Oh, my God! Oh, my God!" She got off the bus at Lime Street.

Another throw of the Morris-Balmer net was directed at everyone who had known the dead woman since the time of her marriage in April 1955. They were obviously toying with the theory that the victim knew her killer. All were willing to co-operate, but none of those who came forward was able to shed the smallest glimmer of light on the mystery.

A promising lead surfaced from the onerous house-to-house interviewing. It came from a young woman in Halewood, who, like Maureen Dutton, had recently had a baby. A man who said he was a doctor called, explaining that he had been asked to examine her. He was dark, with cropped curly hair, a broad nose, horn-rimmed glasses, and was wearing a dark grey overcoat. She judged him to have been aged between 27 and 30. His appearance and demeanour was such that she had felt no reason to doubt his genuineness. It was only after her husband had found out that there was no doctor of the name that he had given in the area that their suspicions were aroused, and they quickly informed the police. The lead petered out.

A theory was then punted that the killing of Mrs Dutton might have been the result of a housebreaking that went wrong; that Leather Jacket was a housebreaker, scouring Knotty Ash for takings under cover of fog. The Thingwall Lane area was a passing prosperous one. Suppose he had knocked at Mrs Dutton's door expecting no answer, but when someone came to the door he resorted to violence. It could be that the agitated Irishwoman on the bus had been Leather Jacket's girlfriend-cum-look-out. When he emerged, covered in blood, she, horrified, terror-stricken, had taken to her heels in panic and pelted all-out for the bus stop.

A theory was also current for a time that the murder had been the work of a madman. Perhaps so. Insanity would explain the lack of motive. But there was not the slightest justification for those who tried to make a specific ascription. St Edward's Orphanage, situated only a short walk away from the scene of the killing, had fairly recently at that time changed its function and become an institution for the housing of mentally ill patients There were irresponsible whisperings … and rumour is no respecter of truth.

As time passed and puzzlement remained, there came about the extraordinary spectacle of down-to-earth detectives planting policemen's flat feet in coffee bars, clubs, record shops, libraries and museums, in quest of Polynesian gods and Polynesian cult worshippers on matter-of-fact

Merseyside. Rumour on the offensive offensive once again! Morris and Balmer had somehow got it into their heads, somehow been persuaded, that Maureen Ann Dutton of Knotty Ash might have been the victim of a ritual sacrifice. They apparently believed that members of a Polynesian/ Hawaiian cult had been at the Dutton home in recent months, and hypothesised from there.

They "discovered" that worshippers "made sacrifices to Tiki during the winter solstice", and Mrs Dutton had been murdered during the winter solstice! The talk was of the God, Tiki, which did not actually make sense, for the word 'Tiki' means 'God'. There are four major Tiki – Ku, Lono, Kane, and Kaualoa. Of these, only Ku, the God of War, has rituals which include human sacrifice.

Then, suddenly, as if by Pacific magic, everything seemed to click into place. A 24-year-old male nurse, resident in Upper Parliament Street, was arrested and charged with the theft of drugs and surgical equipment from three Liverpool hospitals. He was also suspected of having passed himself off as a doctor, and he was tattooed on his right arm with a reversed swastika, the identification mark, according to the police belief, of "a Tiki worshipper".

However, at Liverpool City Magistrates' Court, Mr Rex Makin, solicitor for the prisoner, told the Court that the only drugs which his client had stolen were sleeping pills, mild sedatives, and vitamin K tablets. The nurse was, he said, a man of good character, and had never been in any kind of trouble before. It had been merely a case of the "disadvantage of having a tattoo mark on his arm which had led the police to think that he might be connected with the murder of Maureen Duffy."

The police were back to empty square one. And that, for all their valiant best efforts is where they remained. Sadly, the cruel fate of the young mother, Maureen Ann Dutton, has gone down in Liverpool's history as one more unsolved, unavenged crime.

The Polynesian Tiki theory is ridiculous. *Of course*, it is. But the killing *did* take place; and not the tiniest sliver of guilt has been adduced against anyone; not in the last fifty years.

FACT: At the beginning of the 1960s, the Polynesian cult had a considerable following in Britain, and there were many members in Liverpool.

As Sherlock Holmes somewhere says: 'When you have eliminated the impossible, whatever remains, *however improbable*, must be the truth.'

THE HOPE STREET
CELLAR OF HORRORS

In the twilight of an October evening in the year
1826 a cart is lurching its way through the
gathering gloom of the George's Dock Passage.
Upon this cart are three large Newfoundland oil
casks which are prominently labelled 'Bitter Salts'.
The eyes of the driver seek among the flickers of
dockside lamps for the smack which bears upon
her bows the name *Latona*, for it is his business to
deliver the casks to that vessel. In his pocket there
reposes a note which is addressed to the Carron
Company and which reads as follows :

> *Please ship on board the Latona three casks of*
> *bitter salts, from Mr Brown, agent, Liverpool,*
> *to Mr G.H. Ironson, Edinburgh,*
>
> *J. Brown*

It is not long before the carter has discovered the
Latona, one of the smacks which trade between
Liverpool and Leith, which is lying in the George's
Dock Passage, and, his mission accomplished, is
rumbling complacently homewards. At that time he
has no knowledge of the strange cargo which he has
just delivered, and little thinks that what seems to
him to be the end of a transaction is, in reality, but
the beginning of an extremely unsavoury mystery.
He will hear more of it, much more, but meanwhile

he does not know this, it is getting late and he turns his back upon the darkening waterfront. Nor is the carter the only one anxious to quit the docks. It has been a long day and the crew of the *Latona* feel the urge to abandon ship and escape into the more convivial atmosphere of the Paradise Street taverns. So the casks are hastily slipped betwixt decks, time enough to stow them away tomorrow.

Next morning, however, when the sailors came to deal with the casks they were so overcome by the terrible stench which they gave off, that it was decided that the matter had best be reported to the master. Captain Walker examined the offending casks at once, and, drawing out a plug of straw which had been stuffed into a small hole in the side of one of the barrels, he released so unmistakable an odour of corruption that he made up his mind there and then to investigate further. He ordered one of the bungs to be started and, upon introducing his hand into the barrel, the Captain was horrified to encounter, not the chemical substance which he had anticipated, but the soft tell-tale contours of a human body. Naturally, he immediately sent a message to the Carron Company telling them of his gruesome discovery, and they promptly communicated with the police. The casks were removed forthwith to the old City Deadhouse in Chapel Street, and when opened they proved to contain no less than eleven human bodies packed in salt – bitter salt, indeed !

The police set to work at once to trace the carter who had borne this grisly freight to the *Latona*. The investigation was undertaken by an officer named Robert Boughey, and in a remarkably short space of time he had managed to track down the carter. His name was George Leech and he had a strange story to tell. He had, he said, been with his brother's cart at the stand at the Dry Dock on the previous Monday afternoon. Sometime between three and four o'clock he was approached by a tall, stout man with black whiskers. The stranger, who spoke with a thick Scottish accent, had offered him the sum of two shillings if he would deliver three casks to the *Latona* for him. Leech had agreed to this proposition and was directed to take his cart to No 8 Hope Street. There, he was met by two men who brought the barrels from the cellar and gave him a hand to lift them on to his cart. That same evening he had transported them to the ship, which he understood was bound for Leith. And that, said Leech, was as much as he knew of the matter.

After hearing this tale, Boughey went straight to the house in Hope Street. He found it occupied by the Reverend James Macgowan who ran a small private school there. In reply to the officer's inquiries, Macgowan said that he had let his cellar in the previous January to a Mr John Henderson, a native of Greenock, who had told him that he was a cooper by trade and was engaged in the export of fish-oil. Boughey then asked for the key of the cellar, but Macgowan replied that it was not in his possession. Thereupon, Boughey took a crowbar and announced his intention of breaking the door down. Macgowan became excited and ordered him to desist from damaging his property. When

Boughey seemed disinclined to desist, the reverend gentleman threatened to bring an action against him, but the intrepid Boughey was not to be dissuaded and the door was burst open to reveal in that dusky subterranean place, a scene of horror such as might have been wrung from the tortured imagination of an Edgar Allen Poe. Scattered about in a number of casks and sacks, Boughey found the corpses of twenty-two men, women and children. Here, then, was a sinister riddle. How came all these dead bodies to be gathered together in this frightful basement charnel-house?

It was the police surgeon, Thomas William Davis, who provided the solution. From his examination of the remains he concluded that in every case death had occurred from natural causes, and upon the toe of one young woman he found a significant fragment of thread. This led him to believe that the bodies had been disinterred – probably from the parish cemetery which was situated about a quarter of a mile away from Hope Street, in an area at the foot of what is now Cambridge Street – for it was a common practice in those days to keep the feet of the deceased together by tying the toes. From this small clue, together with the discovery in the cellar of various other pieces of evidence, such as a syringe of the type which anatomists employed to inject hot wax into the veins and arteries of cadavers, he had no hesitation in saying that in the Hope Street basement the police had stumbled upon nothing less than a body-snatchers' warehouse! Moreover, October was that season of the year when the anatomical lectures were just beginning in the Scottish medical schools, and the northern surgeons were always on the look-out for subjects for their dissecting-tables. So vigilantly were the churchyards in Scotland guarded against the depredations of resurrectionists, that the anatomists used to have to send their agents to England, where there was little difficulty in finding men who were quite ready to satisfy their demands at the rate of £10 to £15 per body.

Despite the widespread search which ensued for the Liverpool 'sack-'em-up men,' Henderson, the main actor in that grim little drama, was never brought to justice. Two other men were arrested however. One, Gillespie, was subsequently discharged, but the other, 25-year-old James Donaldson, later stood trial on the charge of "having conspired with divers other persons, lately at Liverpool, and unlawfully, wilfully and indecently disinterred, taken and carried away divers dead bodies."

The trial aroused considerable excitement and not a little horror and indignation. When, at one stage in the proceedings, it was described how a huge barrel containing a number of babies soaked in brine had been discovered, an audible shudder passed through the court and the foreman of the jury was taken ill and obliged to make a hasty exit. Donaldson was found guilty, sentenced to twelve months in the Kirkdale House of Correction and ordered to pay a fine of £50.

On 9 November 1826, a third man, John Ross, was taken into custody for being concerned in the outrage, and also a man named Peter M'Gregor. The circumstances surrounding the arrest are curious. On Saturday, 4 November, a man brought a large box to the White Horse coach-office in Dale Street. Shortly after his departure, the coach-office bookkeeper noticed a very offensive smell coming from the box and, probably recollecting the recent discoveries at Hope Street, he took it upon himself to open the box. Within, was the body of a woman. A day or two later, a man carried a similar box into the Golden Lion inn, also in Dale Street, which was addressed for forwarding to Edinburgh. The bookkeeper, his suspicions thoroughly aroused, managed to detain the man who had brought it until the police arrived. The box was then forced open and, sure enough, yet another human body was disclosed. Both Ross and M'Gregor were committed for trial, charged with having unlawfully opened graves and carried away dead bodies. They were each sentenced to twelve months imprisonment and each had to pay a fine of £21 to the King.

So ended the case of the Liverpool body-snatchers and, although occasional premature resurrections are recorded as having subsequently taken place here, the Hope Street affair stands unique in the annals of the city as the only instance of the existence in Liverpool of an organised company of body-snatchers for the export of corpses to Scotland.

It is difficult for us in these days of well-ordered medical schools to understand the state of affairs which gave rise to the body-snatchers who

254

once purveyed their gruesome merchandise to the centres of anatomical learning. Prior to 1832, the dissection of human bodies was not legalised in the British Isles, but that law which condemned the procuring of a cadaver for purposes of dissection, nevertheless required all medical candidates to have practical acquaintance with human anatomy. In short, those who would fulfil the law had first to break it! Certain provisions were made in that the scant material from the gallows was handed over to the doctors. But demand was far in excess of supply. To remedy this deficiency, an anatomist would periodically gather about him a band of his heftiest students and sally forth on a grave-rifling expedition. Obviously, a busy anatomist could not find time to do all his own cadaver-stealing, and there came into being a new 'professional' class known variously as 'Fishermen', 'Body-snatchers', 'Resurrectionists' and, most descriptively, as 'Sack-'em-up-men'.

The majority of 'Sack-'em-up-men' were blackguards. Often they would sell a body to one anatomist only to steal it back and resell it elsewhere. Another ruse was to deliver a drunk in the corpse-sack, pocket the money and disappear before the deception could be discovered. But the body-snatchers did not have it all their own way, and woe betide any unfortunate fisherman who was caught about his ghoulish activities. A mob would soon gather and he was quite likely to be kicked to death.

On the other hand, as long as things went well there was good money in the business and quite reasonable prices could be obtained for such by-products as teeth. In those days there was no National Health Service to provide plastic dentures and dentists were only too pleased to purchase teeth, torn from the mouths of corpses, which were destined to grace the edentulous mouths of unsuspecting, rich patients!

By 1827, the position had reached its unsavoury climax, but the legislators were still more concerned with the problems of fox-hunting than with the dilemma of the doctors. It took a national calamity, a series of the most brutal murders, to stir the national conscience into belated activity.

The echoes of the horror which was aroused by these terrible crimes, which came to be known as the Burke and Hare murders, still sound in the corridors of memory a hundred and eighty years after their perpetrators have answered for their misdeeds. Parliamentary indifference was swept away before the resultant wave of popular fury and the year 1832 saw the passing of the Anatomy Act, which made adequate provisions for the supply of subjects to properly qualified persons. This measure sealed the death-warrant of the body-snatchers. The golden age of the miners of the cemeteries had passed for ever. Gone now is the fear that sacrilegious hands may resurrect our loved ones before the appointed day, and that the flowers planted upon their graves and watered by the tears of the bereaved may bloom above an empty coffin.

KILLINGS THAT
CHANGED A STREET NAME

You will search the Liverpool street directory in vain for Leveson Street. A hundred odd years ago its name was on everyone's lips. Today, it has vanished without a trace. What is the strange story that lies behind the disappearance of that once-famous thoroughfare? The answer is MURDER – for it was murder most foul that took Leveson Street off the map.

In the early afternoon of 28 March 1849, a terror-stricken errand-boy, running as fast as his little legs would carry him, dashed headlong up Great George Street and into the arms of a patrolling policeman. "Now then; now then," remonstrated that astonished officer, but a glance at the boy's pale face and wide-staring eyes told him that something was wrong. "What's to do, lad?" he queried in more kindly tones.

"Murder!" gasped the breathless boy.

"Now then ..." the constable began again.

"It's true, Mister. I didn't see her killed but she's dead. You come back with me to Leveson Street and see for yourself."

And so the policeman and the errand-boy went together to No 20 Leveson Street. What they found there started a sensation which rocked the whole country, setting a finger to the trigger of terror in many a household, particularly in those where lodgings were let to single men.

It was sometime during the latter part of 1848 that Captain John Henry Hinrichson, the master of a sailing-ship which plied between Liverpool and Calcutta, and his wife Ann, after searching Liverpool for a suitable house, decided to purchase the commodious and comfortable residence at 20 Leveson Street. By the beginning of the following year, the Hinrichsons, together with their two sons, Henry George, aged five, and John Alfred, a three-year-old tot, and a maid-servant named Mary Parr, had settled into their new home. They found the place just a trifle large for their requirements and the Captain and his wife decided that it would be a good idea to let a couple of spare rooms which they had furnished but were not using. The money derived from such a source, together with what Mrs Hinrichson earned by taking in a number of pupils to whom she taught music, would, they thought, help considerably towards household expenses.

Accordingly, a neat card was placed in the front parlour window announcing, 'Furnished Apartments to Let'. Between three and four o'clock in the afternoon of the day when the notice was first exhibited, a well-dressed young man of about twenty-six knocked at the door and asked in an engaging Irish brogue if he might inspect the rooms. He gave the name of John Gleeson Wilson, and said that he was a carpenter by trade and was employed by the Dock Estate. After being shown a front parlour and a back bedroom, Wilson expressed his entire satisfaction with the apartments, paid a week's rent in advance and took possession of the rooms there and then. That this was merely a subterfuge to gain entry to the house became apparent subsequently, for the man already had lodgings in another district of Liverpool.

Having handed over the money to Mrs Hinrichson, Wilson left the house but returned at about eight o'clock that evening, when he retired to his room and, after sending out for a pint of ale at about ten, he went to bed.

Those were the days before 'Dora' had come to put a curb upon the Englishman's drinking habits, and at half-past seven the following morning Wilson was in a public-house in Great George Street, having a breakfast glass of ale. Here, he did something which, in the light of later events, is utterly inexplicable. Calling the proprietress to his table, he asked her if she could supply him with a wafer with which to seal an envelope. The lady said that she did not happen to have one, but brought him a stick of sealing-wax with which he fastened down the flap. He then asked her if she would mind addressing the envelope for him as he was unable to write. The lady of the house summoned her daughter and she addressed the note 'John Wilson, Esq., 20 Leveson Street, Liverpool,' to his dictation.

Wilson then left the tavern and calling a youth whom he saw passing in the street, told him that if he would deliver a letter to a house, to which he would direct him he would earn himself a few coppers. He instructed the lad to watch him into the house in Leveson Street and, when a few minutes had elapsed, to knock with the letter and ask whoever came to the door if John Wilson lived there, adding that he had a letter for him from his (Wilson's) employer. The youth agreed to do this, and, after seeing Wilson disappear into the house, he proceeded, some five minutes later, to carry out his instructions.

The servant, Mary Parr, answered his knock.

"Does John Wilson live here?" he inquired.

"Yes, here he is," the girl replied as Wilson appeared behind her in the doorway. Borrowing some money from Mrs Hinrichson to reward the boy, Wilson took the letter and returned to his room.

Shortly after eleven o'clock Mrs Hinrichson called to Mary Parr that she was going out to do her shopping. She went first to a greengrocer's in nearby St James's Street, where she was a regular customer, and ordered some potatoes. From there she went to a chandler's and bought two jugs. Both these purchases were to be sent to her house by errand-boys.

The boy with the vegetables arrived at 20 Leveson Street first. The door was opened by Wilson, who took the potatoes from him and returned a minute or two later with the empty basket. About twenty minutes afterwards the second boy arrived with the crockery. He put his basket down on the step ... rang the bell ... whistled a popular tune while he waited ... rang again ... still no reply. Next he tried the effect of a thunderous assault on the knocker. The door remained tight shut. Putting his eye to the keyhole, the boy peeped into the hall, where he was startled to see a pair of woman's feet lying across the passageway. Overcome with curiosity, he climbed on to the handle of his basket and, perching himself precariously on the railings, peered in through the parlour window. What he saw in that room drained the colour from his face. The place was swimming with blood and lying there was the battered body of the maid-servant; beside her, his head smashed to pulp, lay the five-year-old Henry. With a shriek of terror, the chandler's boy took to his heels, never stopping till he regained his father's shop. There, he stammered out his story and was sent helter-skelter in search of a policeman.

So it came about that the constable who was gently ambling along on his beat on that ordinary weekday afternoon, when all was so comfortingly quiet and peaceful round about Duke Street, suddenly found himself involved in one of the most sensational Liverpool murder mysteries of the last century.

While the policeman and his young escort were making their way to Leveson Street, things were beginning to happen at that house of death. Scarcely had the chandler's boy fled the scene of horror, when a young lady who was a pupil of Mrs Hinrichson's called for a music lesson. Receiving no reply to her repeated knockings, the girl became alarmed and, convinced that something was wrong, communicated her suspicions to a Mr Hughes who was a neighbour of the Hinrichsons. This Mr Hughes accompanied her to the house and, after looking through the parlour window and seeing the sight which had so unnerved the errand-boy, he broke a pane of glass and forced an entrance into the house.

So it was that when the police-officer and the lad arrived, they found the front-door open and the house swarming with people. His scepticism blasted, the constable turned to the trembling boy: "Down to the bridewell as fast as you can go, young 'un," he shouted, "and get them to send help quickly."

With the arrival of reinforcements, the police began a thorough search of the premises. They found attractive, 29-year-old Mrs Hinrichson, who, by the way, was shortly expecting her third child, mortally injured in the lobby. Down in the cellar lay the three-year-old John, his throat cut from ear to ear. In the parlour was little Henry, also mortally wounded, and poor Mary Parr, who, though badly battered, was still just about alive. Upstairs in Wilson's room was a bowl of bloodstained water in which the murderer had evidently washed his hands, but of Wilson himself there was no sign.

In less than half an hour Mary Parr was in the Southern Hospital with anxious police officials watching beside her bed ready to take a statement should she regain consciousness. She did, briefly, and was able to falter out her story before, a few days later, she died.

Meanwhile, somewhere upon the high seas, Captain Hinrichson was sailing steadily towards home in his ship *Duncan,* blissfully unaware of the terrible blow which fate had struck to rob him of his entire family. Meanwhile, too, a human tiger prowled the drab jungle of the streets as the hunters set to work casting a drag-net to snare him.

Wilson's movements were decidedly odd. He went first to the Figure-of-Eight Pit in Toxteth Park, where he was seen washing his blood-smeared clothes. Next, he made his way to London Road and, after visiting a shop and offering a gold watch for sale, he went to a clothes dealer's in Great Homer Street where he bought a new pair of trousers. He also sold his boots to a poor woman and purchased another pair. After that, he returned to his original lodgings in Porter Street and asked his landlady for a clean shirt. She gave him one of her husband's and noticed that the one which he discarded was heavily stained.

At six o'clock on the evening of the murders, Wilson went to a barber's shop in Great Howard Street and had a shave. He asked the hairdresser if he could sell him a wig. Unable to do so, the man offered to take him to a shop in Oil Street where he could get one. On the way there, after questioning the barber as to the possibility of booking a passage to America for about £3, Wilson suddenly said: "Have you heard about the murder?" and upon the barber's replying that he had not, Wilson remarked: "A terrible affair, two women and two children had their heads bashed in."

"How awful! Did they get him?" asked his companion.

"No," replied Wilson, "not yet."

At that time Wilson had a wife living at Tranmere, and when he left the hairdresser he went over the water and spent the night with her.

Next morning, ignoring the hue and cry, he took

a ferry-boat back to Liverpool and presented himself at the shop of Israel Samuel, a Great Howard Street grocer who also dealt in watches. Wilson showed him a gold watch saying that he wanted £6 for it, but the grocer was not satisfied and before making an offer he called in a policeman. After examining the watch, the constable said he did not think it was one which had been notified as being stolen. Despite this reassurance, however, Samuel was still suspicious, and when the policeman had departed he said that he had not sufficient money on the premises to pay Wilson, but added that if he would accompany his son to his other shop in Dale Street he would be paid there. Before the pair left his shop, old Samuel told his son in Hebrew, "When you are passing the police-station, collar this fellow and give him in charge." The son did as his father told him and so surprised was Wilson that he had been bundled inside the bridewell before he could put up the slightest resistance.

Tried before Mr Justice Patteson at the Liverpool Assizes, Wilson staunchly maintained his innocence. He showed no hint of remorse, refused to speak and while awaiting the verdict displayed "the most brutal indifference and ferocity of disposition". During the time he was in gaol he gave way to fits of uncontrollable rage and on one occasion nearly brained a warder with a hammer. His counsel argued that the evidence against him was wholly circumstantial, but the jury found 'Guilty' without leaving the box. Their verdict was greeted with loud cheers by the huge crowds that had assembled outside the court-house.

Wilson, or, to give him his real name, Maurice Gleeson, who was a native of Limerick, was hanged on 15 September 1849, outside Kirkdale Gaol in the presence of 30,000 spectators. Excursion trains, packed to suffocation, were run to the execution, and the Railway Companies advertised 'Reduced fares for this occasion only'.

On the scaffold, Wilson maintained a pose of stolid indifference and faced the crowd with lips curled in a contemptuous sneer. An eye-witness afterwards wrote: 'A tremendous cheer went up from the vast multitudes when the dangling body of Gleeson Wilson swung from the gallows.'

Ann Hinrichson, together with her unborn child, her two sons and Mary Parr, were all buried in the same grave in St James's Cemetery. History is silent regarding what happened to Captain Hinrichson, apart from the fact that he subsequently gave up the sea and became dock master of Toxteth, Huskisson and finally Queen's Docks.

One last note. Leveson Street, which had become so notorious as a result of Wilson's dreadful deeds, was shortly afterwards renamed Grenville Street.

The Twitching-face Slayer

Back in the 1890s, when the Liverpool waterfront was a spiky forest of masts and spars, old Edward Moyse was a familiar figure at the Pier Head, and the little bookstall which he kept on Mann Island, opposite George's Dock, was well known.

A picturesque character, with a straggling grey beard and a shock of flowing white hair, upon which was always perched a shabby top-hat, old Moyse was something of a recluse. He had few friends and lived alone in his home at 26 Redcross Street, except for 15-year-old John Needham, who helped him at his stall during the day and kept house for him after the shutters had been put up at the kiosk. Despite a certain eccentricity, Moyse seems to have been a good master and a man of markedly religious turn. You could see him every Sunday worshipping at St Nicholas's Church, and his interest in affairs of the spirit extended even into the realms of his daily business, for, apart from dealing in newspapers, magazines and second-hand books, he made something of a speciality of selling bibles.

It was to this harmless old news vendor that, on the night of 18-19 February 1895, death came in no gentle guise.

That evening the stall closed as usual at about 6pm, and John Needham went home alone to Redcross Street as his master had to go to view some books which he was proposing to purchase.

Shortly after 6.30, young Needham, who was busying himself in preparing his supper, was startled by a loud knock at the door. Callers were few at that house, and he was surprised to find upon the doorstep a stranger who told him that he had come to buy some valuable books. The boy explained that Mr Moyse was away from home and was not likely to be back before nine or ten o'clock that night. Upon hearing this, the man said that he would return at nine o'clock, but actually it was just striking eight when he came back, entering the house by means of a back-passage which he evidently knew well.

The stranger, who was subsequently identified as William Miller, a 27-year-old sailor, was obviously well acquainted with Moyse, but the exact nature of their relationship was at the time, and still is, shrouded in mystery. That there was some curious association between them, however, is beyond question.

When Miller appeared for the second time, Needham was engaged in making a pot of tea for himself. He offered the stranger a cup which he politely refused and, seating himself at the table, announced his intention of waiting until the bookseller arrived home. So, as the clock ticked on, these two sat peaceably chatting in the living-room, and the stranger confided that he was a seafarer. Evidently seeking to ingratiate himself with the lad, he promised that he would bring him home a parrot and some 'baccy from his very next voyage to foreign parts, and went on to say that he was due to be paid-off the following day, adding that Moyse's boys used frequently to go errands for him and were always right for two or three shillings. Changing the subject, Miller then made some remarks regarding Moyse's rather peculiar ways of walking and talking, but the lad did not take him up on this and was somewhat non-commital in his reply. For a while the conversation flagged until, suddenly, the sailor demanded: "Where does the old chap keep his money?"

"I don't know," answered Needham.

But Miller was persistent, saying that he thought that the old man was very wealthy and asking Needham if he had never seen any of the cash which he had in the house. "It's very funny that he doesn't tell you where his money is for fear he might die," he Miller suspiciously.

But the boy only shook his head and said they didn't sell enough books to make a lot of money.

Apparently satisfied, Miller reverted to the topic of his impending pay-off, and told the youth that he wanted to give Mr Moyse some sovereigns to keep for him, asking at the same time if he thought that his master would lend him sixpence till the morning. At that very moment, there was the sound of a key in the lock and Edward Moyse came in. That was at five minutes to ten.

The old man shook hands cordially with his visitor, saying as he did so that he had not expected to see him again so soon. Then, turning to Needham, he said, "This is the lodger I had before. He can sleep on the sofa tonight and you can make up the bed in the best bedroom for him tomorrow." The boy was then despatched upstairs to bed. With

Needham's departure, the first scene of the drama came to an end. What transpired between the two men he left sitting amiably beside the living-room fire that night will never be known – only the fearful fate which was to overtake one of them, making front-page news next day and being remembered down the years as the terrible Redcross Street Murder.

It is at 5am on the morning of 19 February 1895, that the curtain rises upon the second act of this real-life tragedy. Upstairs in his room below the eaves, John Needham stirs in his sleep as the nearby clock of St Nicholas's chimes the hour. In the cold and dark of the winter morning, the boy struggles from his bed and lights a candle. He is not the only one abroad in that silent house. Presently, as he is pulling on his clothes, Miller comes into his bedroom. He is without his jacket and boots. He says that he cannot wake the master and that he is unable to find any coal with which to light a fire. The boy tells him that the coal is kept outside on the landing and that the coal-bucket and hatchet are on the floor below. Miller disappears downstairs. There is the clatter of a bucket, the sound of heavy treading, and a minute or two later he is back in Needham's bedroom. Standing in the doorway, he points to an aperture in the ceiling of the landing. "What is that?" he asks.

"It is a manhole," replies Needham.

"Oh!" says Miller," I must have a look up there," and with that fetches a chair, climbs on to it and pulls himself up through the trap. For fully ten minutes he is up there rooting about with his hands on the dusty floor. He does not, it seems, find what he is searching for, and, very quietly, Miller eases his way back through the trapdoor and lowers himself to the landing. Stealthily, he creeps back into Needham's room, extinguishes the candle and deals the boy a vicious blow on the side of the head. Needham slumps on to the bed and, without a word, Miller falls upon him and grips him by the throat until he loses consciousness. When, a few minutes later, the lad regains his senses, he finds his assailant standing over him with a poker. He raises the weapon and brings it down with sickening force upon the youth's skull. Then he leaves the room and Needham, bleeding badly, dimly hears him call, "Good morning," as he passes Mr Moyse's bedroom. The front-door opens, crashes to, and then there is silence. Needham lapses into unconsciousness.

Sometime later, he does not know how long for he has lost all sense of time, the injured boy manages to crawl to his master's room. There, he finds old Moyse dead in his bed, his head battered in, his silky white hair a matted tangle of congealed blood. Weak and dizzy from loss of blood and almost fainting with fright, Needham drags himself out into the street where he is found by a man who is walking through the sleeping town on his way to work. Soon, a little crowd of passers-by has gathered round the stricken boy and one of them identifies him as the youth who works for Edward Moyse. The police are summoned and young Needham is taken away in an ambulance to hospital.

While the doctors tended Needham's injuries, the police made their way to Redcross Street.

There, they found a scene of ghastly confusion. The whole place had obviously been ransacked. There were signs of a severe struggle and the staircase was spattered with crimson sequins of blood. Upstairs, lay the battered corpse of Edward Moyse. The only money in the house was the sum of £8 which they discovered beneath Moyse's pillow. It did not take the police long to decide that this was no chance crime committed by a passing tramp, but the work of a local man who, hearing tales of Moyse's miserly ways, had made up his mind to carry off his rumoured (but actually non-existent) crock of gold.

As soon as he was sufficiently recovered, Needham recounted the story of Miller's visit to the police, but when it came to giving a description of the man he began to realise how very little he really knew about him. That he was aged about twenty-five, dressed like a sailor and talked a great deal about the sea, was not much help in a port the size of Liverpool. But one of the officers happened to ask him if he had noticed anything peculiar about the fellow – strange tattoo marks or something really characteristic like that. The boy thought for a minute. Yes, there *was* one thing: he had a queer way of twitching the right side of his face when excited.

That was more like it. Here at last was something to go on, and this description was immediately circulated to every police station in the North of England.

Time passed, and then one day a woman came to the police and told them that she knew the whereabouts of a man who she thought might be the murderer. He had a nervous twitch of the kind described and seemed loath to venture into the streets in daylight. His name was William Miller, he was a seaman, just back from America, and he was living with his father-in-law in Edgeware Street. A police cordon was thrown around the house. The wanted man was in bed and had no chance to get away. In his room they found a bloodstained shirt. Arrested, Miller protested his complete innocence. "My shirt got covered with blood at the Gill Street slaughterhouse where I had a job for a few days," he said. A reasonable explanation, or so it seemed, until he was taken to the slaughterhouse and told to point out the exact spot where he had been working when he got bloodstained. Without batting an eyelid, Miller said, "I was working just there," and went on to give a detailed account of the animals which had been killed there during his period of employment. They let him talk. When he had finished the superintendent of the abattoir said quietly: "We haven't killed any cattle in this part of the building for months past. Those carcasses you now see were brought over from Birkenhead to be sold here."

The game was up. Miller surely knew as much, but he still tried to bluff his way out. So the police took him to the hospital; to the bedside of the boy he had tried to kill. At first Needham seemed rather doubtful as the police had brought a number of people with them, whom they lined up at the foot of his bed in the style of a regular identity parade. Outwardly calm, Miller must, however, have been inwardly agitated for, very slowly at first, the right-hand side of his face began to twitch. "Look at his face! Look at his face!" screamed the boy and dived in terror beneath the bedclothes. And, as the police-officers closed in upon him, William Miller, his face twitching ever more furiously, was led away to Walton and the gallows, a man whose face had betrayed him as surely as if he had been caught with the bloodstained poker in his hand.

THE GENTLE CHINAMAN

More than three quarters of a century since the hangman's noose despatched him into the arms of his ancestors, the story of the tragedy that overtook Lock Ah Tam is still told in the Chinese quarter of Liverpool. It is a tale, too, that is whispered beneath the gay lanterns of far-away Tai-Ping, of Shanghai, Hong Kong and Singapore. What our bald speech debases to a matter of cold and senseless murder, is, doubtless, in the lilied tongue of the yellow men, elevated to the level of a parable. As they smoke their opium pipes, the oriental philosophers will find in the story of Lock Ah Tam a deep well of proverbial wisdom, and to the poor Chinaman it will seem to justify that wistful dubiety with which he is accustomed to regard wealth.

It was in the high summer of 1895 that 23-year-old Lock Ah Tam decided to abandon his berth as a ship's steward in favour of a clerk's desk in a Liverpool Shipping Office. The move was to prove a wise one, for, possessed of a curiously charming personality, of honest and industrious habits, and speaking fluent English, he advanced rapidly, until, in less than twenty-five years' time, he had become a rich, respected and influential member of the community into which he had moved.

By 1918, Lock Ah Tam had to all outward appearances achieved a happy and well-balanced life. He lived in a delightful home in Birkenhead, which was presided over by his charming English wife, Catherine, who bore him a son Lock Ling, and two daughters, Doris and Cecilia, and had a host of friends whom he loved to entertain at his house.

And if the gods smiled upon him, Tam was not slow to appreciate their favour, and he always tried to share his good fortune with those about him. He contributed most generously to local charities and could always be counted upon to extend a helping hand to anyone who was in trouble. Indeed, he would go out of his way to discover deserving cases and his tenderness towards children was most marked. "I have seen him give half-crowns to little children when we have met them in the street," said one of his friends, "and then he has said "Look at those poor people," and we did not know them, and he would give them half-crowns."

Each Christmas he held a huge party at his own house, to which, irrespective of nationality, were invited a horde of the children of Liverpool's poor. Tam's prestige and influence among Liverpool's Chinese community was immense, for the sympathetic nature of the man was such that he busied himself with all manner of social and political work for the benefit of his fellow-men, not only in the country of his adoption, but also in the land of his birth.

Tam it was who became the European representative of what was virtually a Chinese seamen's trade union. Who but Tam should represent three important shipping lines in this country in all their negotiations with their Chinese employees? Tam was the man who was elected

President of the greatest Republican Society in China, and the British agent of the cause of Sun Yat-Sen.

When the question arose of founding a club in Liverpool where Chinese sailors could meet their friends and enjoy a drink and a game of billiards in comfort and safety from land sharks, was it not Tam who, largely at his own expense, saw to it that that club was provided? In a way it seems likely that it was this club of his which led to Tam's downfall.

One February evening in 1918, shortly before the Chinese New Year, Tam paid a visit to the club to have a drink and a game of billiards. It was while the game was in progress that the door suddenly burst open and the place was invaded by a gang of drunken Russian sailors. Tam ordered them to leave. They started to swear and shout and one of them, a little more drunk maybe than the others, seized a cue and dealt Tam a hefty blow on the head. He fell to the floor, bleeding profusely, but by the time the police arrived on the scene he was sufficiently recovered to walk to his office in the house next door. And later in the night he was able to spend an hour at the police-station and accompany the officers to a nearby lodging-house in order to identify the man who had attacked him.

Nevertheless, it seems that the damage resulting from that chance-struck blow was considerably greater than at first appeared, for thereafter the whole of Tam's character underwent a most distressing change. From being, as we have seen, a kindly, acute and lovable man, he became irritable, absent-minded and morose. Always a moderate drinker, he took to the bottle with a vengeance. Previously, he had confined himself pretty well to whisky, of which he could carry a very considerable cargo. Up to the time of his injury no one had ever seen him drunk, and he always attributed its lack of unfortunate effect upon him to the fact that to every glass of whisky it was his custom to add two teaspoonfuls of salt. Now, however, he started to mix his drinks and tottered upon the brink of chronic alcoholism.

He began, too, to display sudden uncontrollable bursts of maniacal temper on the slightest – real or imagined – provocation. He would flare-up in an instant, stamp his feet, foam at the mouth, and his bloodshot eyes would bulge out from his purple, swollen face like those of a madman. The most trivial thing could send him off into one of those paroxysms.

On one occasion, for example, Tam was entertaining seven or eight friends to supper at his house. One of them, a Mr Jones, who had been his close associate for many years, made some completely innocuous remark. The effect on Tam was terrifying. He sprang to his feet, his face distorted with rage, foaming at the mouth, gabbling and waving his arms about like one demented. Seizing all the glasses on the table, he hurled them one after the other into the fireplace before collapsing, exhausted, into his chair.

Again, one evening Tam invited a taxi-driver into his house for a drink. Thinking to please his generous fare, the driver made some flattering reference to China, whereupon Tam instantly flew into another of his celebrated rages.

In 1922, Tam invested more than £10,000 in a shipping venture. It failed and he lost every penny that he had put into it. Moreover, his business in Liverpool had ceased to prosper, and in 1924 he was made bankrupt. The crowning tragedy of Tam's career came on 31 November 1925. It was his son Lock Ling's twentieth birthday. The boy had only recently returned to Liverpool after nine years absence in China. It was, therefore, an occasion of much rejoicing and Tam was giving a select little dinner-party. Happily, all went well. Tam remained sober and when the last guest had departed at a quarter to one in the morning no untoward incident had sullied the festive pleasantry of the proceedings. About twenty minutes after the household had retired to bed, Lock Ling was distressed to hear stampings, shufflings and shoutings coming from his parents' bedroom. Promptly concluding that his father was ill-treating his mother, he got out of bed and, accompanied by his two sisters, went to her aid. He accused Tam of hitting his mother, an accusation which Tam indignantly refuted. There was a noisy scene and Lock Ling threatened to take his mother next door to spend the rest of the night with Mr and Mrs Chin.

Lock Ling, Mrs Lock, Doris and Cecilia then all went into the sitting-room and Lock Ling said that he was going to get Mr Chin and begged his mother and sisters to go with him. But Mrs Lock refused. So he went off on his own.

Apart from the Locks, there lived in the house

a young woman named Margaret Sing who had for five or six years acted as companion to Mrs Lock. Throughout the trouble Margaret Sing had remained quietly in her room. Now, she heard Tam shouting her name. She went out on to the landing and he told her to bring him his boots. She did so and Tam ordered her to get dressed. Presently, fully dressed, she returned to her employer's bedroom. She found the door ajar and peeping inside she caught a glimpse of Tam's face reflected in a mirror. It was a twisted mask of fury and in his hand he held a revolver.

Silently, Margaret Sing tiptoed to the sitting-room, and told the three women what she had just seen. Swiftly they closed and barricaded the door. It was not a second too soon, for barely had they done so than Tam began battering upon it and screaming that he must be let in. After a few minutes he stopped, and the listening women heard him go back to his room. Very softly they opened the door and crept, trembling, down to the kitchen.

There they found Lock Ling and Mrs Chin. Hearing what had just happened upstairs, Lock Ling again begged his mother to take his sisters and Margaret Sing to the safety of the next door house. Still Mrs Lock refused to do so, and the desperate boy ran off in search of a policeman. The women stood round the kitchen table whispering for a while until Margaret Sing took some crockery into the scullery. The others followed her. The scullery was small and there was not room for them all. Margaret stood together with Mrs Chin and Doris behind the widely open door. Cecilia was by the gas-stove and Mrs Lock remained standing in the doorway.

All at once there was a deafening report and Tam's wife crumpled up on the floor. Then the wicked-looking barrel of a gun slid round the doorway and there was a second ear-splitting explosion. This time Cecilia slumped to the ground and Tam came swiftly and silently into the scullery. Spittle bubbled and trickled from his mouth; he had a revolver in one hand and a rifle in the other. He raised the revolver and shot Doris.

Leaving the three women on the scullery floor, Tam then walked to the telephone, lifted the receiver and said: "I have shot my wife and children. Please put me on to the Town Hall." The operator put him through to Birkenhead Central Police Station: "Send your folks, please. I have killed my wife and children," was all he said.

At his trial, which opened on 5 February 1926, before Mr Justice MacKinnon, Tam was defended by Sir Edward Marshall Hall, who claimed that his client had not been responsible for his crime, but had committed it while in a state of epileptic automatism. Said that great advocate, it was directly due to the injury which he had received in 1918 that the prisoner had committed his crime, for that injury had lead to the gradual deterioration of the man's intellectual and moral character, to a craving for alcohol and to epilepsy.

It took the jury precisely twelve minutes to find Tam guilty.

As the judge passed the death sentence the sound of continuous sobbing filled the court which was crowded with Tam's friends. Only Lock Ah Tam remained calm. He stood there erect in the dock, the faint line of a smile upon his heavy features. Maybe at the end some deep oriental instinct for philosophy had come to his aid. Maybe his mind was far away from that gloomy, panelled courtroom back amid the smiling lotus blossoms of his sun-lit native land.

CORPSE IN THE PARLOUR

Although murder is always horrible, there are some circumstances in which the horror which it provokes is subject to a subtle heightening. For instance, the corpse in the library of the ancient manor-house seems somehow far less out of place than the battered body in the front parlour of the suburban villa. Likewise, murder is always more terrible when it involves average men and women in an everyday setting: one gets the uncomfortable feeling that it could so easily have been oneself.

The matter of murder which is to come under consideration here is one of the great criminological puzzles of all time and has already been used as the basis for no less than three detective novels.

There is nothing to distinguish Anfield's Wolverton Street from any other of a hundred just such streets of neat, red-brick terrace houses which lie about the perimeter of our city. It is not a mean street, nor for that matter is it a particularly prosperous one. It might, perhaps, be best described as an ordinary street; and there, in essence, you have the horror, for it was to this ordinary street, upon a dark January evening in the year 1931, that tragedy came, leaving a bloodstained visiting-card at No 29 – the home of Mr and Mrs William Herbert Wallace.

The story of the murder of Julia Wallace may be said to have begun in the early evening of the day immediately preceding that upon which the actual crime was committed. At the point where Breck Road meets Priory Road there stands a telephone box, and shortly after seven o'clock, on the evening of 19 January 1931, a shadowy figure might have been seen occupying its red-framed interior. In the nearby telephone exchange a signal flashed a call from Anfield 1627. There is some discussion. A man's voice rasps along the wire: "Operator, I have pressed button 'A', but have not had my correspondent yet." The caller is connected with Bank 3581. It is a small incident, a daily occurrence, but it has to be recorded. The operator forgets it: but with the ringing of a telephone it is as if the call-bell for the first act of a tragedy is heard, summoning the actors to the stage. And the bell sounds its echo in the City Cafe in North John Street, where it is answered by a waitress. She does not yet know it, but she is about to speak to a murderer. His strong, metallic voice asks for Mr Wallace. She knows that Wallace is a member of the Liverpool Central Chess Club which holds its meetings in this cafe. A glance tells her that he is not in the room, however, so she calls a Mr Samuel Beattie, who is captain of the Chess Club, to the telephone.

Later that evening Beattie tells Wallace that a man named Qualtrough has rung up and wants to see him on business at 25 Menlove Gardens East, at 7.38pm on the morrow. Qualtrough had regretted that he would be unable to ring back later, as he was busy celebrating his daughter's twenty-first birthday. That, Beattie conjectured, might have something to do with the business matter which he wanted to discuss with Wallace, who was an agent of the Prudential Assurance Company. Wallace seemed puzzled, and several times expressed his ignorance as to the identity of Qualtrough and the location of Menlove Gardens East. Nevertheless, he made a careful entry in his notebook before resuming his interrupted game of chess.

That night, as they sat quietly in their little back kitchen, Wallace doubtless discussed the matter with his wife. The arrangement was vague, even mysterious, but a root-deep instinct whispered the promise of business – good business, perhaps. A daughter's twenty-first birthday party – that might mean a £100 endowment policy, and at twenty per cent commission on the first payment, well, to fishers in small pools, the prospect of such a catch would certainly have appeared irresistible.

There is nothing about the early part of Tuesday 20 January to indicate that it was a day in any way different from any other day in the normal routine of an insurance agent's life. Wallace did his usual round of collecting and returned home at about five past six in the evening. After tea, apparently determined to cast an optimistic net, he gathered together a selection of those forms which he thought appropriate to the type of business which he hoped to transact, went upstairs, washed, brushed his hair and put on a clean collar. Surveying himself in the mirror, he must have seen with some satisfaction the image of a man, neatly attired and carefully toileted; a man conscientiously patterned to create a favourable impression upon a prospective client.

According to his own account, it was about a 6.45 when Wallace left the house. He went out by the back door and made his way down the cobbled entry, which runs behind Wolverton Street, towards the tram stop. Walking down that alley, tall, thin and neat, Wallace becomes for us a figure of enigma. There is nothing in the appearance of this man, who is so soon to step from the respectable shadows of a quiet life into the brief, black limelight of the dock, to suggest that it is a different Wallace who treads a familiar way – a Wallace who has become a murderer. Yet, that is the problem for us to ponder. Is this a callous murderer setting forth through the night to establish a cunningly-contrived alibi, or an innocent man, un-happily victim of a deeply-woven plot ?

The precise hour of Wallace's departure from his house cannot be fixed, but there can be no doubt of the fact that round about 7.10 he was boarding a tram at the junction of Lodge Lane and Smithdown Road, a point which was a good twenty minutes journey from his home.

From this time onwards, Wallace is never lost sight of for very long. There are tram conductors who are able to testify to his fussy progress as far as Menlove Avenue. A clerk, whom he stopped in the street, the householder's wife at 25 Menlove Gardens West, a policeman, whom he met in Green Lane, and the manageress of Allday's newsagent's shop in Allerton Road, are all able to bear witness to Wallace's hunt for the elusive Qualtrough and the non-existent Menlove Gardens East. Weary at last of his unsuccessful searchings, Wallace decided to give up his quest and head homewards.

It was at about 8.45 that Mr and Mrs John Sharp

Johnston, who lived at 31 Wolverton Street, chancing to emerge into the alley behind their house, saw Wallace walking towards his own back-gate. To their amiable "Good evening," he replied with the strange-seeming question, "Have you heard anything at all unusual going on tonight?" He explained that he could not get into his house, having found both front and back doors barred against him. The Johnstons watched while he tried once again to open the back door. This time his efforts met with success. "It opens now," he said, in surprised tones. Wallace disappeared inside. His good neighbours waited outside, just to see that all was well. They heard him call his wife; they saw the flaring-up of gas-jets that betokened his progress through the dark house. Then, suddenly, a tense, white-faced Wallace came rushing out into the yard. "Come and see – she has been killed!" he gasped.

In the front parlour, close to the fireplace, lay the huddled corpse of Julia Wallace. It needed no pathologist to see that murder had been done. The dead woman's skull had been smashed like an egg, and the repeated blows of a frenzied attack had spilled its yoke of brains upon the floor. Everywhere was blood; the sedate sitting-room had become a slaughterhouse, and all about, the dull, red flush of bloodstains sullied familiar surfaces with ugly, alien patterns.

During the next few nightmare hours, that small, undistinguished house became the focus of unaccustomed attention. Police and men of medicine made extensive examinations. But for all their skill, they could deduce nothing beyond the fact that a woman had been brutally done to death in a house which exhibited no signs of having been broken into. And for all their searchings, they could discover no single significant trace of blood outside the confines of that blood-drenched parlour. Despite the fact that nothing but the happiest of relationships could be shown to have existed between Wallace and his wife, suspicion crystallised into accusation, and, on purely circumstantial evidence, Wallace was, on 2 February, arrested and taken to Walton Gaol.

From the windows of the prison hospital he saw the barren trees put on their scanty green coats, and watched the first few flowers poke modest heads between the asphalt cracks. For him, the young sun's pallid promise of summer meant very little, for in his heart he knew that he might never live to see its fulfilment.

His trial opened at the Liverpool Spring Assizes on 22 April 1931, before Mr Justice Wright. It was not long before the line which the Crown intended to take became obvious. The prosecution alleged that on the evening of 19 January, Wallace had telephoned to the City Cafe, and, in the character of Qualtrough, had left the message for himself. On the following evening he had murdered his wife, avoiding contamination by bloodstains by committing the crime either in the nude, or clad only in an old mackintosh (a mackintosh had been found tucked beneath Julia Wallace's body). By the time Mr Hemmerde, the Crown Counsel, sat down, the case against Wallace certainly looked very black.

But Mr Roland Oliver did not seem unduly

perturbed as he rose to open for the defence. He suggested that the crime was the work of an unknown enemy of the Wallaces, who had waited in the vicinity of Wolverton Street to make sure that Wallace was not going to be in the City Cafe when he rang up with his bogus message. It might be that Wallace would recognise his voice. Passing then to the night of the crime, Oliver was able to produce witnesses who stated that Mrs Wallace had been seen alive as late as 6.45. It was, he argued, inconceivable that the prisoner could have committed the crime and washed and dressed himself all in a matter of five, or at the most ten, minutes, as he would have to have done if he was to be at Lodge Lane at 7.10, a fact which was not disputed by the prosecution.

The medical witnesses stated that the murderer was bound to be extensively stained by his victim's blood. Careful examination had revealed neither damp towels nor any signs of a bath having been taken at Wolverton Street, nor did any of Wallace's clothes bear any traces of blood. Oliver was careful to stress the fact that no motive whatsoever had been adduced, and no weapon had been discovered. After an hour's absence, the jury returned a verdict of Guilty.

An appeal was lodged. Public interest waxed high. A special Service of Intercession was held in Liverpool Cathedral that God might guide the Court of Criminal Appeal to a right decision.

And then – the unbelievable happened! For the first time in the entire history of British Law the Court allowed a murder appeal on the grounds that the verdict had been against the weight of the evidence, and Wallace walked out of the Old Bailey into that freedom which he must have almost ceased to believe possible for him.

But the dark forces which had gathered, like so many low, menacing storm-clouds, about Wallace's life were not so easily dispelled. Legally free, he found himself lonely and outcast as any convicted prisoner. Backs were turned upon him, smiles froze and eyes glazed, where only amiable acquaintanceship had been before. He left Anfield and retired to a small cottage in Cheshire and, just two years later, he died in Clatterbridge Hospital of a renal failure at the age of 54. He protested his innocence to the last and it is difficult for us to reach any satisfactory conclusion, for the most extraordinary thing about the Wallace case is that every piece of evidence is capable of bearing two diametrically opposed, yet equally convincing, interpretations – the sinister and the innocent.

It was, perhaps, a very significant comment which was made to me recently by a man who knew Wallace personally, and who was present at the City Cafe on that fateful January evening in 1931. "The more I study the evidence," he said, "the more I am inclined to think that Wallace *must* have done it; and yet the more I think of Wallace as I knew him, the less likely I think that he *did* in fact do it."

It seems that whichever way one turns in the maze of intrigue which surrounds the death of Julia Wallace, the mind finds itself perpetually in check and reason struggles incessantly in the throes of a real-life problem that must always end in an irresolvable stalemate.

MOTIF IN FLY-PAPERS

When first I beheld it in the fast fading light of a late May evening, Battlecrease House looked very much like any other of the solid, respectable relics of the mid-Victorian period which flaunt their nostalgic opulence in the face of austere modernity. Nothing, save the lingering memories of the rearguard of an almost lost generation, now remains to hint at the one-time mystery which centred upon it. All was silence. The old house seemed to know peace at last. I sat within its grounds upon a quaint garden-seat. The mauve of the lilac, the gold of the laburnum, and the emerald-green lawn set in a border of sapphire-blue flowers, all lent an air of perfect tranquillity to the scene. In a nearby bush an evening bird began to voice a vesperal, sharp and clear above the low-pitched insect chorale, droning, insistent and drowse-compelling.

My thoughts began to wander. The mind, all unconsciously, bridged the gap of time back over the dusty irredeemable years of more than a half-century. On such a night as this, tragedy had come to Battlecrease House. Within its foursquare walls a man lay dying. Voices were hushed, anxious faces watched and waited. Suddenly the weak breathing stopped; a sheet was drawn over pale, collapsed features that twitched no longer. Silent figures, moving on toe-tips, left the bedside. A dry rustle quivered upon tense air as the blind was gently pulled down. The drama of a life had seen its climax and its close. It was as if that drawing down of a blind was the signal for the raising of the curtain upon another drama, the terrible drama of a woman's fight for life, for at that very moment the ugly thought of murder was ousting from the minds of the deathbed vigilants the chastening realisation that Death had passed amongst them.

In the next room a young woman lay prostrate, senseless, upon the crumpled cover of her bed. She knew nothing of the passing of her husband, and a merciful oblivion yet screened her from the harsh voices that had begun to cry "Murderess!" in a unison of hate. This is our first glimpse of the 26-year-old widow of the middle-aged Liverpool cotton merchant. A few weeks later she will stand in the dock accused of his murder, and the name of Florence Elizabeth Maybrick will be blazoned throughout the length and breadth of England, the echoes of her shame reverberating through the long, misty corridors of futurity.

Her story is simple enough. A young wife and a husband, 24 years her senior, who is the slave of drug-borne fantasy. He neglects her; she resents it and, being human, seeks solace and understanding in the arms of another. There is the triangle; there the motive. The husband dies in questionable circumstances: she it was, they say, who brought about his death. Nor was opportunity lacking, for it is by no means unknown for the ministering angel of the sickroom to turn assassin and hide beneath the cloak of tender devotion, the swift-despatching poison-cup. Add to this the discovery of her clandestine liaison, and vague suspicion rapidly crystalises into conviction and the dread verdict is pronounced.

What, then, is so unusual about this? Wherefore this nation-wide clamour? It is the old, old story of the delight of the empty-headed vulgar in any revelation of impropriety in high places. The merest crumb of scandal that falls from the regal table affords a veritable feast to the scavengers who thrive upon such carrion. With what interested satisfaction did these despicables learn that the surface calm at Battlecrease House masked but thinly a muddy depth of misery and intrigue. The charming and eminently respectable James Maybrick of the smug suburb of Aigburth stood revealed as a brutal, faithless drug-addict, and his gentle, refined wife as a murderess and, worse than that, the willing paramour of another man! How delicious a morsel to add to the dainty fare at the tables of the chattering bevies of tea-takers in drawing-rooms where the Maybricks had once been honoured guests.

It was in 1881 that James Maybrick's business had taken him to America, and it was upon a liner in the vast Atlantic waste that he came upon his destiny in the pretty face and petite form of the girl who was to become his wife. What helpless puppets were these two in the hands of the strange fate that brought them together. Born the wide world apart, she among Alabama's waving fields of cotton, and he within the forbidding shadow of Lancashire's dark, satanic mills, it was their pre-ordained lot to shape each act and point each wandering step to this inevitable end. Did they, one wonders, ever for a brief moment read beyond life's meaning the omen of death's advent in each other's eyes? Or did they hold but love and promises of an eternal season of wine and roses?

On 27 July 1881, they were married at St James's Church, Piccadilly. For a couple of years they lived in Norfolk, Virginia, returning to England in 1884 to take up residence at Battlecrease House, in Aigburth's Riversdale Road. Here they lived, happily enough for a time, in a manner befitting their substance and station. They moved in the best circles of Liverpool Society, rode, went to the races, dances and soirees. In 1886 a little girl was born (they had had a boy in 1882) and the Maybricks were regarded by all and sundry as an exceptionally happy and well-favoured couple.

But the dark, ragged clouds that precurse the storm were fast gathering upon their horizon. There were many long, lonely nights when the young wife sat alone in the sombre remoteness of her heavily-furnished drawing-room, always listening for the sound of a key in the lock which never came. Gay and vivacious, such solitude weighed sadly upon her spirits. All her efforts to immerse herself in the diversions of reading and needlework were of no avail, and she fell a helpless victim of the toils of *ennui.* It was about this time also that she discovered that the man in whose hands she had placed her life was consistently unfaithful to her, and was, moreover, a drug-addict. Such was the state of affairs when she met young Alfred Brierley.

He was superficially charming, and seemed kind and considerate – the very antithesis of her choleric husband, who was becoming increasingly unpleasant daily. Fickle flattery did its insidious work, the lonely heart fancied that it had found sympathetic companionship at last, and, for a time, rejoiced. But the way ahead was not the primrose path of joy; for her the road of thorns. Her felicity was short-lived, reaching its pathetically sordid crescendo in a daring three-day sojourn with Brierley at an obscure London hotel, whither she escaped in March 1889, on the pretext of paying a dutiful visit to an invalid aunt.

There is no evidence that Maybrick suspected her affair with Brierley, but nevertheless he was the cause of a very unpleasant scene. It came about in this way. On 28 March, Mrs Maybrick returned from her illicit interlude, and on the following day accompanied her husband to the Grand National Steeplechase at Aintree. There, they happened to meet Brierley, and Mr Maybrick appears to have resented the attentions which the latter paid to his wife. A public scene ensued, and upon their return to Battlecrease House, there was a violent altercation, Maybrick so far forgetting himself as to give his wife a black-eye. It seems that he also availed himself of the opportunity to tax her with her extravagance. As a result of this quarrel Mrs Maybrick expressed her intention of leaving the house that very night, but her husband told her that if she did so he would never again permit her to see her children. She decided, therefore, to take no action until the following day. The next morning, however, she went to see the family physician, Dr Hopper, to ask his advice concerning the institution of divorce proceedings. He was opposed to the idea of a separation and agreed to see Maybrick and talk the position over with him. The good doctor's intervention brought about a reconciliation, for James Maybrick undertook to discharge his wife's liabilities to the tune of £1,200, while she for her part, stated that she was prepared to forgive and forget. But there can be little doubt that from this day forward James Maybrick's death-warrant was sealed.

On 13 April, Maybrick departed for London. The purpose of his visit was twofold. He wished to see his brother Michael Maybrick (better known to posterity as Stephen Adams, composer of many popular songs) regarding Mrs Maybrick's financial redemption, and he also wished to consult his brother's physician, Dr Fuller, about the state of his health. It may be mentioned at this point that James Maybrick was pronouncedly hypochondriacal. He was constantly experiencing the most distressing aches and pains which he tended to interpret in even more distressing terms of disease. His pet phobia was creeping paralysis, and a certain numbness in his head and extremities, which he frequently experienced, unfailingly produced the firm conviction that the paralysis had got him at last! He was an inveterate patent medicine swallower, always prepared to advise or be advised on the latest nostrums. Dr Fuller was unable to discover any symptoms of serious organic disorder, attributed Maybrick's discomfort to dyspepsia, and prescribed accordingly. He returned to Liverpool on 22 April, much relieved mentally.

It was on either 23 or 24 April that Florence Maybrick went to the shop of Mr T S Wokes, the local chemist, and bought a dozen fly-papers for sixpence. This purchase was made quite openly and after passing some commonplace remark concerning the troublesomeness of flies in her kitchen, she requested Wokes to send his boy with them to Battlecrease House. These fly-papers were never used for the purpose for which they were supposedly intended. Indeed, we have the evidence of the servants that there were at that particular time no noticeable numbers of flies present in the kitchen.

On or about 24 April, two of the servants observed in Mrs Maybrick's room a basin which was covered with a towel. Curiosity overcoming them, they removed this towel and found beneath it another smaller basin, also covered by a towel, which proved to contain some fly-papers soaking in a quantity of water. This fact becomes very significant when we learn that each of these fly-papers contains somewhat over two grains of arsenic, which can be extracted quite easily by the simple expedient of soaking them, and that two grains constitutes a fatal dose of that substance.

A day or two later, Mr Maybrick is coming downstairs; a horrible faintness overcomes him; he reels, his head begins to swim, and he feels that dreaded numbness in his legs again. He grits his teeth and sets off for his office. Somehow or other he gets through that morning, and by lunch-time he is feeling so much better that he decides to attend the Wirral races. In view of the inclemency of the weather, this was rather rash, and when he arrived home that evening he was wet through. Nevertheless, he insisted on keeping a dinner engagement with some friends. The dinner was not a success as he felt very poorly. He was home before 9 o'clock and went to bed. As he was no better in the morning, Dr Humphreys was summoned and he advised the discontinuance of some medicine Maybrick was taking, which contained strychnine. The next day Mrs Maybrick made another of those curious purchases of fly-papers for non-existent flies. This time she went to the shop of Mr Christopher Hanson in the neighbouring district of Cressington. Here she bought a bottle of cosmetic lotion and a further two dozen arsenic-impregnated fly-papers.

Mr Maybrick is now on the mend, and by the evening of 30 April, is so far recovered that his wife is able to attend a private Domino ball at Wavertree with her brother-in-law, Edwin Maybrick. This ball is an important event in the history of the case, for it was claimed by Mrs Maybrick to supply the motive for her bizarre shopping. She said that from her earliest childhood she had suffered from a most unfortunate periodic irritation of the skin of her face which she believed to be due to some gastric disorder. When she was at school in Germany, a friend had given her the receipt for a face lotion which would swiftly remove many of the little blemishes which were so ruinous to her complexion. One of the ingredients in this lotion was arsenic, but her school-friend had told her that the very small quantity required could be extracted quite easily from soaked flypapers. At the time of the Wavertree Domino ball, her face was in a state of uncomfortable irritation, and it was in order to prepare the balming lotion that she had procured the fly-papers.

By Mayday, James Maybrick was sufficiently recovered to return to his work, but as he still felt rather too weak to wander round cafes he took with him for his lunch some Barry's 'Revalenta Arabica', a farinaceous food for invalids, which the cook had prepared for him in a jug given to her by Mrs Maybrick. This made him sick and he ascribed his indisposition to the cook's having put some inferior sherry in the mixture. Traces of arsenic were subsequently found in that jug. The next day he again lunched on the Revalenta and was again violently sick. By the evening of 3 May, he was in great pain and Dr Humphreys was summoned once more. During the next three or four days, Maybrick's condition was very unsettled. At first it seemed as though he was going to recover, but by the 7th he was so much worse that Mrs Maybrick called in a Dr Carter for a second opinion. She also telegraphed for a nurse.

It was on that afternoon that the children's nurse, Alice Yapp, saw her mistress apparently pouring medicine from one bottle to another. This struck her as being very peculiar and she began to regard Mrs Maybrick with something akin to suspicion. The next day she had a hunt around and

298

found a packet which was labelled 'Arsenic' in Mrs Maybrick's trunk. Its presence in that house is one of those mysteries which was never solved. Yapp communicated the discovery to a Mrs Briggs, an old friend of James Maybrick's, who was not slow to apprise his brother Edwin of the fact that in her opinion all was not well at Battlecrease House.

Thus were the seeds of suspicion sown and they were speeded in their germination by a letter which Mrs Maybrick gave to Yapp to post on the afternoon of 8 May. This letter was addressed to A Brierley, Esq. The nursemaid opened it and found that it contained the ominous words: 'He is sick unto death'. In view of the fact that the doctors were not unduly perturbed by the patient's condition at this time, it was surely a rather curious statement. The letter was handed to Edwin Maybrick and from that time onwards Mrs Maybrick was not permitted to attend her husband.

It was on the evening of 11 May that James Maybrick died. His relatives had all been summoned that morning. The doctors abandoned hope, yet he lingered on throughout that May day, and it was not until 8.30pm that he breathed his last. Mrs Maybrick had fainted before the end came and remained unconscious for many hours. The corpse had scarce grown cold before a search was made for further arsenic. Arsenic there was, and in abundance. They found traces in Mrs Maybrick's clothes, among the dead man's effects, and in medicines, where, according to the prescriptions, no arsenic should have been. On 14 May, Mrs Maybrick was arrested. Until then she had been too ill to be charged. She was taken first to the little old-fashioned police station which still stands in Lark Lane, and thence to Walton Gaol to await her trial, which opened on 31 July 1889, at St George's Hall, Liverpool. The trial lasted for seven days. Sir Charles Russell, QC was briefed for the defence.

The evidence of the servants and the chemists told strongly against Florence Maybrick, as did that of her brother-in-law, Michael Maybrick. She herself gave evidence from the dock and explained about the face lotion, swearing that it was for this purpose that she had endeavoured to extract the arsenic from the fly-papers. A number of witnesses testified as to the drug-swallowing propensities of the deceased and stated that no one could be reasonably surprised at anything which was found in his stomach, one witness referring to it as a "druggist's waste-pipe". The medical men disagreed too. The Home Office expert, Dr Stevenson, said that there was no doubt that Maybrick had died of arsenical poisoning, whilst another eminent toxicologist was equally emphatic that arsenic had nothing to do with his death. In view of all this conflicting testimony it seems extraordinary that the jury should have brought in a verdict of guilty, but it was undoubtedly the judge's summing-up which turned them against the prisoner. Before sentence was passed upon her, Mrs Maybrick, in a tensely dramatic moment, cried out, "I was guilty of intimacy with Mr Brierley, but I am not guilty of this crime." The judge donned the black cap, and the dread words of the death sentence echoed through the strained silence of the court. Then Florence Elizabeth Maybrick was led away to Walton Gaol to await the execution of that sentence upon her. Up to the time of the passing of sentence, opinion had been very much against Mrs Maybrick, but no sooner had pronouncement been made, than it veered in her favour in the most astounding way. The judge was jeered and cat-called as he left St George's Hall, newspapers throughout the country condemned the conduct of the trial, protest meetings were held and petitions for a reprieve poured in to the Home Secretary. As a result of this nation-wide clamour she was reprieved from the gallows, which she had heard being erected at Walton. Her sentence was commuted to one of life imprisonment, and she spent fifteen years in Aylesbury and Woking prisons.

On her release in 1904, she went to America and produced a book entitled *My Fifteen Lost Years* – surely the only book of its kind ever written.

On 24 October 1941, Mrs Maybrick died, aged 80, at South Kent, Connecticut, but not before she had revisited Liverpool and seen the Grand National in 1927. Now, the last of the actors in that memorable Victorian tragedy is dead, but there will be no hurried forgetting of her name. She rests, we hope, in peace, and has taken her secret with her. There will be no rest for us who remain, for the problem of whether she was a woman who did wrong, or a woman wronged, lingers still to tantalise the minds of those who find an interest in such mysteries.

Gradually my mind came back to the present. I began to feel a wind that blew a little chill.

Evening had slipped into the cloak of night as surely and silently as the heat and haze of high noon fade into the mellow glow of late afternoon. Nightfall, and I was alone in this isolated place, the domain of ghosts, and yet I felt no fear, only peace. Gone was the babble of curious tongues; gone the jostling throng of morbid sightseers. Before me stretched the long gravel drive down which the body of James Maybrick was carried in the great hearse, with its waving black ostrich-plumes, on that final journey to the last abode of crumbling mortality at Anfield. All this had happened so long ago that the veneer of horror seemed to have been worn off by the restless hand of time. The wind rustling the leaves of a copper-beech murmured secrets that no man can know. A few wisps of fog from the nearby river swirled among the trees and made ghost-like wraiths upon the yellowing facade of Battlecrease House. Somewhere in the distance a dog barked, a fog-horn moaned the pleading of a ship's soul. I drew my coat closer about me and stepped forth into the darkness, leaving the old house to the vague entities that seem still to cling to its brooding walls on such a night.

HOW DEATH CAME
TO FLORENCE MAYBRICK

On 7 August 1889, a woman stood in the dock of the Crown Court at St George's Hall and heard the dread sentence of the law passed upon her. The woman's name was Florence Elizabeth Maybrick and she had been accused of the murder of her husband at their home in Aigburth. Her story has been told and retold many times, but over the years it has gathered about itself that aura of fascination which frequently attaches to things which belong to the past. Moreover, it bears a burden of nostalgia which in these hectic days recalls pleasurably a leisured age of crinolines and carriages when Aigburth was virtually a country village which the brick tentacles of Liverpool had yet to engulf.

Was Mrs Maybrick guilty? That was the question which, one hundred and twenty years ago, divided all England. A jury decided that she was, but the great British public felt that there was some doubt in the matter. Petitions, signed by thousands of people, began to flood into the Home Office. Largely as a result of this agitation, the Home Secretary was persuaded to re-examine the evidence, and, on 22 August 1889, he commuted her sentence to one of penal servitude for life.

As prisoner P29, Mrs Maybrick served fifteen years in Woking and Aylesbury prisons. Her term of imprisonment, with full remission for good conduct, was due to finish on 25 July 1904. In the

303

January of that year she was released on the condition that she spent the next six months in a convent at Truro. At the end of those six months she left England and joined her mother, the Baroness von Roques, at Rouen. Three weeks later she travelled to Belgium and embarked from Antwerp on the steamship *Vaderland* for America. On 23 August 1904, just twenty-three years after she had set forth on that fatal voyage in the course of which she had met James Maybrick, she sailed into New York harbour. The girl from Mobile, Alabama, was home.

In the December of 1904, Mrs Maybrick published in America a book – *My Fifteen Lost Years,* today a collector's piece. For a while after her return to the States, she tried to lecture, chiefly about conditions in English prisons. But it did not go down too well. A new world had grown up during the long years that she had spent in prison; a world that was not specially interested in the misfortunes of Florence Maybrick. Eventually, tiring of publicity, she settled down in Florida. Sometime later she moved to Highland Park, Illinois, and then she just disappeared. Now, as a result of certain information which chance has put into my hands, I am able to tell the full story of how, more than half a century after she was condemned to die, death came to Florence Maybrick.

The year is 1923. The scene shifts to a tiny, three-room shack in the woodlands of the Berkshire Foothills, between the villages of Gaylordsville and South Kent, Connecticut. A stranger has just moved into this little rural community. A small, thin, bent woman, with a face as wrinkled as a walnut. She calls herself Mrs Florence Chandler. Shortly after her arrival, a neighbour, Mrs Austin of Gaylordsville, does her several kindnesses. Mrs Chandler is grateful and makes her a present of a dress. One day Mrs Austin is shaking that dress and from the shoulder-padding there drops a cleaner's card. Upon it are written the tell-tale words 'Mrs Florence Maybrick, Highland Park, Ill'. The secret is out. But, for once, that luck which seems so rarely to have favoured Mrs Maybrick, is attending her. Mrs Austin tells her sister of her discovery and together they consult a local woman probation officer. There is a family council, just the three ladies and the husbands of the two sisters. Gallantly they resolve to forego the temptation to release upon the church socials and the staid bridge parties the juiciest morsel of gossip of a lifetime.

So it was that five charitable people made a vow of silence and Mrs Maybrick was permitted to spend the last twenty years of her life unrecognised and unpersecuted.

As the years slipped by, the shy, scurrying little old lady became a well-known character of the local scene. They nicknamed her 'Lady Florence'. She spent most of her time on the campus of the South Kent School, a quaint figure in her one, indestructible, brown straw-hat, a gunny sack slung over her meagre shoulder. Into this sack were stuffed newspapers – old copies of the *New York Times* and an occasional *Bridgeport Sunday Post*

– which, salvaged from academic dustbins, made up her only reading. The sack also contained little titbits for cats, for Mrs Chandler had developed an immense passion for those creatures and her days were mainly devoted to looking after their welfare. Indeed, she was known to successive generations of South Kent boys as 'The Cat Woman'.

From time to time there were rumours, rumours of the sort that always circulate about lonely old ladies who live secluded lives, that she had been left a vast fortune. Perhaps she did receive some small legacy, for in 1927 she was able to revisit Liverpool and attend the Grand National. It seems fairly certain, however, that towards the end she was very poor, having nothing but an old-age pension. With advancing age she became rather eccentric. No one was ever allowed to enter her shack, which was always in a state of dirt and disarray. And all through the night she kept burning a single, twinkling light. It was as if she feared ghosts which the darkness might raise from out the grave of a past which she wished to bury. Latterly, she showed scant regard for personal hygiene and amused acquaintances by recalling how she tied a loose tooth to the one next to it with a piece of string so that she would not lose it!

It was the neighbour who supplied Mrs Chandler with the milk to feed her innumerable cats, who first discovered her death. Peering through a fly-spotted window into the dusky interior of the hut, this person saw the crumpled little body lying amidst the grimy chaos where several hungry cats nosed at the empty milk saucers. The date was 24 October 1941, and Mrs Maybrick was in her eighty-first year.

They buried her, in accordance with her last wish, on the South Kent Campus, and five of the students – boys of good American stock – acted as her pall-bearers, bringing a final touch of quondam respectability to her end. It is strange to think that that frail, wasted body had outlived her prosecutors and her defenders, and even harder to realise that the dowdy little walnut of a woman, who died surrounded by cats in an American backwood shack, was Florence Elizabeth Maybrick, as remote-seeming in time and circumstances as we ourselves from the pretty, Victorian young woman whose life was irreparably shattered with the drawing down of a blind one long-ago May evening in distant Liverpool.

THE BARBAROUS SEA-CAPTAIN

If ever Captain Bligh of the *Bounty* had a rival, it must surely have been Captain Henry Rogers, master of the *Martha and Jane,* whose ferocious and brutal treatment of an unfortunate seaman named Andrew Rose was to lead him to a dry dock somewhat different from those to which he had grown accustomed in the course of his maritime life – that of the Crown Court in St George's Hall, Liverpool, where, on an August day in 1857, he stood at the bar to answer a charge of Murder on the High Seas.

It was towards the end of April 1857, that Rogers and Rose joined the barque *Martha and Jane,* then lying off the Barbados, the one as captain and the other as a lowly member of the crew. Rogers, who took command of the vessel, was 37 years old. A native of Aberdeen, he had spent 23 years at sea and had earned a reputation as a reliable master. Rose, on the other hand, was "an amiable, quiet man who would harm no one, but a little weak in the head." He claimed that he had had more than twenty years experience of the sea and was signed on as an able seaman. As a matter of fact he seems to have been anything but able. Almost as soon as he came aboard, Rose was put to work by Charles Seymour, the second mate, and such a hash did he make of the job that the mate beat him most severely. Indeed, so savage was the beating that Rose's fellow crew-members advised him to run away. He did so, but was caught and brought back 10 May. Rose was immediately put in irons and on 11 May the *Martha and Jane* weighed anchor and set sail for Liverpool. Then began an orgy of senseless cruelty which it is terrible to contemplate.

On 12 May Rose was thrashed by Captain Rogers, William Miles (the first mate), and Seymour; and thereafter never a day passed but he was kicked and flogged with a rope-end or whip. In the end, the floggings seem to have lost all meaning or relation to events, a sort of blood lust took hold of the Captain and his unsavoury mates and at any hour of the day or night when they felt so inclined they would pitch into the luckless Rose.

One Sunday morning when the voice of Rose, who had a fondness for singing, was heard raising itself piously to the heavens in the Primitive Methodist hymn 'Oh Let Us be Joyful' the effect on Rogers was extraordinary. He descended, cursing, to where Rose lay in irons trying to be joyful, and shouted, "I'll make you sorrowful." He then ordered the mate to fetch a large iron bolt. This he forced into Rose's mouth, the mate tying it in with yarn. The bolt was left in the choking man's mouth for an hour and a half.

As the voyage wore on, the Captain introduced further refinements into his blackguardly treatment of Rose. He had on board a dog which he used to set on him with the command, "Bite that man". The dog entered into the spirit of the thing and eventually whenever Rogers came forward with his whip the dog would automatically fly at Rose and savage him, tearing great pieces of flesh from his legs, thighs and arms. His body became black and blue all over and covered with dozens of festering wounds, running sores and ulcers.

By way of infusing a little variety into the proceedings, he would sometimes be sent aloft naked to furl the sail, the mate following him up the mast with a whip, lashing him until the blood spurted from his body. For several days he was kept entirely without clothing, exposed to the cold sea-winds and finding what cover he could at night. On yet another occasion, in order to "cure him of his filthy habits," Captain Rogers forced Rose to eat his own excrement and plugged his nostrils with it.

Then, the Captain dreamed up another little torture. He knocked the end out of a water-cask, forced the hapless Rose into it, headed it up again and spent a few merry hours rolling it up and down the deck. Finally, he had it lashed to the side of the ship and Rose, cramped, stifling and with only the bung-hole to breathe through, was kept there for twelve hours. Some of the crew, taking pity on him, gave Rose a little pea-soup and some water, but one of the mates, discovering this concession to ordinary humanity, became so furious that they dared not interfere again.

It was when the *Martha and Jane* was seven days out from Liverpool that the final act of cruelty was perpetrated. After all he had endured, it is hardly to be wondered at that when the Captain said roughly, "Rose, I wish you would either drown or hang yourself," the man answered in despair, "I wish you would do it for me". Hearing this, Rogers and the two mates seized Rose and led him to the mainmast. They got a rope, made a timber-hitch in it, slipped the noose round his neck and hoisted him up.

For fully two minutes Rose remained suspended by his neck a couple of feet above the deck. His face turned black, his eyes and tongue protruded, and he began to froth at the mouth, and when at length he was let down he fell flat upon the deck and lay there like one dead. The Captain was heard to say to one of the crew that if he had been kept hanging half a minute longer he would have been finished.

After that, the crew managed to get Rose down to the fo'c'sle, but he had become unhinged by all he had undergone and was so crazed that they were obliged to tie his hands. He remained in the crew's quarters a day or two, and on the morning of 5 June, he was taken up on deck again in order that he might wash himself. By this time, however, he was so weak that he could scarcely crawl and he lay upon the deck with his head towards the forward hatch and the water washing over his legs. And there, some hours later, he died. Such was the state of his body, a festering mass of evil-smelling and maggot-infested wounds, that the crew were loath to touch it. They dragged him aft with a rope and by the Captain's order the corpse was thrown overboard. When, on 9 June, the *Martha and Jane* arrived at Liverpool, information was laid by the crew, and the Captain and the first and second mates were arrested.

Captain Rogers, on being taken into custody, said that he had almost expected it for he had heard "that villain Groves" (a seaman on board and one of the principal witnesses for the prosecution) wanted to get up something of the kind against him in order that he might get ten shillings a day for attending the police-court. He further alleged that he had seen Groves ill-use Rose and said that when he first came aboard Rose was covered with sores as a result of sleeping out in the fields in Barbados. He also stated that he himself had never done Rose the slightest harm apart from whipping him for being dirty.

The trial of Henry Rogers, William Miles and Charles Edward Seymour took place at St George's Hall on 19 August 1857, and when the jury announced a verdict of guilty the court was startled by a succession of loud cheers from the crowd which was assembled in the large hall outside. All three were sentenced to death, but a recommendation to mercy was acted upon in the cases of the two mates, who were subsequently reprieved.

During the time he spent in Kirkdale Gaol, an amazing change came over the barbarous sea-captain – a transformation which, it must be remarked, takes place extraordinarily frequently in the cases of cornered bullies and captured murderers. He turned wholeheartedly to the consolations of religion. He began to lament the neglect of his religious duties in early life and there was a touching little scene when, before taking his final leave of his two mates, he insisted upon praying with them and bestowed upon them the benefits of a great deal of pious and kindly advice. Indeed, his demeanour was such that, when it was all over, the chaplain volunteered: "He has been in the constant habit of praying, even when I have not been with him, very beautifully and very fervently and in a most delightful manner, which gave me much pleasure."

In the circumstances, one feels that the good padre was just a trifle carried away when he added: "He had a very feeling heart." And although Mr Wright (the prison philanthropist) claimed: "I never met one more so," one has the distinct impression that Andrew Rose might have ventured to disagree with their pronouncements!

On the morning of his execution – 12 September 1857 – Captain Rogers, after bidding farewell to his wife and five children, who had come up from their home in Swansea in order to be near him, remained in the prison chapel engaged in religious exercises until a few minutes before twelve noon. Outside the gaol milled a great crowd, twenty or thirty thousand strong, of thieves, prostitutes, vagabonds, the residents of vile courts and cellars, such as were invariably attracted to the scenes of public executions. The women were for the main part disreputable and abandoned characters who "seemed by their conversation and manner highly delighted at having an opportunity of seeing a man hanged." But apart from the usual assemblage of human riff-raff, there could be seen, not only many in the unmistakable dress of the common seaman, but also a number of those holding higher positions – such as ships' captains and mates. According to Mr

Wright, the aforesaid philanthropist, Captain Rogers was "sadly frightened of facing the crowd," and before walking out to the scaffold expressed his deep obligation to the chaplain and the governor for their kind and charitable feelings, and also to all the prison officers, adding, somewhat incongruously all things considered, that if he lived for a thousand years he should not forget their kindness.

The mood of the crowd may be gauged from the remark of a sailor who, looking up at the gallows, said with a leer, "My word, he'll be a different man on *that* quarter-deck than he was on the quarter-deck on the *Martha and Jane.* He will look more like a cook than a captain." This last referred to the white cap which is pulled over the eyes of the hangman's victim.

When, shortly after twelve o'clock, Captain Rogers appeared on the platform, he carried himself with great courage and dignity and, until the white cap covered his face, he stood gazing over the sea of heads below him, across the city to where the ships were riding the Mersey. In a matter of minutes, Mr Hangman Calcraft had despatched him, and Able Seaman Rose was avenged.

Within four days of his death, a model of Captain Rogers was on display in the Chamber of Horrors of Mr Alsopp's Crystal Palace Waxworks in Lime Street. The waxen effigy, 5 feet 7 inches in height, was that of a stoutish, handsome, florid man, with sandy hair and light blue eyes set in a long face, to which a sharp nose and the absence of one of the upper teeth lent a slightly sinister aspect. Clad in the actual clothes which he had been

wearing when he was executed – which Alsopp
had purchased from Calcraft – the likeness was
said to be first-rate and for many, many years it
remained one of the greatest bogeys in the
waxworks. But time, which alters all things,
brought about the closure of both Mr Alsopp's and
nearby Reynolds's waxworks, where the Captain
had also a place of horripilatory honour, and the
memory of his dark doings and the price he paid
for them passed away.

To this day, however, you will still hear, in
maritime circles, bated talk of the barbarous sea-
captain whose terrible history is here set forth, and
the record of whose deeds is perhaps the greatest
blot on Liverpool's brave history of those who go
down to the sea in ships.

The Borgia Sisters
of the Liverpool Slums

The hearse, together with the line of empty mourning coaches, stood, that grey October afternoon one hundred and twenty-six years ago, forlornly in the roadway outside the house in Ascot Street. Inside, behind the drawn blinds, a group of middle-aged women in rusty black dresses was clustered about a coffin in which lay the body of the husband of one of them, and the clinking of glasses, mingled with the plangency of drunken laughter, sounded unpleasantly irreverent in that tiny room of death. There was not, you might think, much of grief there. The grisly party was reaching its climax when suddenly, without a word of warning, three men entered the house. As if by magic, the noise stopped. With a little cry of fear, one of the women bolted for the back door and fled up the alley.

"I am the coroner's officer," said a quiet voice," and these two gentlemen are doctors. I have an order to stop the funeral. Which of you is Mrs Higgins?" Margaret Higgins stepped tremulously forward. "The dead man Thomas Higgins was your husband?"

"Yes."

"Well, I'm afraid the burial won't be able to take place today, Mrs Higgins; there's going to have to be a post-mortem."

There's going to have to be a post-mortem! Those eight words sealed the fate of 44-year-old

Margaret Higgins, a charwoman, and her 54-year-old sister, Catherine Flannagan, described as a lodging-house keeper, as surely as those other eight words which were to be pronounced by Mr Justice Brett just four months later: "Hanged by the neck until you are dead."

The game was up and they both knew it. It was only a matter of time now before the doctors would discover those tell-tale red patches on the stomach, and the chemists recover the death-dealing powder of arsenic from the viscera of the late Mr Thomas Higgins.

The story of the crimes of Margaret Higgins and Catherine Flannagan, those two ruthless poisoners of the Liverpool slums, is a sordid one. There is nothing of grandeur about it. All that they did was mean and petty. It was murder most mercenary, and no less than four innocent people lost their lives to sate an overwhelming greed.

The commencement of this cold-blooded partnership in crime dates back to the year 1880. At that time Mrs Flannagan and her sister were occupying a house in Skirving Street. Both were widows, women of drunken and morally dubious character, and they shared the house with five other people – John Flannagan, the Widow Flannagan's 22-year-old son; Thomas Higgins, a lodger, who was later to commit the grave indiscretion of marrying Margaret Higgins; Mary Higgins, the aforesaid Thomas Higgins's 8-year-old daughter; another lodger named Patrick Jennings, who was a dock labourer, and Jennings's 16-year-old daughter, Margaret.

The first of the many deaths which were to decimate this household of seven occurred in the December of 1880, when John Flannagan died and his grieving mother lost no time in collecting the eleven pounds eight shillings, for which he was insured with no less than five societies.

Towards the end of the following year, Margaret took Thomas Higgins, the lodger, who was a bricklayer's labourer, for her second husband (her first had been a Mr Thompson), and, in the November of 1882, little Mary Higgins died, and her stepmother made haste to draw the twenty-two pounds ten shillings club money.

Two months later, Margaret Jennings was dead. She, too, had been heavily insured, and, a couple of days after the unfortunate girl's death, Mrs Flannagan claimed the insurance money.

Thus far, three people had died within the space of two years and two months. No awkward questions had been asked and a reasonable profit had been forthcoming, but you couldn't go on having people die in your house without the neighbours starting to talk. For a time you might succeed in countering wagging tongues by actually prophesying the death of your victim from the time you had marked him down. Mrs Flannagan had done that in John's case. "My son is very ill," she had said to a neighbour. "He's in consumption and will go off like all the other cases. He will never live to comb a grey hair." And when he obligingly fulfilled her gloomy forebodings no one was a whit surprised.

Again, it was not policy to strike when your intended was in the best of health. Far better to be patient and wait until some trifling ailment provided the opportunity to administer, under the guise of devoted nursing, the fatal dose. That way you also had less difficulty in getting the doctor, who had been attending the invalid anyway, to issue a death certificate. Still, three deaths in one house were enough however you looked at it, and so the ghoulish sisters and the two remaining members of their menage removed to 105 Latimer Street. They remained there until the following September and, strange to relate, there were no further deaths.

In September, however, when the household removed once more, this time to 27 Ascot Street, a fresh victim was selected in the person of Thomas Higgins, and the Borgia-like sisters made careful plans to ensure that their fourth killing should prove worthwhile. Mr Higgins had policies effected on him to the tune of nearly £100. An attempt to secure a further policy for £50 was made by Mrs Flannagan, but the company in question insisted that any person insured for such a sum should undergo a medical examination. An agent, accompanied by a doctor, called on Thomas Higgins and their reception by that worthy, who happened to be drunk and had in any case heard nothing of the matter, was not exactly friendly. Actually, it was this final piece of greed which was to prove the women's undoing. For when, on 2 October 1883, Thomas Higgins died, of what his doctor certified as dysentery due to excessive drinking, it was his brother Patrick, who, having in all probability heard from Thomas of this unsuccessful attempt to insure his life, began, on the day after his death, to make certain inquiries.

He visited a number of insurance societies and found that the life of his deceased brother had been insured with several of them and that the money had been already drawn. He went also to see the doctor who had attended Thomas Higgins, told him of his suspicions, and together they approached the coroner, with the result that the funeral was stopped, a post-mortem ordered, the arsenic in Thomas Higgins's corpse discovered and Mrs Higgins arrested.

Mrs Flannagan, the woman who had fled from the house in Ascot Street, was arrested a few days later. She had been moving from one lodging-house to another but was finally cornered through the information of a woman who took pity on her , but whilst entertaining her to tea suddenly recognised her as the person for whom the police were searching.

On 16 October, both sisters were formally charged with murder. With the two women safely under lock and key, the police set to work to build up the case against them. The house in Ascot Street was searched and a flask-shaped bottle containing a turbid whitish fluid, a mug, and a spoon were found. There was also a 'market pocket' which Mrs Higgins had been wearing at the time of her arrest. The liquid and the pocket both contained traces of arsenic. The bodies of Margaret Jennings, Mary Higgins, and John Flannagan were all exhumed and in each case the remains of fatal doses of arsenic were recovered.

It subsequently became apparent that Mrs Flannagan had really been the leading spirit in the macabre partnership, but she did her best to foist the blame on to her younger sister, and actually offered to turn Queen's evidence in order to save her own neck. The offer was refused.

The trial, which opened at St George's Hall on 14 February 1884, lasted three days, and after an absence of forty minutes the jury returned with a verdict of guilty against both prisoners. Catherine Flannagan listened to the words of the death sentence unmoved. In the dock beside her, her sister was practically prostrated.

When three clear Sundays had elapsed, they were hanged. It was on the morning of 3 March 1884, and it was in a snowstorm, that the two Irish sisters, to whom must go the credit for having invented the method (adopted without acknowledgement by Mrs Maybrick just five years later) of obtaining arsenic by soaking fly-papers in water, paid, as it were, the patenting fees upon their murderous invention in the execution shed of old Kirkdale Gaol.

CYLINDER OF DEATH

Appropriately enough, it was on Friday the thirteenth that they made the gruesome discovery: Friday, 13 July 1945, to be precise. It was a little group of children playing on a blitzed-site at the corner of Fulford Street and Great Homer Street, that first stumbled upon the cylinder. It lay among the spilled red bricks of the waste land, strangely black-looking in the bright sunlight. A game of hide-and-seek was in progress and the fun was at its height. Nine-year-old Tommy Lawless crouched, laughing, behind the cylinder. "Ready!" he shouted. And then, he saw the boot. It was projecting from between the compressed, leaden lips of the open end of the cylinder. He called to his playmates. Excitedly, they gathered round while Tommy eased the boot from the narrow gap. All at once there was a gasp of horror, for, as the boot came out, they saw within the dark interior of the cylinder the stark, white bone of a human leg. Even upon that brilliant July morning, so tight a grip of fear fastened about those young hearts, that, in a single instant, they overcame a lifetime's nurturing in fear of 'bobbies' and ran helter-skelter in search of one.

It was just 11.45am, when a terrified boy ran up to Police Constable Robert Baillie, who was on duty at the junction of Great Homer Street and Kirkdale Road, and breathlessly told him of his discovery. The officer accompanied the lad to the waste ground, examined the cylinder and had it removed to the mortuary. That was the beginning.

The mystery opened its dark bud in the City Morgue. When, at 1.10pm, the cylinder was officially deposited in the mortuary, it must have seemed just another routine job. Certainly, there was nothing to indicate just how strange a corpse lay hidden within it. Its arrival was duly recorded and it was prosaically described as a riveted, sheet-iron cylinder, approximately 6 feet 9 inches long and nearly 19 inches in diameter, sealed at one end with an iron lid, riveted in position, and the other end closed by pressing together. At about 3 o'clock that afternoon an engineer was sent for and the cylinder was cut open with an acetylene blowlamp. What was then revealed must have astonished even the accustomed eyes of Dr Charles Vincent Harrison, at that time senior lecturer in pathology at Liverpool University, who had come to perform a post-mortem examination on behalf of the coroner. There, stretched upon a rough bed of sacking, his head resting on a kind of pillow formed of a brick covered with a sack, was the corpse of a man clad in tattered Victorian clothing. He wore a braid-edged morning-coat with cloth-covered buttons, narrow, striped trousers, and elastic-sided boots. They laid the cadaver upon a dissecting-slab and there, amid the clean, white tiles, Dr Harrison began his autopsy. What he found left him in no doubt that the body had been dead for a long time. The remains were those of an adult male, the state of whose bones indicated that he had been more than twenty-five years of age when he died. On the other hand, since the teeth were fairly well preserved and a quantity of hair adhering to the skull was brown and not grey, it was unlikely that he was of more than middle age. Harrison calculated his height as having been about 6 feet, and added that there was no way of ascertaining the cause of death.

Naturally, this extraordinary discovery excited considerable curiosity when it was reported in the press. On the face of it, it seemed impossible to learn anything more about the man in the iron cylinder. Who was he? How came he to be in that great metal canister? These were questions which appeared likely to remain unanswered. But the police are accustomed to having to find answers to apparently hopeless questions and their determination, together with what the coroner was subsequently to call "the astonishing perseverance of the Liverpool CID," led to the unearthing of certain facts which went a long way towards solving a unique mystery.

The first thing the police did was to call in that great forensic expert, Dr J B Firth, director of Preston's Home Office Forensic Science Laboratory. Dr Firth came to Liverpool and made an exhaustive examination. In the main he agreed with Dr Harrison's conclusions, though he put the man's height at about 5 feet 7 inches. He took possession of certain clues including a number of keys, a penknife, a gold signet-ring, set with a bloodstone and bearing the hall-mark for London, 1859, and two monthly diaries for July 1884, and June 1885, respectively. Most important of all, however, Firth recovered from the tail pocket of the right half of the morning-coat, a small wad of papers. This wad was a solid mass of adipocere (a peculiar waxen substance which forms during the decomposition of bodies, especially when they have been in contact with moisture) and it was only after a great deal of work, which involved treating the bundle with organic solvents and carefully separating its constituents with a spatula, that Firth was able to isolate and render legible thirteen documents. They proved to be the vital clue, for many of them related to T C Williams & Co, of Leeds Street, Liverpool. They also included a postcard addressed to Mr T C Williams himself.

Meanwhile, on 19 July 1945, the inquest was opened by the Liverpool Coroner, then Dr G C Mort, and was adjourned for one month. On 16 August, it was further adjourned to 31 August, to enable the police to complete certain inquiries.

Once he had the name T C Williams to work with, Detective-Inspector (later Chief Inspector) John William Morris, who, under Superintendent (later Assistant Chief Constable) A W Fothergill, was in charge of investigations, really got busy. He found that in the year 1883 there was a firm of Oil Merchants, Paint & Varnish Manufacturers trading under the name of T C Williams & Co, and with the business address of 18-20 Leeds Street. The principal of this firm was a Mr Thomas Cregeen Williams, who lived at what was then 29 Clifton Road, Anfield. Williams had originally been a commercial traveller and had later set up in business on his own account. He was born somewhere about 1830, and married Elizabeth Lea,

325

who died at 29 Clifton Road, aged 42, and was buried, as Elizabeth Williams, at Anfield Cemetery at 10am, on 25 May, 1878. There was one child of the marriage, Thomas Lea Cregeen Williams, born about November, 1858. Inspector Morris also discovered that in 1884 a T C Williams, with a paint works in Leeds Street, was undergoing an examination, handled by a well-known firm of Liverpool accountants, in connection with his business. This Mr Williams was extremely worried over his affairs. Significantly, maybe, Inspector Morris could trace no record of the death of T C Williams, nor, after 1884, could he find any mention of the firm in any Liverpool trades directory. Furthermore, a careful search failed to reveal any official bankruptcy.

There, matters had perforce to remain, and, on 31 August 1945, the coroner closed the inquest by recording an open verdict on the death of an unknown man.

That the 'Unknown Man' was Thomas Cregeen Williams seems more than probable : that his death took place *circa 4* July 1885, is generally accepted, but the cause of that death remains a complete mystery. The bones and clothes were analysed by Dr Firth for poisons but none were found. Nevertheless, the experts felt that there was a strong likelihood of the man's having committed suicide. In charity, however, we must not entirely dismiss the possibility that Williams – if it *was* Williams – finding himself in financial difficulties, was keeping away from home in order to evade his creditors. He may have crawled into the cylinder to sleep, and in so doing shut out the air and asphyxiated himself. It could well be that his disappearance caused no sensation at the time, as in those days it was not unusual for debtors to flee their creditors by boarding a ship and working their passage abroad. The whole story is a bizarre one teeming with fascinating possibilities.

In 1945 I was in Italy, and the circumstances first came to my attention through a batch of news-cuttings which were sent out to me. I was profoundly interested then and I have remained so ever since. Back in England in 1949, I listened to an intriguing radio play, 'The Black Cap Has to Wait,' by, H R Jeans, based upon the Liverpool cylinder case. But ten years had to elapse before I was able to fulfil a long-standing ambition to make a few-inquiries of my own.

In a quiet street off Stanley Road, I found Mr William Pemberton, who used to be the caretaker at the Methodist Church in Boundary Street East. Mr Pemberton was 79 at the time and was the man who first saw the cylinder in the summer of 1943. "The American soldiers were clearing the site at the back of our church," he said. "There was a large bomb-crater and the cylinder was in the crater with the open end downwards. I saw the spade of a mechanical navvy crush the cylinder in its efforts to dislodge it. About a couple of months later, another navvy managed to get the cylinder out and laid it on the level ground. The boys used to roll it about all over the place and I have seen gypsies sitting on it in the sunshine making their artificial flowers."

By a stroke of good fortune I also succeeded in finding Tommy Lawless. He was then nineteen, a tall, dark-haired young man, who went into the army the week after I met him. He remembered finding the cylinder because when he saw the boot sticking out of it he thought he was in luck. "I'd never had a pair of boots in my life," he told me, "and when I saw a smashing pair like that I thought my days of running round barefoot were at an end." Tommy took me along to Fulford Street and showed me where the cylinder used to lie. The blitzed-site had disappeared and a bright crop of pre-fabs stood where it had once been. Mr and Mrs Robert Foy's home covered the exact spot where Tommy made his alarming discovery, and when I told them about it Mrs Foy said with a laugh, "Well, it's no wonder that we've had no luck, is it?" Still, she was very proud of the spick and span little house and I don't think she would have liked to have to leave it.

The next day I went to see Dr Firth at his Preston laboratory and had a long talk with him about the case. He had preserved portions of the original documents which his skill and patience had seen extracted from that fatty mass and which did so much to dispel the mystery. He also had a series of lantern-slides illustrating various aspects of his investigations and was kind enough to give me a little lecture all to myself on how he had read the hidden clues in the cylinder.

I also visited the late Chief-Inspector J W Morris and heard from his own lips many interesting sidelights on what he described to me as "one of the most interesting cases that I have ever had to deal with." At the time though, he had his leg pulled quite a bit about it.

"You worried about the question of identity?" asked one of his friends. The inspector admitted that he was rather. "It's obvious," came the reply, "Nothing to worry about. The fellow is undoubtedly a boiler-maker who got too wrapped up in his work!"

And last of all I went to Anfield Cemetery, where an obliging young lady showed me what was perhaps the most fascinating of all the things that I saw in my search. She produced a great, dusty, blue volume, its leather binding crumbling with age. It was an old receipt book which people had signed more than a hundred years before, when they received the deeds of a grave. And there, over the date 21 December 1878, in brown and faded ink, I beheld the name Thomas Cregeen Williams. Unreasonably perhaps, I was certainly certain that it was the autograph of the man in the cylinder.

DEATH IN THE
TEMPEST MANICURE LOUNGE

Among sundry surviving quaint nooks and corners of old Liverpool, there linger still in the Tithebarn Street area two narrow, dagger-thrust-straight passageways, really more like alleys, known by the ancient name of 'hey' – Hackins Hey and Tempest Hey, respectively. It is with the latter, named in commemorative tribute to the early nineteenth century family of Plumbe Tempest, owners of considerable properties in these parts, that we are presently concerned. For it was here, in the year 1946, that a somewhat curious establishment known as Bobby's Gents' Manicure Lounge, run by a shady lady by the name of Mrs Ella Staunton, became the scene of a singularly grisly, not to say lethal, incident.

Born in 1905, Ella Valentine French had in her youth been eye-catchingly lovely, slim with a delicate complexion and generously tumbling cascades of Titian hair. A beauty queen at 15, a ballroom dancing champion at 22, Ella had gone on to travel the world as a dancer and manicurist, with spells as a salesgirl in an exclusive New York gown shop, and lazing away halcyon holiday hours on the sun-drenched Carribean beaches of Cuba.

In 1934, at the age of 29, she had married Thomas Staunton, of Crosby, importing to the altar with her a child of a previous, unsanctified, liaison. The marriage with Staunton was short-lived – four years – and unblessed with progeny. Not too long after the separation, Ella elected to throw in her lot with that of a Dutch naval captain. Whether or not that union would have prospered there is no knowing, for in the early days of the Second World War the gallant captain went down with his ship.

It was, indeed, during those first months of the war that Ella decided to go into business. She and a friend and partner, Gladys Henderson, set up shop in Rumford Street – a premises which was rapidly identified by the sharp-eyed Liverpool constabulary as what was vernacularly spoken of as a 'knocking shop', to wit, a brothel. They set about collecting the necessary evidence in earnest. The condemnatory dossier waxed fatter and fatter. Then ... Mrs Henderson was killed in one of the terrible air raids of the 1940 May Blitz, and the authorities decided to proceed no further with the ripening investigation. Ella Staunton was off the hook.

However, having had a taste of easy money, by May 1946, Ella was once again reaping the fringe benefits of sporadic prostitution. She had opened another business premises, within a stone's throw of Rumford Street, Bobby's Gents' Manicure Lounge, situated in a basement in Tempest Hey. But fresh tidings of bawdy behaviour in Mrs Staunton's premises had come to the ears of the police, and on the afternoon of 20 May 1946, a surveillance of her suspect basement was initiated.

Arrangements had been made with the owner of the small engineering workshop which occupied the ground floor immediately above the suspect manicure lounge, and this was to be the vantage point from which, peering through a ventilation grille exposed below a lifted portion of floorboard, a pair of peeping 'Jacks' could keep a watchful eye on the antics in Bobby's subterranean lair.

It was at 4.15pm on that Monday afternoon that Detective Constables Anderson and Ballam took up their position and commenced observations. Voices from below they could hear clearly, but their view through the spy-hole was prescribed, restricted. They could see only part of the salon, albeit that part where Ella greeted her clients, sat them down on arrival, and offered them a hospitable drink. What they could not see were the interiors of the curtained alcoves, into one of which, in due course, the client was ushered. If, however, the proprietress followed the client into the alcove bearing with her a basin of water, the assumption must be, they decided, that this was a visit for legitimate cosmetic purposes.

As Anderson and Ballam steadfastly looked and listened, they could no longer see Mrs Staunton and the man whom she had just admitted, but they could hear a peculiar, disturbing sort of noise which they recognised as that of a distinctly unpleasant struggle going on. They began to feel uneasy. "It sounds like he's giving her a good hiding," said Ballam.

They agreed that they had better check out exactly what was going on down there. They dashed over to the connecting staircase, practically tumbling down it into the basement and hammered on the salon door. There was no response. No one came to open it. What they did then was to hasten up the street to Exchange Station, from where they telephoned the establishment. Again, no response. The line was engaged. So they made their way back to Tempest Hey, where they arrived just in time to see a man leaving Bobby's Lounge, closing the door behind him. They approached the man and, identifying themselves as police officers, asked him to provide some identification. He thereupon produced a medical card, bearing the name Thomas Hendren and the address 9 Roe Street, Birkenhead. As Anderson was knocking again at the salon door, Hendren told him that he was wasting his time.

"There's a man in there. She won't answer for a quarter of an hour or twenty minutes," he said, adding with a smirk, "You know what Ella is. She's a prostitute."

This was not news to the detectives, although later, when it all came out, it was a considerable shock to her relatives, and greeted with shock, horror and disbelief by the neighbours in respectable Ullet Road, where she lived. Having supplied the detectives with his personal details, and saying that he was in rather a hurry to get back to Birkenhead, Hendren was permitted to go on his way.

Determined now to find out just what mischief was afoot in Bobby's salon, Anderson and Ballam returned once more to Exchange Station to put through another phone call. Still engaged. Back they trudged to Tempest Hey and began knocking really thunderously on the door of the manicure lounge. It was only then, at about 4.50pm, that they discovered to their embarrassment that the door was not locked. It had been open all the time! They pushed their way in and stepped into a narrow passage, the carpet of which, they noticed, was quite severely displaced and rumpled up. As they entered the lounge itself, they stopped abruptly. Just inside the doorway, eerily illuminated by the light of a large standard lamp, lay a woman's body. She was supine. Her head was covered with blood. There was a length of electric light flex knotted round her neck. It was Ella Staunton. The walls and carpet of that cellar of death were spattered with blood. In a small kitchen opening off the lounge they found a bloodstained box-opener, shaped like a miniature pickaxe.

This was surely a unique case. The detectives had missed by a hair's breadth actually witnessing the murder. Leaving Anderson to keep guard over the corpse, Ballam rushed off to telephone through to police headquarters and to send for an ambulance.

A post-mortem carried out later that night brought a surprise discovery. It had been generally assumed that Ella Staunton had been strangled or had died as the result of injuries inflicted by the box-opener. Not so. The pathologist found that death had resulted from a wound to the heart, most likely brought about by a stabbing with a knife.

In view of the unexpected turn which events had taken, Mr Thomas Hendren's credentials and activities presented with a whole new and possibly sinister significance. A rapid riffling through official documents had revealed that the 31-year-old man was "less than a good 'un". Light fingers were his particular affliction. They had indeed provided him with a record. He had been arrested on 3 May 1946, and charged with stealing property from the Birkenhead factory where he worked. He was remanded on bail with further charges pending. These concerned thefts perpetrated in his own home, where he lived with his parents. He had forced open a savings box which he had found in his sister's room, stealing money from it, and taking also a quantity of National Savings Certificates. It was his mother who had discovered this latest of his turpitudes, and her errant son had left home after being warned that if he did not restore the stolen property his aggrieved sister would press charges against him.

The usual mitigations were trundled out by his anxiety-ridden mother, who stated that, formerly a ship's baker, he had always been well-behaved and law-abiding, but because of illness he had had to leave his last ship. That was in January 1945. Since then he seemed to be unable to hold down a job, and things had gone from bad to worse when his fiancee, a Miss Johnston, a post office worker in Salford, had broken off her engagement to him in the spring of the same year. It transpired that the young woman suspected him of having given her a dose of venereal disease.

Severely depressed, Hendren had, in June 1945, been found by his mother with his head in the gas oven. In a second bid to take his own life he had swallowed 120 Aspirins. Convicted of attempted suicide, he had served a short sentence in Walton. Released under medical supervision, he had remained unemployed until he found the factory job from which he had recently been dismissed for theft.

Facing what she regarded as a painful duty, his mother informed the police that her son had in his possession a frightening-looking nine-inch knife. He had told her that it had been given to him by a Mexican who he had met during one of his voyages. It was his habit to carry this formidable weapon about with him.

There was by now little doubt in the minds of the police that the man they had allowed to slip through their hands as he left the murder scene was the killer. But where was he now? He had not been seen at his Roe Street home since storming out after a family argument eleven days ago.

The first clue came from a Liverpool taxi driver. He said that at around five o'clock on the evening of 20 May he had picked up a man matching Hendren's description – 5ft 9in tall; well set-up shoulders; small, clean-shaven, thin-featured face; brown eyes; fair hair, thin on top; wearing a brown check suit, brown trilby hat, black shoes – at The Ocean Club, in Lord Street. The fare had at first said that he wanted to go to Birkenhead. Then he had changed his mind and asked to be driven to Huyton railway station. He had insisted on their going there via Wavertree, saying that he wanted to buy a raincoat there.

"I told him that he'd do better buying one in the city centre," said the cabby, "but he said he wanted a second-hand one."

The passenger went into a gents' outfitters in Wavertree and purchased a cheap macintosh.

Checking at the shop later, detectives made the significant discovery that the clothes coupons surrendered for the mac were in the name of Staunton. The police scoured Huyton, but found neither sign nor clue as to the fugitive's whereabouts.

Then, another lucky break. Hendren telephoned his sister in Llandudno. The call was traced to a telephone box in St Helens, and the hunt was switched to that town. The foreman at St Helens' Shaw Street railway station remembered that a man who had struck him as being in a state of considerable agitation had asked him the times of the trains to Leeds. "I told him 6.20am and 9am, and his next question was, 'Where's the porters' room?' I told him he could not stay on the station all night, and with that he walked off the platform." Next morning a porter found papers bearing Hendren's name stuffed away behind a toilet bowl.

A message had gone out to the police at Salford warning them that the wanted man might try to pay a visit to his former fiancee.

It was 6am when two Salford policeman, entering the public toilets in Albert Park, found a man sitting in a cubicle. Suspicions aroused, they asked him to identify himself. He said his name was Johnston – the name, it will be remembered, of Hendren's fiancee – and explained that he was on his way home after spending the night with a woman. "I believe that your name is not Johnston but Thomas Hendren," one of the officers, Sergeant Vaughan, told him.

Hendren immediately dropped all pretence. "Yes, Sergeant," he admitted. "They want me for Ella."

Arrested and searched, he was found to have a number of items, including a fountain-pen, a cigarette lighter, and a wallet, which had belonged to Mrs Staunton. "I took them out of her handbag after I had done her with the box-opener," Hendren told the detectives. The existence of the box-opener had deliberately not been mentioned in any of the newspaper reports.

When the police escort arrived at Manchester to take him back to Liverpool, Hendren told them, "All I want to say is that I did it". And in the course of the journey to the Liverpool bridewell he confided to Detective Superintendent T A Smith: "She's had plenty out of me – over a hundred pounds in the five years I've known her. When I asked her to lend me a couple of quid, she wouldn't. So it happened. I got about ten pounds out of her handbag, a five-pound note and five ones. I bought a box-opener in Lewis's that morning. I thought of breaking in somewhere."

His trial for murder opened at Liverpool Assizes on 27 June 1946, before the formidable Mr Justice Oliver, whom I had often seen in action. An old friend of mine, Mr Basil Nield, KC, MP, defended, and Mr HI Nelson, KC appeared for the prosecution. Hendren was smiling as he stepped up into the dock at St George's Hall and pleaded not guilty.

The defence was that at the time of Ella Staunton's murder the prisoner was insane. Mr Nield called several of Hendren's relatives to testify to his flaring temper, and to his love for reading comics as witness to his immaturity. The, to me unconvincing, cause of his alleged insanity was said to date from his wartime service in the Merchant Navy. The ship on which he had been serving was one of the last to leave Singapore at the time of the Japanese invasion, and Hendren had been among those ordered to go ashore to help to bury the dead. There had, however, been too many corpses for burial to be possible in the very short time available, so the bodies had been piled up to create a human bonfire, which had been set alight after spraying with petrol. The resultant stench of the repugnant conflagration had been overwhelmingly sickening and, Hendren had told his parents, the experience had haunted him ever since.

The tale did not convince Mr Nelson either. He pointed out that, far from being insane, Hendren had shown admirable presence of mind in his purchase of a raincoat to conceal the bloodstains on his suit. Moreover, neither were the prison medical officers, who had examined the prisoner while he was awaiting trial and failed to discover the smallest symptom of insanity, convinced. The jury, however, was convinced … of Hendren's guilt.

Thomas Hendren was executed at Walton Gaol on 17 July 1946. What the gas stove and the bottle of Aspirins had failed to do was achieved mercifully swiftly at the practised hands of another of my friends, the late Mr Hangman Pierrepoint.

AND WHAT ABOUT LIVERPOOL JACK?

In August 1993, Stewart Evans, one of the world's leading authorities on the Jack the Ripper murders mystery, paid me both a visit and a compliment. At a time when it was top secret, he confided to me his completely new evidence as to the possible identity of one who was, without question, a prime contender for the bloodstained laurels of that Victorian bogeyman, the Whitechapel murderer, who passed by the n*om de meurtre* of Jack the Ripper. I can still recall walking up the zigzag path to bosky St Ann's Well, with its perpetually bubbling fountain of crystal-clear Malvern water, while he unfolded his startling discovery. He knew then that it was going to be big, and indeed it was.

Back in my study, he also laid before me for my inspection his newly-acquired treasure – a letter written, on 3 September 1913 by former Detective Chief Inspector John George Littlechild, who was at the time of the Ripper murders head of the Special Branch at Scotland Yard, to the celebrated journalist, George R Sims, author, incidentally, of that famous sentimental Victorian ballad, *It is Christmas Day in the Workhouse*. In that letter, Inspector Littlechild names a man whom he describes as 'a very likely' suspect. And that man had very strong Liverpool connections.

The first association of Jack the Ripper with Liverpool can be traced back to 1927 – thirty-nine years after the East End crimes – when a London journalist, J Hall Richardson, who covered the Whitechapel murders for the *Daily Telegraph*, published his autobiographical volume, *From the City to Fleet Street*. It is here that we can find the following:

The Police and Press received many letters from the 'Ripper', mostly written in red ink, and I give one:

Liverpool
29th inst.

BEWARE I shall be at work on the 1st and 2nd inst. in "Minories" at 12 midnight and I give the authorities a good chance but there is never a Policeman near when I am at work.

Yours,
Jack the Ripper
Prince William St., L'pool.

What fools the police are I even give them the name of the street where I am living.

Yours,
Jack the Ripper

Prince William Street, by the way, still exists. It escaped the bombs of the Second World War in the Great May Blitz of 1940, and stands, very little changed, running between Hill Street and Warwick Street, in Liverpool 8.

We next come upon reference to this letter in *The Identity of Jack the Ripper*, by Donald McCormick, published thirty-two years later, in

1959, when McCormick refers to what Richardson described as *one* letter ('and I give one') as *two* letters from Liverpool. He also dates that which he identifies as the first letter as having been written on 29 September – the month being gratuitously substituted for the abbreviation 'inst'.

In Stewart Evans and Keith Skinner's definitive volume, Jack the Ripper: Letters From Hell, Evans, who has examined and recorded every one of the 210 letters and postcards 'which purport to have come from the murderer' in the Metropolitan Police files, and the 'substantially fewer in the preserved City of London Police letters file', states that the original Liverpool letter, or letters, cannot be traced. He adds: 'The only mention of this Liverpool correspondence prior to McCormick was by J Hall Richardson. The inevitable conclusion is that McCormick must have used Richardson as the source for the Liverpool letter(s).'

McCormick further complicates the matter by his assertion that 'Dr Dutton ... confirms that the Liverpool letters were in his [the Ripper's] hand.' For the said Dr Dutton and his 'lost' diaries constitute a very dubious factor in the whole equation! This Dr Thomas Dutton, of Westbourne Villas, Bayswater, is claimed by McCormick to have: '... compiled over a period of sixty years three volumes of handwritten *Chronicles of Crime*, based on his experience as a doctor. Prior to the East End murders he had been a leading figure in the Chichester and West Sussex Microscopic Society and had specialised in micro-photography.'

Possibly with the exemplar of the sleuthing

doctor as represented by the very genuinely concerned and involved Dr Forbes Winslow in mind, McCormick proceeded to develop Dutton as a leading protagonist in his book, according him especial stature as a student of the Ripper correspondence. He quotes Dutton's alleged statement: 'I made micro-photographs of 128 specimens of the alleged correspondence of 'Jack the Ripper' to the police and other institutions and individuals. Of these at least 34 were definitely in the same handwriting.'

As a result of all this, Tom Cullen, in good faith, perpetuated in his *Autumn of Terror: Jack the Ripper His Crimes and Times* (1965), the McCormick myth of *two* letters from Liverpool – and another Ripper legend was born!

One of the keenest proponents of a Liverpool lad for the role of Jack the Ripper was a Mr John Morrison, of Leyton, East London. It was back in 1986 that I paid him a visit, and sitting in his Ripper Murder Hunt HQ – the living-room of 21a Goodall Road – surrounded by books and gruesome wall-charts of victims and slaying sites, the then 60-year-old, out of work lorry driver told me, "'Mad Jack' has kept me sane". For when, four years before, he lost his job, he remembered the Duke of Edinburgh's glib advice to the mounting thousands of work-hungry unemployed: "Don't just waste the time on your hands. Use it to do something you've always wanted to do." And what John had always wanted to do was to discover the identity of Whitechapel Jack. After four years of dedicated ferreting, he was convinced that he had solved the mystery; run the Ripper to ground.

A fanatical enthusiast, eyes shining, tongue flailing, he rocket-launched into a breathless monologue on the topic that had become the most important thing in his life. As I stood by, he feverishly excavated a paper mountain of research data 'filed' under the sideboard, and surfaced triumphantly waving a single page document. "Here's a quote from the private notes of Inspector Joseph Chandler, who was actually on the case." He read it out to me, voice trembling with excitement.

> The man we are seeking once murdered in a house in Liverpool, was sent to an asylum and escaped just prior to the commencement of these crimes. I doubt if we'll catch him, he's such a cunning devil.

John Morrison told me: "Chandler was talking about a man named James Kelly." That, he said, was the name of the Ripper ... and it came to John in a dream.

> I dreamt I was in court. They were trying Jack the Ripper. Lord Hailsham was the judge. He called for the evidence, and they produced a *Guinness Book of Records*. And it was a dream that came true! Next morning I went along to the library and looked it up in the Guinness book. And there it was. James Kelly was listed as the longest-ever escapee from Broadmoor. He had murdered his wife in Liverpool and been declared insane.

Wife-killer Kelly went over the wall on 28 January 1888. Just 65 days later, the Ripper murders began.

The story that John Morrison pieced together was one of "terrible vengeance" and "a scandalous cover-up in the highest places". He told me: "The name of Jack the Ripper's last victim was Mary Kelly. She came from Liverpool, where she had had a passionate affair with a man so infatuated with her that he killed his wife. This man was James Kelly. He and Mary were lovers. She even took his surname. By the time he was convicted of wife-murder, Mary was carrying his child. Desperate to erase all traces of him from her life, she fled to London, had an abortion, and went on the streets. It was a mistake. Kelly found out where she was."

But why would he have wanted to kill and mutilate her? Morrison explained: "The insane Kelly saw Mary's desertion and rejection of him as vile treachery. Getting rid of their child made it worse. And he couldn't bear the thought of her selling herself to other men. He escaped, made his way to London, started to scour the East End. He killed ten women before he finally tracked Mary down. He would ask each prostitute victim if she knew where he'd find Mary Kelly – then slay her to silence her. By the time the last of the ten died – a woman named Kate Kelly – the police were hot on the Ripper's trail. For a while the killings stopped.

"Then Scotland Yard received a letter from Liverpool admitting the murders. It was signed 'Jack the Ripper'. James Kelly had gone home. He returned to London soon afterwards, went straight to Mary Kelly's Whitechapel hideout, and, literally, ripped her to pieces. This last killing was the absolute confirmation the police needed. Now the Yard knew that Kelly was their man. They wanted to raise the alarm, put out a hue and cry for him. Then, to their amazement, the Home Office said, 'No'. Why? I'll tell you. Because officialdom was embarrassed by its own incompetence at having failed to make the obvious connection between the dangerous homicidal lunatic at large and the Whitechapel slayings. Police Commissioner Sir Charles Warren was ordered either to obey the clam-up command, or resign. He resigned."

Sheer fantasy?

"I have proof," said John Morrison. "Inspector Chandler's mistress wrote a book about the case. It is disguised as fiction, but it reveals so much of the mechanics and details of the police work that it just has to be the inside story of the truth."

Morrison said that he knew the identity of the woman. She was a well-known person, highly connected and married to an eminent writer on *The Times*. Her name and all the facts were, he informed me, in the safe-keeping of his solicitor.* Morrison continued: "Early in 1889, the New York City Police complained to Scotland Yard that they had experienced a couple of murders identical to those in Whitechapel. And, later, Paris police reported Ripper-style killings."

Then he brought out what he clearly regarded as the clincher: after an adventurous life in New York, Paris, and at sea, James Kelly surrendered to the police in April 1927, and after an absence of thirty-nine years was returned to Broadmoor, where

346

he died in 1930, but, according to Morrison, "not before confessing that he was Jack the Ripper".

There are, I have to say, glaring inaccuracies in John Morrison's more detailed narrative, but it was nevertheless accepted in principal by James Tully as the basis for his book on the case, *The Secret of Prisoner 1167: Was This Man Jack the Ripper?* (1997).

Tully got the facts right. In the second half of 1859, Sarah Kelly, an illiterate, 15-year-old, working-class Liverpool girl found herself pregnant without benefit of matrimony. The father of her, as we now less barbarously term it, love child, was a free-ranging clerk by the name of John Miller, who promptly abnegated his responsibilities and deserted Sarah. Fortunately, her family stood loyally by her, and she was despatched by her mother to Preston, most likely, the home of her aunt, Mary Motler, to have her baby. The child, a boy, named James, was born on 20 April 1860, at 43 St Mary's Street, Preston. Mother and son returned to Liverpool, where James was handed over to be brought up by his grandmother, who, Sarah having gone off, he believed to be his mother.

In 1870, the missing Sarah suddenly turned up with a husband, John Allan, a master mariner with a share in his ship, who lived at 76 Aubrey Lane, in Everton. After their marriage the couple moved out to Southport, where they occupied 95 Manchester Road. Their union was childless, and on 16 May 1874, while voyaging to foreign parts, John Allan died, at Pisagua, in Peru.

The widowed Sarah returned to Liverpool. She was ailing, in constant pain from an affliction of the liver, and was looked after by John Munro, a victualler and friend of her late husband's, at his home, 10 Walker Street, Low Hill. Her health deteriorated rapidly, and on 29 July 1874, she died. In a will she made provision for the future of James. He had left school at 13 and been apprenticed to a firm of upholsterers, Messrs Ray & Miles, of London Road, but now, in accordance with the terms of his mother's will, he went over the water to attend Dr Robert Hurworth's Commercial Academy, at 1 Albert Terrace, Egerton Street, New Brighton. He left the Academy when he was 17, found a position with the pawnbroker, Isaac H Jones, at 102 West Derby Road, and went into lodgings at 49 Fielding Street. It was while he was there, lonely and brooding in the evenings in his room, that he began, gradually, to exhibit symptoms of mental instability. There was madness on his mother's side. A cousin had become insane. James developed a positive obsession that he must get out of Liverpool. He moved to London, and it was there that he was to meet the girl whom he was to marry and to murder, Sarah Brider. It was as a result of his furious and fatal knife attack upon his wife that James Kelly was to be sent, in August 1883, to Broadmoor Criminal Lunatic Asylum.

That, as John Morrison, reports, Kelly escaped from confinement there, and remained at liberty for nearly four decades, is indisputable, but that he was, as Morrison and Tully affirm to be their belief, the veritable Jack, seems, after a careful study of all the concommitant circumstances, highly unlikely.

Let us turn now to the very different constellation of suspicious factors surrounding the man with the very strong Liverpool connections whom Detective Chief Inspector Littlechild put tentatively in the frame.

He was Dr Francis J Tumblety. His family origins were Irish, and he was born, the youngest of 11 children, in Ireland in 1833, although the family moved very shortly afterwards to Rochester, New York. He seems early to have displayed a streak of sexual disreputability, for at the relatively tender age of 15 he was, as they say, turning a fast buck, peddling pornographic books and papers on the local canal boats. His first taste of medical practice was only slightly less dubious, doing odd jobs for the highly suspectable Dr W C Lispenard, specialist in a gallimaufry of sex nexus afflictions. Following in the good doctor's somewhat scabrous shoe-prints, Tumblety had, by the time was 24, established quite a reputation for himself as a great herbal healer.

The path of the true pioneer is never, or seldom, straight, and Tumblety's corkscrew progression was pock-marked with deaths and brushes with the police, but his footwork was of the finest, and his agility as a side-stepper truly remarkable. Setbacks set adroitly aside, his fortune grew.

Coffers bulging, his first descent on the Old World would seem to have been in 1869. He was back again across the herring pond in 1874, and that was the year when, in his role as herbal doctor, he set up his therapeutic tent in Liverpool. Here he met, and enjoyed a Uranian relationship with, a young bisexual writer, Hall Caine, who was to achieve outstanding literary success as the author of such novels, set in the Isle of Man, as *The Deemster* and *The Manxman*. Caine suffered from chronic neuralgia, and it was as a patient that he first came into contact with Tumblety.*

Throughout the next dozen or so years, Tumblety was constantly back and forth between America and England, and on Friday 31 August 1888, when Ripper-shed blood fell on the cobbles of Bucks Row, he was assuredly in London. That was the very day that he committed an act of gross indecency there with one Arthur Brice. Twice more he was similarly caught out, on 14 October and on 7 November, when he was arrested. He was out on bail on the night of 8-9 November, when Mary Kelly was unpicked at the seams in Miller's Court. He appeared again before the magistrate at Marlborough Street on 16 November, was further remanded on bail, and fled from England, sailing on 24 November from Le Havre to New York.

Supporting the theory that Francis Tumblety was the Whitechapel murderer, Stewart Evans and Paul Gainey have discovered that when he reached New York, two American detectives shadowed him to his lodgings, and, in December, Inspector Walter Andrews, one of the original three Ripper hunters, arrived in Manhattan in quest of Jack the Ripper. But nothing came of it.

Tumblety lived on for another fifteen years, dying on 28 May 1903, a Roman Catholic, ultimately groomed and garnered for salvation by the nuns who ran the institution where he breathed his last, St John's Charity Hospital, St Louis.

He left a living link in the Liverpool area – Mrs Margaret Brady, who resided at 20 Frederick Street, Widnes. She was the daughter of Dr Tumblety's sister, Bridget. Another tie with Liverpool was a namesake uncle Tumblety, who had been connected for more than twenty years with the Cunard Line. By an odd coincidence, it turned out that a Captain Anderson, serving in the Royal Navy, whom Dr Tumblety, when he was living in Boston around 1863, had got to know, knew Tumblety's Liverpool relatives. They had got it into their heads that Dr Francis had joined the United States Army and been killed in action. On one of his trips, Captain Anderson took a daguerrotype of Tumblety to his Liverpool uncle to convince him that Francis was still in the land of the living.

But was Francis Tumblety Jack the Ripper? Evans and Gainey are of the opinion that he very likely was. But what was the official police conclusion at the time? Littlechild wrote to Sims that there was a large dossier on him at the Yard. There is absolutely no trace of it. It has simply vanished into thin air. And, here is the oddest thing of all. There is a total absence of the name of Francis Tumblety, not only from the English newspapers, but also from the official documents. He rates not a single mention in the police files or in those at the Home Office. Tumblety's name exists nowhere amid the acres and acres of bureaucratic paperwork. What are we to make of this blanket of silence – a deliberate shroud for the Liverpool Ripper?